Identity, Culture, and Chinese Foreign Policy

This book assesses the role of identity and Chinese face culture in Chinese foreign policy by analyzing China's political and economic retaliation against South Korea's deployment of the THAAD (Terminal High Altitude Area Defense) system on its soil.

By examining the history and military action of China, Japan, and North and South Korea, the book argues that China's divergent responses were caused by different expectations according to whether states had a perceived identity as a friend or a rival. The author demonstrates that Chinese face culture shapes China's reaction to others through three dynamics of seeking, saving, and losing face. This book shows how identity and culture have worked in the relationship between China and neighboring countries through three case studies exploring North Korea's Taepodong-2 missile launch and first nuclear test in 2006, South Korea's decision to allow the United States to deploy the THAAD around 2016, and Japan's decision to deploy two U.S. X-band radars in 2005 and 2014.

A timely analysis of the importance of identity and culture in international relations, the book will be of interest to scholars of Chinese foreign policy, Sino-South Korean relations, Sino-North Korean relations, Sino-Japanese relations, Korean Politics, Asian Politics, and International Relations.

Kangkyu Lee is a research fellow at the Korea Institute for Defense Analyses (KIDA), the Republic of Korea.

Routledge Studies on Think Asia
Edited by Jagannath P. Panda, Institute for Defence Studies and Analyses, India

This series addresses the current strategic complexities of Asia and forecasts how these current complexities will shape Asia's future. Bringing together empirical and conceptual analysis, the series examines critical aspects of Asian politics, with a particular focus on the current security and strategic complexities. The series includes academic studies from universities, research institutes and think-tanks and policy oriented studies. Focusing on security and strategic analysis on Asia's current and future trajectory, this series welcomes submissions on relationship patterns (bilateral, trilateral and multilateral) in Indo-Pacific, regional and sub-regional institutions and mechanisms, corridors and connectivity, maritime security, infrastructure politics, trade and economic models and critical frontiers (boundaries, borders, bordering provinces) that are crucial to Asia's future.

1 **India and China in Asia**
Between Equations and Equilibrium
Jagannath P. Panda

2 **Northeast India and India's Act East Policy**
Identifying the Priorities
Edited by M. Amarjeet Singh

3 **The Korean Peninsula and Indo-Pacific Power Politics**
Status Security at Stake
Edited by Jagannath P. Panda

4 **Conflict and Cooperation in the Indo-Pacific**
New Geopolitical Realities
Edited by Ash Rossiter and Brendon J. Cannon

5 **Chinese Politics and Foreign Policy under Xi Jinping**
The Future Political Trajectory
Edited by Arthur S. Ding and Jagannath P. Panda

6 **Identity, Culture, and Chinese Foreign Policy**
THAAD and China's South Korea Policy
Kangkyu Lee

URL: https://www.routledge.com/Routledge-Studies-on-Think-Asia/book-series/TA

Identity, Culture, and Chinese Foreign Policy
THAAD and China's South Korea Policy

Kangkyu Lee

LONDON AND NEW YORK

First published 2021
by Routledge
2 Park Square, Milton Park, Abingdon, Oxon OX14 4RN

and by Routledge
52 Vanderbilt Avenue, New York, NY 10017

Routledge is an imprint of the Taylor & Francis Group, an informa business

© 2021 Kangkyu Lee

The right of Kangkyu Lee to be identified as author of this work has been asserted by him in accordance with sections 77 and 78 of the Copyright, Designs and Patents Act 1988.

All rights reserved. No part of this book may be reprinted or reproduced or utilised in any form or by any electronic, mechanical, or other means, now known or hereafter invented, including photocopying and recording, or in any information storage or retrieval system, without permission in writing from the publishers.

Trademark notice: Product or corporate names may be trademarks or registered trademarks, and are used only for identification and explanation without intent to infringe.

British Library Cataloguing-in-Publication Data
A catalogue record for this book is available from the British Library

Library of Congress Cataloging-in-Publication Data
Names: Lee, Kangkyu, author.
Title: Identity, culture, and Chinese foreign policy : THAAD and China's South Korea policy / Kangkyu Lee.
Other titles: THAAD and China's South Korea policy
Description: London ; New York, NY : Routledge/Taylor & Francis Group, 2021. |
Series: Routledge studies on Think Asia | Includes bibliographical references and index.
Identifiers: LCCN 2020028490 | ISBN 9780367553302 (hardback) | ISBN 9781003095095 (ebook)
Subjects: LCSH: China—Foreign relations—Korea (South) | Korea (South)—Foreign relations—China. | China—Foreign relations—Japan. | Japan—Foreign relations—China. | National security—China. | National characteristics, Chinese. | Terminal High Altitude Area Defense Weapon System.
Classification: LCC DS779.47 .L44 2021 | DDC 327.5105195—dc23
LC record available at https://lccn.loc.gov/2020028490

ISBN: 978-0-367-55330-2 (hbk)
ISBN: 978-1-003-09509-5 (ebk)

Typeset in Times New Roman
by codeMantra

Contents

List of figures		vii
List of tables		ix
List of abbreviations		xi
Acknowledgments		xiii
1	Introduction	1
2	Identity and Chinese foreign policy	11
3	Chinese face culture and foreign policy	52
4	Case study: Japan's THAAD radar deployment	78
5	Case study: South Korea's THAAD system deployment	88
6	Case study: North Korea's Taepodong-2 launch and the first nuclear test	110
7	Conclusion	130
	Bibliography	143
	Index	177

Figures

2.1	Frequency of Usage of "Great Power" in CFMSA	22
2.2	Pie Chart of Chinese Proclaimed Identities	23
2.3	Usage of the Term "Responsible Great Power" in the *People's Daily*	25
2.4	Usage Frequency of "Responsible China" or "China Great Power" in Korean Newspapers	26
2.5	Trade Volume Between China and South Korea, 1979–2018 (US$ Millions)	38
2.6	Chinese Visitors to South Korea, 1984–2017	39
3.1	Relationship Between Dynamics of Chinese Face Culture	61
5.1	Chinese Tourists to South Korea (2010–2017)	97
7.1	Fluctuations in Sino-South Korean Relations	135
7.2	Fluctuations in Sino-North Korean Relations	135

Tables

1.1	China's Puzzling Behavior at a Glance	3
1.2	Three Cases	8
2.1	Identity of North Korea to South Korean Governments	18
3.1	Examples of Chinese Face Culture in Chinese Foreign Policy	69
3.2	*Mianzi/Lian* in CFMSA Database	71
4.1	Japan's Description of North Korean Missile Threat in the Defense White Papers	79
5.1	China's Official Statements on South Korea as a Friend (2016–2017)	100
5.2	High-Level Meetings Between China and South Korea (2008–2017)	101
5.3	Chinese Core National Interests Appearing in the *People's Daily* (2008–2018)	105
5.4	Types of Chinese National Interests Relating to THAAD (2015–2018)	106
6.1	High-Level Visits Between China and North Korea (2000–2010)	118
6.2	China's Official Statements on North Korea as a Friend (2006)	119
6.3	Mentions of *Hanran* (悍然) in Official Press Conferences (2001–2018)	125
6.4	Chinese Core National Interests That Appeared in the *People's Daily* (2004–2007)	127
6.5	Chinese Core National Interests in CFMSA (2004–2007)	127
7.1	Hypotheses of the Book	132
7.2	Test Results of the Hypotheses	137
7.3	Features of the Three Cases	138

Abbreviations

AN/TPY-2	Army Navy/Transportable Radar Surveillance
APEC	Asia-Pacific Economic Cooperation
ARF	ASEAN Regional Forum
ASEAN	Association of Southeast Asian Nations
BIGKINDS	Korean Integrated News Database System
BMD	Ballistic Missile Defense
CCP	Chinese Communist Party
CCTV	China Central Television
CFMSA	Chinese Foreign Ministry Spokesperson Archive
DPRK	Democratic People's Republic of Korea
FPA	Foreign Policy Analysis
FTA	Free Trade Agreement
GDP	Gross Domestic Product
GSOMIA	General Security of Military Information Agreement
IAEA	International Atomic Energy Agency
IR	International Relations
KADIZ	South Korea's Air Defense Identification Zone
KAMD	Korea Air and Missile Defense
KCNA	Korean Central News Agency
KIDA	Korea Institute for Defense Analyses
KMT	Kuomintang
KTC	Korea Trade Commission
MOFE	Ministry of Finance and Economy
NACF	National Agricultural Cooperatives Federation
NKPA	North Korean People's Army
NPT	Treaty on the Non-Proliferation of Nuclear Weapons
PAC	Patriot Advanced Capability
PLA	People's Liberation Army
PRC	People's Republic of China
ROC	Republic of China
ROK	Republic of Korea
SCO	Shanghai Cooperation Organization
SDI	Strategic Defense Initiative

xii *Abbreviations*

SM	Standard Missile
SPT	Six-Party Talks
THAAD	Terminal High Altitude Area Defense
UNSC	United Nations Security Council
USFK	United States Forces Korea
WTO	World Trade Organization

Acknowledgments

This book would not have been completed without the support of many people. I am particularly indebted to professors at Seoul National University (SNU), my undergraduate and graduate school. Special thanks go to Yong-duk Kim and Jong-Ho Jeong, my advisors at SNU, for their unwavering support. I am appreciative of Young-Rok Cheong, Young Nam Cho, and Geun Lee for their intellectual inspiration. I would like to thank my professors and colleagues at the University of Denver. Above all, I express my sincere thanks to Suisheng Zhao, my dissertation director, for his continuous support and encouragement throughout my study in the United States. I am also deeply grateful to my committee members: Haider Khan, Paul Viotti, and David Goldfischer. Without their fruitful advice, this book would not have come into being. Also, I am indebted to the Honorable Christopher R. Hill for his warm support. Many thanks to Minsun Ji for her guidance during my stay in Colorado. I would like to recognize my excellent colleagues at the KIDA, too – especially Jina Kim for her warm encouragement. I thank the editors at Routledge, including my friend Jagannath Panda, for helping me refine my manuscript. No words can fully express my gratitude to my grandmother Soon-rye Hong and my parents, Ki-Heung Lee and Song-in Sook, for their unconditional love. Most importantly, this book is dedicated to my beloved wife, Namhee Park, and my beautiful kids, Kyuhee and Taejay, who provide unending love, sacrifice, support, and encouragement.

1 Introduction

On February 19, 2020, while the world was caught in the thick of the novel coronavirus pandemic, the People's Republic of China (PRC) expelled three *Wall Street Journal* reporters – Josh Chin and Chao Deng, both U.S. nationals, and Philip Wen, an Australian – over a headline. Earlier in the same month, the newspaper had published an opinion piece that called China the "sick man of Asia" (Mead 2020; Stevenson 2020), which is interpreted by China as a reference to the crippled dragon during the country's "century of humiliation." Although it is true that the column blamed China for its failure to prevent the spread of the virus, some people were bewildered by the Chinese government's overreaction to the headline. The explanation lies in the concept of *face* in Chinese culture that is characterized by the reluctance to lose face, which may ultimately result in retaliation.

China's overreaction to losing face, however, is not just limited to journalists.

China's international behavior has sometimes appeared contradictory to outside observers. And its rise to a great power has only compelled states to examine and understand how China thinks and behaves in the international arena. In particular, the Republic of Korea (ROK or South Korea), China's closest neighbor, has been very concerned about China's policy toward both the Democratic People's Republic of Korea (DPRK or North Korea) and South Korea, because it is one of the most important variables influencing security on the Korean Peninsula.[1] However, South Korean leaders have failed to develop a clear understanding of China's behavior, despite almost 30 years of relations with China after diplomatic normalization in 1992.

When South Korean President Park Geun-hye took office in 2013, she began to pursue pro-Chinese policy, unlike her predecessor, President Lee Myung-bak, who was well known for his strong pro-American policy.[2] China welcomed the shift in policy and eulogized the relationship between the two states as the best period in history. The peak of this "best relationship" was President Park's participation in China's military parade on September 3, 2015, which was held to celebrate the 70th anniversary of the victory over imperial Japan. In this event, President Park was seated close

2 Introduction

to Chinese President Xi Jinping on the platform, as well as in the photo session. China clearly perceived South Korea as a close friend.[3]

However, this intimacy did not last long. One year later, China began to retaliate strongly against South Korea, economically and politically, in response to South Korean's decision to deploy the Terminal High Altitude Area Defense (THAAD) system. China argued that the THAAD system, especially its X-band radar, gravely infringed on Chinese core national interests and posed a threat to its security: on February 7, 2016, South Korea and the United States announced talks aimed at "the earliest possible" deployment of THAAD, which is "a system designed to shoot down short-, medium-, and intermediate-range ballistic missiles using interceptor missiles, launchers, a radar, and a fire-control unit" (Swaine 2017, 1). After months of subsequent discussions, on July 8, Ryu Jae-seung (the South Korean deputy minister for National Defense Policy) and Thomas Vandal (the commander of the U.S. Eighth Army in South Korea) formally announced that the THAAD system would be deployed in South Korea (Choe 2016). In retaliation for the decision by the South Korean government to deploy THAAD, China immediately suspended all government-level exchanges with South Korea (Swaine 2017, 2). Along with an expression of outrage in the political sector, China also imposed economic sanctions in the private sector. In addition to the pullback of Chinese tourists, the South Korean company Lotte's business in China took a hit, while sales of Korean restaurants in the Beijing area plunged by a third year-on-year and sales of Korean automakers Hyundai and Kia Motors fell by half (Tselichtchev 2017). Even though Chinese State Councilor Yang Jiechi, who was the top official responsible for the Chinese foreign policy, repeatedly assured that China would withdraw major retaliatory measures from South Korea in 2017 and 2018; still, by the end of 2018, no substantive actions were taken by China to reduce the economic pressure (Jo 2018).

Similarly, no one had expected China to cut off oil supply to the DPRK, its so-called best friend, in response to North Korean provocations in 2006: the launch of the Taepodong-2 missile and its first nuclear test. China harshly denounced North Korea for the nuclear test by using the term *hanran* (悍然), which means "flagrant" or "brazen." This dramatic term is seldom used in diplomatic and official statements. The Chinese Foreign Ministry spokesperson said that "the DPRK flagrantly conducted a nuclear test. The Chinese government is strongly opposed to this act" (Ministry of Foreign Affairs of China 2006b).

In contrast to the above cases, Japan's deployment of the THAAD radars did not lead to any retaliation by China. In recent years, Japan has deployed two X-band radars in Shariki and Kyogamisaki. However, there was no attack by China when Japan announced its deployment of the Shariki radar in 2005 and activated it in 2006. When it came to the radar installation in Kyogamisaki, China simply expressed its concern: "Neighboring countries pushing forward the deployment of anti-missile systems in the

Table 1.1 China's Puzzling Behavior at a Glance

Cases	South Korea Case	Japan Case
Relationship to China	Friend	Rival (or potential enemy)
Issue	Deployment of the THAAD system (esp. X-band radar)	Deployment of the X-band radar
Outcome	Excessive retaliation by China	No retaliation

Asia-Pacific and seeking unilateral security is not beneficial to strategic stability and mutual trust in the region" (Chinese Foreign Ministry Spokespersons Archive 2014).[4] The reason China gave for its fiercer retaliation against South Korea's THAAD deployment was that the South Korean radar could monitor and detect China's territory, including sensitive missile facilities. The truth, however, is that the radars in Japan have a longer detection range than those in South Korea, and theoretically, the former's system could be a more serious threat to China. These incidents are typical examples of China's complex behavior, which perhaps appears to outsiders as bewildering (see Table 1.1).

Further, China often attacks other states on the grounds that it is protecting its core interests.[5] When French President Sarkozy met with the 14th Dalai Lama in 2008, Chinese Premier Wen Jiabao removed France from the list of countries during his "journey of confidence" in 2009, and China canceled the contract to purchase 150 Airbus planes from France. Similarly, China canceled many investment plans in the United Kingdom when the latter treated the Dalai Lama as an honored guest in 2012.[6] Also, China imposed a ban on the import of Norwegian salmon when Chinese dissident Liu Xiaobo won the Nobel Peace Prize in 2010.

This chapter attempts to understand China's unexpected retaliation against South Korea following the THAAD deployment; and in doing so it aims to open the discussion on China's irregular behavior with other states in terms of its face culture. The underlying cause of retaliation is explained using two variables: China's perception of South Korea's identity (friend) and China's face culture (losing face). For this purpose, it compares the three aforementioned cases: Japan's THAAD radar deployment, South Korea's THAAD system deployment, and North Korea's Taepodong-2 missile launch and first nuclear test discussed in detail in Chapters 4, 5, and 6, respectively. The last two sections of this introductory chapter outline the aims and the general structure of the book.

Any insight from existing studies?

Scholars have undertaken numerous studies on the relations between China and North Korea; in contrast, the relationship between China and South

4 *Introduction*

Korea has not been widely examined. In particular, there are very few studies on this subject in Western International Relations (IR). The topic is mainly examined by some Korean and Chinese scholars, and focuses on Sino-South Korean relations or the dynamics among the two Koreas, China, and the United States (Zhao 2004c; Chung 2007; Snyder 2009; Lee 2010; Friedberg 2012; Jin and Jun 2012; Nathan and Scobell 2012; Harding 2013; Yu et al. 2016; Ye 2017). Even though such scholarships are very informative, and sometimes insightful, the problem is that they often lack a theoretical base and much focus is directed on great powers such as China and the United States, rather than the two Koreas.

As many scholars pay attention to the matter of identity in IR and foreign policy study, research that explores identity as a factor shaping China's behavior has also been recently emerging (Rozman 2012; Shambaugh 2013; Boon 2018). South Korean China watchers have paid more attention to the relations between China's identity and North Korean nuclear crises (Kim 2004; Lee 2013). Although they explain how China's identity is formed or changed (i.e., how China perceives itself), and how that influences its behavior, they only address one side of identity (namely, the endogenous identity). This book approaches it from two sides, arguing that China's perception (or definition) of the identity of others influences its foreign policy too. I contend that state identity and national interests are socially constructed (Wendt 1999). Therefore, other states' identities, as perceived and understood by China, can be changed by social construction and can influence Chinese foreign policy.

Scholars who want to explain Chinese foreign policy through its culture often rely on Chinese views of exceptionalism, nationalism, and traditional values, or such ideologies as Marxism, Leninism, and Maoism (Lai 2012, 191). Similarly, although there are not many works that have taken note of Chinese face culture in foreign policy, some scholars do argue along these lines. For example, Huang and Bedford (2009), Nathan and Scobell (2012), and Ho (2016) all believe that the concept of face is uniquely influential in Chinese society, and important in explaining Chinese behaviors with other nations. In addition, Gries (2004) explains Chinese nationalism and its influence on foreign policy with reference to face culture. He believes face culture is a significant component of contemporary Chinese nationalism, in that it helps to explain the interplay of reason and passion that is essential to nationalism and the way in which Chinese national identity is reshaped by international pressure (Gries 2004, 23–25). Other researchers also view Chinese face culture as shaping Chinese pursuit of prestige in relations with other states. For instance, China has made efforts to be treated as a global power in the international community (Cheng and Ngok 2004; d'Hooghe 2005; Brady 2015). Although it does not always result in any practical gains, China often takes actions to save its face in the international community (Amako 2014).

Introduction 5

Many works on Chinese face culture and on foreign policy are useful in providing insights and theoretical groundwork for the research question of this study. Nevertheless, they are insufficient to explain China's erratic behavior – this book's main puzzle. First, most of them focus on how Chinese culture is extraordinary, rather than on how this culture works to shape foreign policy. Second, these studies often seem to confuse between the goal and the cause of Chinese behavior when they use face to explain the same. In other words, is *face* the goal of its errant behavior? Or does the prospect of losing face compel it to act a certain way?

A new approach to identity and culture

No existing research can clearly explain the reason behind China's divergent responses to South Korea and Japan, keeping in mind that the former is a friend and the latter a competing power, post THAAD deployment in both the countries. It is widely accepted, and perhaps more reasonable, to treat a friend less aggressively than, say, a non-friend when both have given equal reasons to be angry about. However, China has defied this implicit rule, seemingly followed by the majority of the world.

To address this behavioral riddle, additional attention must be paid to the concept of identity and how it shapes foreign relations. It may be that China behaved differently toward the two nations in keeping with the Chinese perspective, which differs from the approach mentioned above. In other words, China perceived South Korea as a friend, believing the feeling to be favored, and expected it to treat China as such. But ROK's THAAD deployment contradicted China's expectation of a friend, causing a loss of face to China. Hence, the aggressive response was warranted from China's perspective. In contrast, Japan being a non-friend, China had no expectations. Hence, for China, Japan's deployment of the THAAD radar was understandable even, because it did not cause any loss of face. In short, China's divergent responses toward South Korea and Japan could be explained through these understandings of national identity, from the Chinese perspective.

Identity matters in various relations including inter-state relations. Constructivist Alexander Wendt explores how states interpret actions of another country depending on the meaning they hold for them. For example, even though Canada and Cuba are located next to the United States, U.S. military power has a very different meaning for Canada than for Cuba (Wendt 1992, 397; 1999, 25). Or, 500 nuclear weapons in the possession of the United Kingdom versus five weapons in North Korea have very different significance for the United States (Wendt 1995, 73). Furthermore, changes in state identity affect not only a state's foreign policy but also the policy of other states toward it. For instance, in 2017, U.S. President Donald Trump threatened to unleash "fire and fury" against North Korea if it endangered the United States in the midst of a discussion regarding the horror of nuclear

6 *Introduction*

bombs (Baker and Choe 2017). Just one year later, however, President Trump said that he fell in love with North Korean Leader Kim Jong-un because of Kim's beautiful letters (Rodrigo 2018). All of a sudden, fury changed into love, and the U.S. military's threatening policy toward North Korea changed into a negotiating policy through talks.[7]

Aims and objectives of this book

Against this backdrop, two questions need to be examined:

1 Did China identify South Korea as a friend and Japan as a non-friend, to begin with (as also during the period around the THAAD deployment)?
2 Did South Korea's identity change from friend to non-friend in China's perceptions following the deployment?

If China did not have those differing perceived identities in its approach to South Korea and Japan, my argument should be rejected from the outset. Moreover, if South Korea's or Japan's identity vis-à-vis China had changed from friend to non-friend or vice versa following the THAAD deployment, the distinction between friend or non-friend would be meaningless.

Regarding the first question, to explain the matter of identity in shaping relations between China and South Korea, or between China and Japan, two types of identities are proposed in the book: *proclaimed identity*, which is an identify asserted by a state itself, and *perceived identity*, which is how a state's identity is understood by others. Proclaimed identity is important to understand the influence of Chinese face culture. Perceived identity, in this book, is mostly the phenomenon of whether a nation perceives another as a friend or a non-friend. To explore the extent of this identity, this study uses three measurements: social bonds, social exchanges, and expressions of intimacy.

If the answer to the second question is not in the affirmative, it is curious that China retaliated with such fury, rather than simply showing disappointment. The book argues that Chinese face culture promotes fury rather than soft expressions of disappointment, especially when Chinese leaders feel disrespected by a close friend, and eventually this fury translates into harsh actions.

Three dynamics of Chinese face culture are developed in the book to explain the mechanism that converts fury into retaliation: *seeking face, saving face*, and *losing face*. These three dynamics are closely intertwined. The purpose of seeking face is to actively make its own image in relations with others. It is related to the proclaimed identity of the Chinese state as a great state that should not be disrespected by its friends. Saving face is a defensive mechanism to avoid losing face. When confronted with a negative situation, the dynamic changes from seeking face to saving face. When saving face fails, it leads to losing face. When that happens, an actor may attempt to

Introduction 7

restore face in two ways: seeking another face and/or retaliation to overcome frustration and humiliation.

The book further explores the second North Korean nuclear crisis and the Garlic War, which serve to produce a hypothesis that China's lost face is the cause of its assertive behavior. Although the two events are discussed in detail in Chapter 3, some important observations are as follows:

1 *North Korea's second nuclear crisis.* It was triggered by a North Korean official's confirmation when the U.S. Assistant Secretary of State for Asia and the Pacific James Kelley, during his visit to Pyongyang in 2002, asked North Korean counterparts about the rumor that Pyongyang was covertly developing nuclear weapons by using enriched uranium (Sanger 2002). Furthermore, North Korea announced that it would restart three nuclear reactors with plutonium reprocessing, expelled International Atomic Energy Agency (IAEA) inspectors who had been monitoring the freeze of nuclear programs at the end of 2002, and eventually announced its withdrawal from the Treaty on the Non-Proliferation of Nuclear Weapons (NPT) in January of 2003 (Fu 2017, 8; Nikitin et al. 2017, 7). To tackle this crisis, China played an active role in establishing the Six-Party Talks (SPT) regime, which comprises China, Japan, North Korea, Russia, South Korea, and the United States. When North Korea was reluctant to participate in multilateral negotiations to discuss the issue, China stopped its supply of oil to North Korea for several days (Shin 2005, 37).

2 *The Garlic War.* It was a trade dispute between China and South Korea which lasted from 2000 to 2003. It began when the South Korean government took a safeguard action by increasing tariffs on Chinese garlic imports from 30 to 315 percent to protect Korean farmers, because South Korean farmers blamed cheap Chinese imports for a 30 percent drop in garlic prices in the South Korean market. In response, a week later, China imposed a ban on imports of South Korean mobile telephones and polyethylene, which is used to make a wide range of plastics (Kirk 2000). After two months of negotiations, South Korea and China agreed that South Korea would increase the import of Chinese garlic, and China would lift the ban on importing Korean mobile phones and polyethylene. However, China's retaliation was unreasonably excessive because Chinese garlic exports to South Korea amounted to only about $9 million, whereas exports of South Korean mobile phones and polyethylene were worth approximately $510 million altogether.

Furthermore, the book analyzes the aforementioned three cases using a mixed system approach that combines the *most similar* cases with the *most different* cases to allow the researcher to draw causal inferences from the selected cases (see Table 1.2). Thus, this design uses both the method of agreement and the method of difference (Frendreis 1983; Hage and Meeker 1988).

8 *Introduction*

Table 1.2 Three Cases

	Sino-Japanese Relations	*Sino-South Korean Relations*	*Sino-North Korean Relations*
Category	Most similar cases	Most different cases/ most similar cases	Most different cases
Case	THAAD deployment	THAAD deployment	Missile launch and first nuclear test in 2006
Outcome	No retaliation by China	Retaliation by China	Retaliation by China

Thus, this book aims to explain China's inconsistent, and often contradictory, international behavior. It ultimately seeks to provide new insight for understanding Sino-South Korean and Sino-North Korean relations, which will allow South Korea to establish a definitive strategy for maintaining security and peace on the Korean Peninsula. My argument is that China's varying perceptions of other nations' identities result in its divergent behaviors and that these behaviors are strongly influenced by Chinese face culture. In other words, unexpected and unfavorable action by a state that China believes to be a friend leads to humiliation (loss of face), anger, and eventually excessive retaliation.

Overview of the book

The book is divided into seven chapters, including this introductory chapter and a concluding chapter. Following the Introduction, Chapter 2 explores the theoretical foundations for exploring the effects of identity on foreign policy. It examines two types of identities – proclaimed and perceived – and explains how they might shape Chinese foreign policy toward the two Koreas and Japan. Furthermore, it suggests three measurements to identify a friend: social bonds, social contacts, and friendly expressions. Based on these theoretical foundations, this chapter explores the brief history of the Sino-North Korean, Sino-South Korean, and Sino-Japanese relations, and develops the propositions that are tested through the case studies in later chapters. It also discusses the mainstream realist approach, including an overview of its limitations in developing understanding of some state behaviors. The realist approach serves as the counterargument to my propositions about the influence of culture and identity on foreign policy, and this realist approach is tested as a null hypothesis in this chapter.

Chapter 3 delves into the effect of culture on foreign policy by focusing on Chinese political culture, especially its culture of saving face. By tracing the long tradition of Chinese culture, it explores the psychological underpinnings of China's behavior. The main theme of this chapter is how the concept of face shapes Chinese people and society, and influences decision-making at the state level. It examines three dynamics of Chinese face culture: seeking face, saving

Introduction 9

face, and losing face. Drawing from observations regarding the 2000 Garlic War between China and South Korea, and the second nuclear crisis prompted by the North Korean nuclear weapons development in the early 2000s, it elaborates on the hypothesis regarding the effect of Chinese face culture on its foreign policy.

Chapters 4–6 discuss case studies.[8] Chapter 4 briefly touches on Japan's introduction of radars that are integral to the THAAD system. It describes China's relatively lukewarm response to the radar installation, compared to the ROK.

Chapter 5 covers China's retaliation against South Korea in response to its THAAD deployment in 2016. By using process-tracing and content analysis, it examines the remarkable change in the relationship between China and South Korea.

Chapter 6 deals with China's changed position toward North Korea following its Taeopodong-2 missile launch and first nuclear test in 2006. A process-tracing method, supplemented by historical and content analysis, shows how China's proclaimed identity of a responsible great power operated to shape its actions, and how the dynamics of Chinese face culture led to China's retaliation against its longtime friend.

Chapter 7 concludes the book. Based on findings from the previous chapters, it summarizes the results of the analysis. It also highlights the contribution of the study in terms of theory, empirical insights, and policy recommendations. Lastly, it provides suggestions for future study.

Notes

1 Hereafter, the People's Republic of China is referred to as PRC or China, the Democratic People's Republic of Korea is referred to as DPRK or North Korea, and the Republic of Korea is referred to as ROK or South Korea.
2 The surnames have been written first for all Chinese, Korean, and Japanese individuals mentioned in this book.
3 When attending a South Korean conference, Yang Wenchang, former Chinese vice foreign minister, and Yan Xuetong, one of the most influential scholars in Chinese foreign policy, asserted that Sino-South Korean relations were much more important than Sino-North Korean relations because the former was a strategic cooperative partnership, whereas the latter was only a normal inter-state relationship (Han 2009, 2).
4 The Chinese Foreign Ministry Spokesperson Archive (hereafter CFMSA) has a database of manuscripts of regular press conferences held by Chinese Foreign Ministry from 2001 to 2018.
5 There is a controversy over the definition of Chinese core interests among scholars, politicians, and policymakers. In 2009, Dai Bingguo, then Chinese state councilor responsible for foreign policy, defined Chinese core interests to include three components:

> 1) preserving China's basic state system and national security(维护基本制度和国家安全); 2) national sovereignty and territorial integrity (国家主权和领土完整); and 3) the continued stable development of China's economy and society (经济社会的持续稳定发展)."
>
> (Swaine 2011, 4)

For details of the controversy, see Zeng et al. (2015).

10 *Introduction*

6 Chinese leaders think that meetings between foreign leaders and the Dalai Lama and support for dissidents who are against the CCP infringe on China's core interests (Swaine 2011, 2).
7 Of course, this changed dynamic alone might not be the evidence of North Korea's changed identity to the United States, because many Americans still saw North Korea differently according to the survey by YouGov, which showed that almost half of the respondents considered North Korea as the enemy (Frankovic 2018). Nevertheless, it is noteworthy that the rate of perceiving North Korea as an enemy was diminished from previous years and there was evidence of increased support for Trump's handling of North Korea as a possible ally or even friend.
8 Chapters 4–6 have a similar structure that consists of recounting the historical background and developments of the events, together with analysis of the effect of China's losing face as these events unfolded. The analysis section of each chapter includes verification of the identity hypothesis (including the influence of Chinese face culture), as well as analysis of the null hypotheses, or the mainstream realist hypotheses, and their focus on Chinese national core interests.

2 Identity and Chinese foreign policy

Identity can be used by political scientists to understand a variety of actors, including individuals, nations, corporations, governments, and states.[1] Identities are the understandings and expectations about one's self that are acquired by interacting with or defining the self in relation to an "other" in the context of social relationships, shared meanings, rules, norms, and practices (Viotti and Kauppi 2012, 287). Furthermore, one can perceive a certain identity of the *other*, regardless of the other's real identity. Despite the probability of misperception, a state must develop its understanding of the identity of other states because each state must try to predict how other states will act, and how other states will be affected by one's own state actions in determining how to behave (Jervis 1968, 454). Therefore, I argue that proclaimed identity (which is identity that is perceived or pursued by one's self) should be distinguished from perceived identity (which is how one's identity is perceived by others).

This chapter discusses the influence of these two identities on a state's behavior and the applicability of this identity theory to understanding Chinese foreign policy.

Identity and foreign policy

Identity in foreign policy analysis

When it comes to how identity influences state behavior, a prominent challenge has been made by constructivism to neo-/structural realism in IR theory. The key to the constructivist social theory is that "people act toward objects on the basis of the meaning that the objects have for them" (Wendt 1992, 396–397). In this sense, states are not as alike as the structural realist Waltz (1979) posits. He believes that the international system is a kind of self-help system because it is anarchic in the absence of a world government, and thus states are alike in that they all seek the same goal of survival (Waltz 1979). According to constructivism, however, states can have different identities and national interests of their own. Wendt (1992, 397; 1995, 73; 1999, 25) gives examples of how U.S. military power is perceived differently by

12 *Identity and Chinese foreign policy*

different nations, and how nuclear weapons in the United Kingdom versus in North Korea have totally different significance for the United States (for details, refer to Chapter 1). Therefore, for the United States, the difference in perceived identities of other nations will have a bearing on the U.S. policies toward them. Furthermore, the U.S. perception of DPRK's identity can also explain the recent dramatically changed situation between the United States and North Korea: dialogue has replaced the traditional hostility due to the changing identities of the two countries toward each other.

Despite the usefulness of this approach, the effects of identity on foreign policy were overlooked by scholars during the Cold War and have only come to figure prominently in Foreign Policy Analysis (FPA) since the 1990s, after the Cold War was over (Kaarbo 2003; Grove 2010; Hudson 2014; Vucetic 2017). Identity in FPA requires researchers to ask how people within a nation-state answer the questions "who are we?", "what do we do?", "who are they?" (Hudson 2014, 118), and sometimes "what does who they are mean for what we do?" (Grove 2010, 765). Based on these questions, the FPA on identity has evolved with several trends (Grove 2010, 766–769). First, some works focus on a specific region or country (Pye 1985; Campbell 1992; Shaffer 2006). Second, other studies, especially comparative politics studies, take a more systematic approach to measurement, including attempts to measure the supra-culture of the elite and the subculture of mass (Ebel et al. 1991). Third, other studies look into the demographic makeup of a state and pay attention to the various ethnic groups in the state by focusing on how multiple cultures and identities of these ethnic groups affect foreign policy (Wilson 2004; Hill 2007). Fourth, still other studies investigate the uses of culture and identity by politicians to manipulate particular groups to support their foreign policies, such as through the "rally-round-the-flag" effect (Baum 2002).

Even though many researchers utilize identity theory and try to define identity, there is no satisfactory single definition of identity in the social sciences or in the humanities (Fearon 1999). The concept of identity is too fragmentary, contingent, and malleable (Vucetic 2017). IR constructivist Wendt (1999) suggests four kinds of identities: personal or "corporate" identity, which is constituted by the "self-organizing and homeostatic structures" that distinguish self from the other; "type" identity that is placed within the "site" of personal/corporate identity and refers to a "social category"; "role" identity that depends upon culture and shared expectations and as such exists "only in relation to Others" and cannot be enacted solely by the self on its own; and "collective identity" that leads to the "identification" of self with other through blurring the distinction between them (221–230). Similar concepts of identity are also found in other FPAs (Jepperson et al. 1996).

Proclaimed and perceived identities

To explain state behaviors in terms of state identity, I reduce Wendt's four kinds of identities, particularly role identity and collective identity, to two

Identity and Chinese foreign policy 13

more simple and intuitive kinds of state identities: proclaimed identity and perceived identity.[2]

Let us first consider an example: suppose you come across a person holding a sushi knife (which is a weapon of choice of Korean and Japanese gangs) on a dark street, you might feel threatened by the person. You may be relieved if the person wielding the knife self-identifies as the sushi chef at a restaurant where you are a regular. However, you may still feel fear if you do not believe the self-identification. Your "imagined" security depends on whether you believe your perception of the person's identity or the proclaimed identity.[3] The same drives your reaction too.

Proclaimed state identity means the identity proclaimed and pursued by a state itself. This proclaimed state identity can be a clear signal of state policy and behavior because it is usually declared through an official channel, including by qualified individuals. However, a proclaimed identity is not always solid because this identity is not always accepted by others. For example, North Korea declared itself a "nuclear state" in its constitution. In the "Kim Il-sung–Kim Jong-il Constitution," which was the new constitution revised in 2012, North Korea stipulated that it was "an undefeated country with strong political ideology, a nuclear power state, and invincible military power" (Kwon 2012). However, this proclaimed identity of North Korea being a nuclear state or an invincible military power has not been welcomed or accepted by other states. South Korea promptly disapproved it on the grounds that North Korea could not be a nuclear state because it was not a signatory of the NPT that comprises only five nuclear powers, namely, the United States, the United Kingdom, France, Russia, and China (UPI 2012). Similarly, despite arguments from experts that the United States should accept North Korea's nuclear status (McKeon and Thalheimer 2017; Narang and Panda 2018), Washington's position has not changed (Kim 2017d).[4]

A proclaimed identity can be formulated not just for describing the present status but also for announcing future goals. For instance, Japanese Prime Minister Abe Shinzo proclaimed Japan's identity to be a "normal state" (*futsu no kuni*, 普通の国) in the future, by relentlessly attempting to revise its constitution so that it could become a military power (Yellen 2014). Although there is no official definition of what "normal" exactly means, *normal state* means a state that has the basic authority and capability to exercise autonomy in the management of its economic and security affairs (Inoguchi 2005, 135).[5] In other words, the core of this identification of Japan is to allow itself to fully remilitarize. The advocates for *normal* Japan think that Japan is not normal because it has not responded adequately to structural factors, including the need to develop Japan's own security in the international system (Tadokoro 2011, 45; Hagström 2015, 138), while the opponents argue that Japan has been and should be a "peace state" (*heiwa kokka*, 平和国家) under the pacifist constitution forced by the United States after the Second World War (BBC 2015; Lind 2016, 2–3). These varying proclamations and controversies are all a matter of Japan's changing identity (Akimoto 2013; Hagström 2015).

14 *Identity and Chinese foreign policy*

Moreover, some leaders of states want to formulate their own identity to achieve a perceived identity that is desirable for them internationally and to achieve political goals such as regime legitimacy domestically. Proclaiming an identity assumes there is an audience, who is listening to the proclamation. As seen from the examples of North Korea and Japan, mentioned earlier, the aim of such an announcement of state identity is twofold: first, an extroversive effect on other states. For North Korea, the proclaimed state identity of nuclear power can contribute to securing the survival of North Korea as well as Kim's regime, which is of greatest concern to North Korean elites. Given that the presence of nuclear weapons is a game changer in the international security structure, the identity of nuclear state can guarantee the survival and preservation of the poor and hermit Kingdom, and of Kim's dynasty to a considerable extent.[6] Similarly, Japan's proclamation of normal state identity not only brought it to the attention of other states, including its neighbor countries that are concerned about Japan's assertive behavior, but may also help Japan to more effectively handle territorial conflicts with China.

Second, it also has an introversive effect. North Korean leader Kim Jong-un needs a prominent achievement to consolidate his power domestically. Even though he has the "Mount Baekdu bloodline,"[7] this charismatic source of origin for legitimacy is not sufficient to ensure the young leader's power. Leaders in authoritarian regimes are usually faced with the lack of powerful authority (Svolik 2012). Kim Jong-un is no exception. This is the reason he proclaimed North Korea's achievement of the nuclear power status to his people. All North Korea media are required to propagate Kim Jong-un's greatness, and such related claims as North Korea could only become a dignified nuclear power thanks to the dedication of Chairperson Kim who made achievements in the parallel development of economic might and nuclear weapons (Cho 2018).

Similarly, Japanese Prime Minister Abe enjoyed his second term by politicizing the concept of "normal state" in elections (Nagy 2014, 8; Dobson 2016; Hornung and McElwain 2017). When he won the election for his third consecutive three-year term as the head of the ruling Liberal Democratic Party in 2018, which took him closer to becoming Japan's longest-serving Prime Minister, Prime Minister Abe said that "I feel I received a strong push to exert strong leadership for another three years, based on the results of my economic, diplomatic and national security policies so far" (Reynolds and Nobuhiro 2018).

Contrary to proclaimed identity, the perceived identity of a state is the identity perceived by other state(s), regardless of the state's will. In this sense, perceived identity has similarities with the reputation discourse in IR.[8] Many students in IR think reputation can influence cooperation and conflict among states (Schelling 1960; Mercer 1996; Copeland 1997; Sartori 2005; Tomz 2007; Crescenzi 2018). For example, the reputation of a state improves or aggravates the commitment problem and lack of information that

Identity and Chinese foreign policy 15

are critical to cooperation and conflict. Moreover, the reputation of a state is related to signaling a state's competence, and thus a state's reputation for competence can increase the likelihood of cooperation, while a reputation for incompetence can raise the possibility of war (Crescenzi 2018, 80). Furthermore, reputations influence a state's behavior. States do not want to have a bad reputation by violating international rules because they are afraid to be excluded by other states from future opportunities that can be beneficial to them (Brewster 2009).

In addition, the perceived identity of a state can be relative, and thus can vary according to how other states perceive the identity of a given state. In other words, one state may have several different perceived identities by other states. For example, when the United States counted North Korea as part of the "axis of evil" along with Iran and Iraq, South Korea viewed North Korea as a partner in cooperating for peace on the Korean Peninsula based on its engagement policy toward North Korea. So, North Korea had conflicting identities vis-à-vis the United States and South Korea at the same time. In the same manner, the United States might view Japan's quest for normal state status as creating a more reliable ally to check the rise of China; however, the same quest reminds South Korea and China of the resurrection of militarist Japan due to their memory of the past (Moon and Suh 2018).

Although the formation of proclaimed and perceived identities is not the primary concern of this book, it is a topic worthy of brief analysis.[9] First, the process of forming identity is similar to the process of making foreign policy, in that identity is made rather than given and both proclaimed and perceived identities can change. Changes in identity include formation of identity because change is the replacement of an old identity with a newly formed one. Even though Wendt (1992, 397) thinks that identity is relatively stable, it does not necessarily mean that identity is unchangeable.[10] Because identity is socially constructed (Wendt 1999), the process of change in identity occurs naturally through social interaction involving values, norms, beliefs, role conceptions, attitudes, stereotypes, and other cognitive phenomena (Chafetz et al. 1998, 10). This social interaction leads to the breakdown of the old identity, a critical reexamination of old ideas and practices, and the construction of a new identity (Larson 2011, 60). After all, there are no permanent friends or enemies in IR.

Second, individuals, especially national leaders and policy elites, are most influential in the process of change. Of course, national leaders and policy elites are not the only factors to make or change foreign policy or identity, because institutions are not just a neutral channel through which leaders project their unmitigated influence on state behaviors. For example, states try to conform to international law on many issues, irrespective of a leader's personality (Mitzen 2006, 352–353). Nevertheless, leaders are very influential in forming state identity and shaping foreign policy based on this state identity. In the history of U.S. foreign policy, presidential power and

16 *Identity and Chinese foreign policy*

policy-elite preferences have played a significant role in swinging its foreign policy between peaceful engagement and containment (Viotti 2010). For example, it is the influence of President Trump that has pushed the United States to pursue an engagement policy with North Korea, despite oppositions and skepticism from his staff and many in the international community (Sullivan 2019).

Third, both proclaimed and perceived identities are foundational to the foreign policymaking of a state. However, the roles of the two identities are somewhat different. Proclaimed identity has more influence on the proclaiming state's behaviors and consequently affects the other state's perceived identity of the proclaiming state, while perceived identity has more influence on one state's reaction to another state's behavior, whose identity is being perceived.

A good example of the importance of proclaimed and perceived identities in shaping a state's foreign policy is the case of South Korea. South Korea has been swinging between hard-line and soft-line policies toward North Korea, depending on the nature of the government in power. Thus, "[v]ariation in state identity, or changes in state identity, affect the national security interests or policies of states" (Jepperson et al. 1996, 52).

Before democratization in 1987, authoritarian governments of President Rhee Syngman, Park Chung-hee, and Chun Doo-hwan had regarded North Korea as the principal enemy. All these governments placed great importance on anti-communism for their legitimacy. There had been some exchanges and dialogues with North Korea intermittently, but they did not change the governments' view on the identity of North Korea. Even though the Roh Tae-woo government is not taken as fully democratic, Roh's regime did take a different foreign policy stance toward communist countries, including North Korea, shifting from the previous authoritarian governments' hard-line stances in pursuit of detente after the Cold War.[11] The Roh government established diplomatic ties with the Soviet Union (later Russia) and China. It also pushed ahead with dialogue with Pyongyang (Cotton 1993; Kang 2012; Kim 2014b). In subsequent civilian governments, conflicting North Korean policies emerged, which have also been controversial in South Korea. President Kim Young-sam was criticized for inconsistent policy toward North Korea: there was a rapid change from a policy of economic cooperation (separating economic cooperation from political differences) to a policy of coercion in which both political and economic conflicts were heightened (Lee 1997; Park 1998; Paik 2012).

President Kim Dae-jung, who was awarded the Nobel Peace Prize for his "sunshine policy," pursued an engagement policy, assuming that North Korea would be willing to cooperate and have dialogue (Bae and Moon 2014; Lee 2015c). Thanks to the policy, the first-ever inter-Korean summit was held in Pyongyang in 2000 between Kim Dae-jung and the North Korean leader Kim Jong-il. The Kim government pursued this engagement of

Identity and Chinese foreign policy 17

"sunshine policy" despite the second North Korean nuclear crisis and the skirmish in the West Sea.[12] His successor, President Roh Moo-hyun, too, held a similar view on North Korea, carrying on Kim's engagement policy. He also participated in the second inter-Korean summit in 2007.

Two conservative presidents, Lee and Park, followed the two liberal presidents (Kim and Roh) and had a different view on North Korea from their predecessors. They basically thought that the engagement policy toward North Korea for the past ten years allowed North Korea to develop nuclear programs (Park 2008; Suh 2009; Kim 2014b; Kim 2017b, 254–256). Thus, President Lee Myung-bak and President Park Geun-hye regarded North Korea as a security threat rather than as a cooperative partner. During the Lee government, in addition to the nuclear tests, there were two significant military provocations by North Korea. And even though the Park government's North Korea policy could not become concrete because of her impeachment, it was not much different from that of the previous conservative government – the hard-line measures included the shutdown of the Kaesong Industrial Complex jointly operated with North Korea.

Liberal President Moon Jae-in brought the engagement policy back in inter-Korean relations, similar to his liberal predecessors. He asserted that he and his government would continue President Kim Dae-jung's and President Roh Moo-hyun's efforts for reconciliation and cooperation between the North and the South (Chung Wa Dae 2017). Furthermore, he made clear that South Korea did not have a hostile policy toward North Korea (Chung Wa Dae 2017). Based on the perceived identity of North Korea as South Korea's possible partner, the Moon government pushed for a dialogue with North Korea patiently, despite missile launches and a nuclear test by North Korea.

As shown in Table 2.1, the South Korean governments have carried out their policy toward North Korea according to their perceptions of North Korea's identity. Liberal presidents have employed engagement policy toward North Korea, while conservative presidents have taken a hard-line policy, particularly since democratization (Kim 2017b). These changing identities of North Korea can be found in defense white papers of South Korea, which reflect the changing identity of North Korea according to differing South Korean perceptions. For example, the *Defense White Paper 1995* stipulated North Korea as a major enemy but this notion was removed in the *Defense White Paper 2004* (Ministry of National Defense of Republic of Korea 1995; 2006).[13] The perception of North Korea as enemy reappeared in the *Defense White Paper 2010* with the expression that "the North Korean regime and its military [armed forces] will remain [as our] enemy." This phrase was retained in the recent *Defense White Paper 2016* (Ministry of National Defense of Republic of Korea 2017, 41). As expected, however, this expression was crossed out from the *Defense White Paper 2018* – the first defense white paper under the Moon government (Ministry of National Defense of Republic of Korea 2018).

Table 2.1 Identity of North Korea to South Korean Governments[14]

Govt.	Rhee Syngman (1948–1960)	Park Chung-hee (1963–1979)	Chun Doo-hwan (1980–1988)	Roh Tae-woo (1988–1993)	Kim Young-sam (1993–1998)
DPRK identity	Communist enemy	Communist enemy	Enemy and partner	Partner	Partner → enemy
DPRK policy	Use of armed forces	Development before unification → development after unification	Non-retaliation and dialogue	Nordpolitik and engagement policy	Appeasement → coerciveness

Govt.	Kim Dae-jung (1998–2003)	Roh Moo-hyun (2003–2008)	Lee Myung-bak (2008–2013)	Park Geun-hye (2013–2016)	Moon Jae-in (2017–
DPRK identity	Partner	Partner	Enemy	Enemy	Partner
DPRK policy	Sunshine policy (reconciliation and cooperation)	Peace and prosperity policy (engagement)	Denuclearization opening and 3,000-dollar vision (coerciveness)	Trust-building process on the Korean Peninsula (coerciveness)	Moon Jae-in's policy on the Korean Peninsula (engagement)

In sum, state identity can be divided into the two identities of proclaimed identity, by the state's own self, and perceived identity, which is how a state is perceived by other states. Both identities can play a role in making and conducting foreign policy: active foreign policy emerges largely from proclaimed identity, and reactive foreign policy stems largely from perceived identity. The identities are advantageous, *inter alia*, to individuals, including national leaders, who use them to influence policies. Chinese foreign policy should not be an exception to this theory of identities. Therefore, the following hypothesis can be produced:

H1: *China's foreign policy is influenced by its proclaimed identity and by the perceived identities of others by China.*

Chinese proclaimed identity: great power (Daguo, 大国)

The notion of great power in Chinese tradition

China's proclaimed identity is closely related to its positioning in world politics (Shambaugh 2013, 13; Pu 2017; Hoo 2018, xvii). A great power's identity focuses on "the country's past, present, and future in IR, concentrating its capacity to project power in comparison to other countries with their own ambitions" (Rozman 1999, 384). Since China has extremely unbalanced development levels in many areas, it sometimes wants to be treated as a developing country, especially on the world economy stage;[15] other times, it wishes to be treated as a powerful state in the political arena (Wu 2004, 58–59; Editorial Board 2018). Despite its preference to be treated as a developing country (with favorable treatment in terms of international trade rules), China also wants to be a seen as a great power nation that is different from other developing countries. The conception of great power (*Daguo*, 大国) underlies these contradictory goals and is one of the longest lasting and most influential notions in China.

The notions of great power status and the dichotomy of big and small states have had a long history in Chinese thought. For example, when asked if he had a formula for diplomacy with neighboring states, Mencius (2016, 27) answered that "[o]nly a man of humanity is able properly to put his large state at the service of a smaller one...Only the wise man is able properly to put his small state in the service of a larger one." The notion of big and small countries is also found in the works of other ancient Chinese great thinkers like Confucius and Lao-Tzu. In the *Analects*, Confucius' student Zilu used the term "great states," saying "[l]et there be a state of a thousand war chariots, wedged between great neighboring states" (Confucius 2015, 56). It is more obvious in *Daodejing*, where Lao-Tzu (2010, 28–29) explains that "when the large state takes the lower position it controls the small state. When a small state takes the lower position, it places itself under the control of the large state." The discourse of great power and the obligations of a

20 *Identity and Chinese foreign policy*

small state toward that power have been reflected throughout Chinese history. For example, in his letter to King Injo of Chosun dynasty, Hong Taiji, founder of the Qing Dynasty, said, "How dare you, small state, disobey great power of mine!" (Jangseogak Royal Archives). Furthermore, his successor, Emperor Qianlong, called his empire the Celestial Empire (天朝大国) – called *daguo* (大国) in the original Chinese – in a letter to Lord Macartney of Britain's East India Company in 1793 (Peyrefitte 2013, 288–292).

As Confucius divided the grade of states by the number of war chariots, the notion of great power originated from conceptions of national power rather than the size of a state. As time passed, the word *daguo* (great power) became associated with assumptions of state virtues like generosity and responsibility, especially by Confucian political elites. For example, in most contexts *daren* (大人) and its opposite *xiaoren* (小人) do not, respectively, mean a tall and a short person. Instead, *daren* indicates a gentleman who is respectable, whereas *xiaoren* refers to a person who is narrow-minded and petty. Similarly, a great power should act like a gentleman under Confucian tradition. Consequently, it is reasonable that the Chinese concept *daguo* (大国) is often translated as "great power" rather than "big country," because the term implies greatness in non-material aspects, rather than greatness in territory and population. This notion of great power in Chinese thought has developed into Sinocentrism that pursues influence through education and transformation (*jiaohua*, 教化) of other states, rather than through conquest and subjugation with armed forces (Zhang 2015; Hoo 2018, 2–3).

The notion of "great power" has a long history, tracing back to ancient times. Furthermore, it has been deep-rooted in Chinese society. Thus, the traits are easily found in contemporary Chinese politics. In fact, China's proclaimed identity of great power was severely damaged by the "Century of Humiliation" in modern China, which began with China's defeat in the First Opium War and the loss of Hong Kong to Britain in 1842, and was followed by Japanese invasion (Gries 2005, 45–47). The discourse of great power revived with the end of the "Century of Humiliation" that was accompanied by China's participation in the victory of the Allied Forces over imperial Japan in 1945, followed by the establishment of new China in 1949 (Gries 2005, 56–57; Kissinger 2011, 58).[16] It is not surprising that Mao Zedong, who was the founding father of the PRC and had a profound understanding of Chinese traditional thoughts, also expressed the notion of great power (Shen and Xia 2015, 101). In his *On Protracted War*, he reiterated this notion:

> We shall not be able to convince them merely by stating that Japan, though strong, is small, while China, though weak, is large....There is the additional factor that while Japan is a small country with a small territory, few resources, a small population and a limited number of soldiers, China is a big country with vast territory, rich resources, a large population and plenty of soldiers, so that, besides the contrast

Identity and Chinese foreign policy 21

between strength and weakness, there is the contrast between a small country, retrogression and meagre support, and a big country, progress and abundant support. This is the reason why China will never be subjugated.

(Mao 1938)

Mao had the ambition to re-position China in the world as a great power. This goal is well reflected in his renowned speech, "The Chinese People Have Stood Up," in which he was very confident that China "shall be able to win speedy victory on the economic front" and "shall emerge in the world as a nation with an advanced culture" because "[t]he Chinese have always been a great, courageous and industrious nation" in addition to having the very favorable conditions of large population and territory (Mao 1949).

The current Chinese President Xi Jinping, oft-mentioned to be reminiscent of Mao (Zhao 2016), also has the notion of great power. He came up with a "new type of great power relations (*xinxingdaguoguanxi*, 新型大国关系)" and has been trying to construct relations with the United States based on this notion. This concept of China having "great power relations" among major states has gradually developed since the late 1990s (Zeng 2016), but the idea only attracted attention during Xi's visit to the United States in 2012 when he was still the vice president of China. The idea, based on the framework of his predecessor Jiang Zemin, states that "the major powers are the key, surrounding areas are the first priority, developing countries are the foundation, and multilateral forums are the important state" (Shambaugh 2013, 14).[17] Furthermore, President Xi declared his new foreign policy by focusing on "major country diplomacy with Chinese characteristics (*Zhongguotesedaguowaijiao*, 中国特色大国外交)."[18] Although China stresses that its diplomacy advocates equality among all countries regardless of their size (Wang 2013), this statement does not mean that Chinese leaders do not maintain a notion of "great powers," which have unique power and responsibilities in the world. During his visit to Brunei in 2018, President Xi wrote an opinion piece in a Brunei newspaper that included the phrase "countries of different sizes" in the English version; a more faithful translation of the Chinese original, however, would be "big and small countries" (Xi 2018b). This notion of great power based on the differentiation between a country with substantial power, and a small and weak country is well summarized in a remark by Shen Dingli, a Chinese professor at Fudan University: "China is a Big Power; we can handle any country one-on-one. No one should try to lead us; no one should tell us what to do" (Shambaugh 2013, 15).

The notion of great power has moved through Chinese thought from ancient times to the present. The continuing influence of the concept is supported by qualitative content analysis of the Chinese Foreign Ministry Spokesperson Archive (CFMSA). The term *daguo* – referring to great power – was found 554 times in the CFMSA, and most times it was used to address China itself. According to the usage of this term in the CFMSA, China is a

22 Identity and Chinese foreign policy

great power in terms of economics, production, consumption, population, development model, and military power.[19] As seen in Figure 2.1, the use of term *daguo* has been increasing over time. Moreover, it has sharply risen since Xi became the president of China. Meanwhile, it is noteworthy that China uses the term *daguo* in Chinese, but not all uses of *daguo* are translated into "great power" in English. For example, China addressed Brazil as a great power in the developing world, and Mexico as a great power in Latin America, but in the English translation Brazil was called a "major developing country" and Mexico a "major country."

The more specific identity proclaimed by China is captured using various expressions to modify descriptions of the country by spokespersons of the Ministry of Foreign Affairs of the PRC – hence, they are official. Among these descriptions, "responsible great power" has been used the most (see Figure 2.2): it was used 78 times in the CFMSA database that I consulted.[20] It was followed by the phrase "great power of developing," which appeared in several English translations of Chinese statements, and appeared 40 times in the database. However, China rarely addresses itself as a "global great power" (four times), a "nuclear great power" (one time), or a "globally influential great power" (one time).

The rise of responsible great power

Though China is only one of the many large-sized countries in the world, it has carved its niche by attaining the status of a nuclear power and a

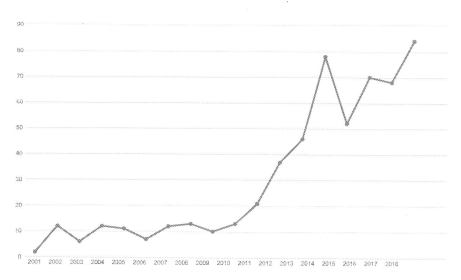

Figure 2.1 Frequency of Usage of "Great Power" in CFMSA.
Source: CFMSA.

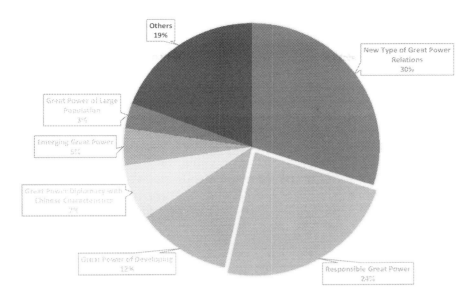

Figure 2.2 Pie Chart of Chinese Proclaimed Identities.
Source: CFMSA.

permanent membership in the United Nations Security Council (UNSC). In spite of its low Gross Domestic Product (GDP) per capita, China is expanding its influence over other states in economic, military, and cultural realms too, and has consequently become a great power. But, what kind of great power will China be? This question has been hotly debated in China: high popularity of TV documentaries such as the Rise of the Great Powers (*Daguojueqi*, 大国崛起) and the Road to Revival (*Fuxingzhilu*, 复兴之路) is evidence of this debate (Mueller 2013).

As briefly discussed earlier, in official proclamations, the answer to the question is typically "Responsible Great Power" (*fuzerendaguo*, 负责任大国). Even though the concept of the responsible great power of China has attracted great attention in recent years, the discussion can first be traced back to the 1990s when the rise of China came into the spotlight.[21] For example, Deng Xiaoping, known as the architect of Chinese reform and opening up, stated in his speech "Seize the Opportunity to Develop the Economy" that "we cannot simply do nothing in international affairs. We have to make our contribution. In what respect? I think we should help promote the establishment of a new international political and economic order" (Deng 1990).

Following Deng, Jiang Zemin, too, put emphasis on the notion of responsible great power during his term. In April 1997, President Jiang used the term officially in his speech before the State Duma of Russia.[22] He stated that both China and Russia, as great powers and permanent members of

24 Identity and Chinese foreign policy

the UNSC, had an important responsibility to safeguard world peace and stability (Larson 2015, 337). In accordance with such claims, the notion of responsible great power became an important goal of Chinese foreign policy in the 1990s (Xiao 2003, 47).

As evidence of its commitment to behaving as a responsible great power, China did not devalue its currency during the Asian financial crisis in 1997 despite the risk of its own economic loss due to decreased exports (Chan 2001, 55). The result was a double positive effect on China's image: China demonstrated economic robustness in bearing the loss of trade and was seen as a responsible great power, preventing another round of crisis by sacrificing itself (Kim 2003a, 63). Accordingly, Tang Jiaxuan, then foreign minister, ranked this case as one of the examples of China fulfilling its great power responsibility in foreign policy during Jiang's era (Tang 2002). Even though in the era of Hu Jintao, Jiang's successor, China seemed to be more reluctant to take on active and broad international responsibilities (Zhao 2012), the notion of responsible great power continued to shape China's foreign policy goals (Cho and Jeong 2008, 469). For example, Chinese Foreign Minister Yang Jiechi put stress on acting as "a responsible big country" (big in terms of power), despite his emphasis on holding onto a low-profile foreign policy at the same time (Zhao 2013, 119).

President Xi brought the notion of responsible great power back into the core of Chinese foreign policy, which had been relatively neglected during Hu's era. Xi has repeatedly emphasized China' role as a responsible great power. For example, in his speech at the Boao Forum for Asia in 2015, he asserted that "being a big country means shouldering greater responsibilities for regional and world peace and development, as opposed to seeking a greater monopoly over regional and world affairs" (Xi 2015). His emphasis on the notion of responsible great power status is also found in his major country diplomacy with Chinese characteristics. China is a great power, he claims, so it should have great power's "way of thinking (心态), sense of responsibility (担当) and manner (气度)" (Hu 2019, 2). Furthermore, in the dimension of diplomacy, China, as a great power, believes that a great power is responsible for providing public goods (Su 2018). In an article that explains the meaning of such diplomacy, Chinese Foreign Minister Wang Yi said that "as a permanent member of the UNSC and a developing country, China needs to consider and contribute to global wellbeing, shoulder its due international responsibilities and play its role as a great power in promoting common development." In addition, he added that China will "continue to act as a responsible great power to contribute to world peace, promote global development, and uphold the international order" (Wang 2018; translated by Li).

Given such emphasis by Chinese national leaders, the notion of responsible great power is one of the most significant identities proclaimed by China. The attention to this concept can be gauged by the number of articles in the *People's Daily* containing the term "responsible great power" (*fuzerendaguo*, 负责任大国); in the body or main text, this usage has been constantly increasing over the past two decades (see Figure 2.3). According to the database of the *People's Daily* (人民日报图文数据库), which provides articles from 1946, the term "great power" appeared in the main text and the headline for the first time in 1998 and 2008, respectively. The article in 1998 celebrated the 20th anniversary of China's reform and opening-up policy, and the one in 2008 applauded the Chinese Navy for successfully completing a mission to protect ships in the Gulf of Aden. Moreover, the number of articles with "responsible great power" in the title or body has dramatically increased since 2008. Interestingly, the world was in the grip of two financial crises in 1998 and 2008: the Asian crisis (1997–1999) and the global economic crisis (2007–2008). Thus, it can be assumed that the role of China as a great power was more vigorously discussed in the times of the financial crises. However, the number of articles with *responsible great power* in the title alone shows no significant change.

The trend of an increasing number of *People's Daily* articles referencing responsible great power can also be found in Korean newspapers. Using the Korean Integrated News Database System (BIGKINDS) of the Korea Press Foundation, a keyword search was run in 55,530,070 Korean newspaper articles from the 1980s to the present for the following combinations: 중국 (China) & 책임 (responsibility) or 중국 (China) & 대국 (Big country). This search, too, resulted in a very similar tendency of a rapid increase in the number of articles mentioning Chinese great power (see Figure 2.4).

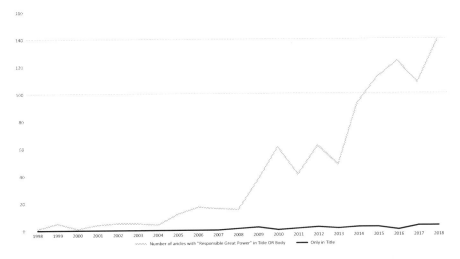

Figure 2.3 Usage of the Term "Responsible Great Power" in the *People's Daily*.
Source: Database of the *People's Daily* (人民日报图文数据库).

26 *Identity and Chinese foreign policy*

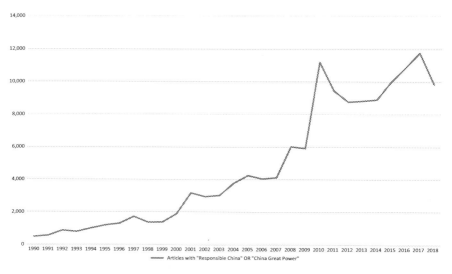

Figure 2.4 Usage Frequency of "Responsible China" or "China Great Power" in Korean Newspapers.
Source: BIGKINDS.

The proclaimed identity of responsible great power emerged due to a nexus between China's own needs and other states' request for greater Chinese responsibility in the world, especially requests from the United States. In terms of meeting China's own needs, the discourse of responsible great power began to be actively discussed when the rise of China in the 1990s was seen as a threat in the West (Broomfield 2003). China was not happy with this perception; it wanted to enjoy its robust development period for a longer time so as to achieve its goal of realizing a *xiaokang* (小康) society in China, which means a moderately prosperous society where all Chinese people are well-off, without worries about the necessaries of life. So, China needed to address the West's perception of China as a threat by playing a "responsible great power" role in international affairs in order to reassure Western nations, and thereby not upending diplomatic and trade relations, which might slow down Chinese growth. At the same time, international society came to expect China's increasing role in international affairs in terms of burden-sharing and responsibly engaging with the international system. For example, in his remarks to the National Committee on U.S.-China Relations in 2005, the U.S. Deputy Secretary of State Robert B. Zoellick responded to an article titled "China's 'Peaceful Rise' to Great Power Status" in *Foreign Affairs* by Zheng Bijian, who was an influential theorist to China's leaders. Zoellick proposed that "[w]e need to urge China to become a responsible stakeholder in the international system. China has a responsibility to strengthen the international system that has enabled its success" (Zoellick 2005).[23]

Due to these double driving forces of domestic needs and international expectations, the proclaimed identity of responsible great power has increasingly been the center of Chinese foreign policy. Even as China has embraced a proclaimed identity as a responsible great power, the country has disappointed the international community on some issues, including perceived inadequate action to address climate change. In fact, China artfully employs its contradictory identities, i.e., it claims status as a developing country on the issue of climate change, so as to avoid the great power's responsibility to lead the way in adopting environmentally responsible growth practices. Even though there might be controversy over the actual extent of Chinese responsibilities, China has demonstrated a commitment to responsible great power status through its behavior during the Asian financial crisis and by joining important treaties for world peace such as the Chemical Weapons Convention and the Biological Weapons Convention. In the same way, China's proclaimed identity as responsible great power is likely to affect its policy toward North and South Korea, which leads to the following hypotheses:

H1a: *China's proclaimed identity of great power or responsible great power influences its policy toward North Korea.*

H1b: *China's proclaimed identity of great power or responsible great power influences its policy toward South Korea.*

H1c: *China's proclaimed identity of great power or responsible great power influences its policy toward Japan.*

Perceived identities of three neighbors by China

Perceived state identity is literally how a state is perceived by other states. It may be the same as a proclaimed identity or different from it. For example, socialist China wants to project an image of a responsible great power that promotes democracy in IR (Wang 2014a), but other nations do not necessarily accept this proclaimed image. In another instance, the United States designated North Korea as a state sponsor of terrorism despite North Korea's repeated claims of not supporting terrorism. South Korea also has confused proclaimed and perceived identities. For example, South Korea often proclaims that it adopts "middle power diplomacy" in its foreign policy, and South Korean elites often present their country as a middle power (Kim 2016c; Robertson 2018). According to a survey by the U.S. News and World Report (2019), however, South Korea was ranked at the tenth place among the most powerful countries of the world and at the 22nd place among the overall best countries in 2019. These examples show the reality of how perceived identities can vary among nations, and conflict with a nation's proclaimed identity.

28 Identity and Chinese foreign policy

How does China perceive the identities of North Korea, South Korea, and Japan? One possibility is that China imagines South Korea as "a former tributary periphery, a US ally, a democratic market economy, and a rising but ambivalent regional power" (Lee 2018a, 35). Although this view might be plausible in explaining the fact-based identity of South Korea, it lacks depth in explaining the psychological perception of South Korea that might exert influence on foreign policy, especially at the level of influencing individual leaders.

For perceived identity, it is often not important what others really are, but how they are perceived. The identities of the two Koreas and of Japan vis-à-vis China can be simply split into "friend" and "non-friend." Even though there might be conflicts between "friends" in state relations, there should be no war between them. Put simply, China is willing to treat North Korea, South Korea, or Japan as friends when it perceives them to be friends, and vice versa. The perceived identity of a nation as a friend or a non-friend reasonably shapes foreign policy toward a nation. This insight gives rise to the following hypotheses:

H1d: *China behaves according to its perceived identity of North Korea in Sino-North Korean relations.*

H1e: *China behaves according to its perceived identity of South Korea in Sino-South Korean relations.*

H1f: *China behaves according to its perceived identity of Japan in Sino-Japanese relations.*

To identify the level of friendship in Sino-North Korean, Sino-South Korean, and Sino-Japanese relations, three measurements are used in the case studies: social bonds, social contacts, and expression of intimacy. The notion of national friendship has relatively recently been introduced to IR and foreign policy (Hoef and Oelsner 2018). Despite the increasing interest in relations between friendship and foreign policy, most studies only focus on the types of friendship at the international level or the possibility of peace through friendship (Gartzke and Weisiger 2012).

Measurements of friendship have usually been developed in psychology. Nevertheless, studies in psychology mostly put emphasis on developing various scales to measure friendship by using survey methods, completely relying on individual respondents (Parker and Asher 1993; Sharabany 1994). However, this type of measurement is not feasible for states because states cannot be surveyed, and in any case the degree of friendship as measured on a psychology scale is not of interest to this study. In fact, for this study, the three measurements mentioned earlier (social bonds, social contacts, and expressions of intimacy) are simple but sufficient to determine whether two states are friends or not.

First, the measure of social bonds indicates any binding or alliance between states. Alliance is a strong evidence of these social bonds (Gartzke

Identity and Chinese foreign policy 29

and Weisiger 2012). However, examining only evidence of formal alliance is too strict threshold for China, in that China has not officially pursued alliances with other nations. So, pieces of evidence of diplomatic ties are also considered to demonstrate social bonds at a minimum level in this study. Second, social contacts are measured through evidence of meetings and exchanges of leaders and political elites between two states. In general, if two states are not friends, they do not have summits or top-level meetings between leaders because a summit is generally accompanied by a high political burden. Last, expressions of intimacy imply words or behaviors that reflect friendship. One state's positive expression of relations with the other state and one's actions that benefit the other are regarded as expressions of intimacy.

North Korea: from "blood alliance" to strategic asset and liability

The building of "blood alliance"

China has never used this term "blood alliance" officially.[24] However, it has long been used to describe Sino-North Korean relations because of its symbolic wording for the very close relationship between the two countries.[25] China uses "traditional friendship" to describe relations with North Korea.[26] In contrast, North Korea often describes its relations with China as "forged in blood." For example, the North Korean party newspaper, *Rodong Sinmun*, recalled Chinese Premier Zhou Enlai's gift of a flower to North Korean leader Kim Il-sung as the symbol of the alliance forged in blood (Shim 2018a). Similarly, South Korea and the United States also use this expression of "forged in blood" to describe their alliance (U.S. Army 2017). Thus, whether the term is officially used by China is not critical at all. Whatever it is called, the relations between China and North Korea have been very close, like a "blood alliance."[27]

This close relationship can be traced back to the 1910s when Chinese and Korean forces engaged together in armed struggles against imperial Japan. In particular, Korean and Chinese communists in Northeast China helped each other with anti-Japanese activities, set up their communist organizations together, and carried out communist revolution against the Kuomintang (KMT) by providing personnel, weapons, and other war materials (Lee 2016). For instance, at least three competent combat units of the Chinese Army mostly comprised ethnic Koreans (Chen 2003, 4; Jin 2015, 110; Shen and Xia 2018, 28). So, they had very close relations at all levels of individuals, communist parties, and states (Shen and Xia 2018, 15–17). Kim Il-sung, who later became the North Korean leader, formed personal relationships with Chinese leaders and political elites through this process (Chen 2003, 4). Based on these relationships, China established diplomatic ties with North Korea on October 6, 1949, by mutual state recognition (Wertz et al. 2016).

30 *Identity and Chinese foreign policy*

This close relationship was consolidated by brotherhood through the Korean War.[28] With a goal to "Resist U.S. Aggression and Aid Korea," China decided to participate in the Korean War. Mao Zedong had described North Korea's relationship with China as being as close as "lips and teeth": if the lips were gone, the teeth would be cold.

The two countries signaled the building of "blood alliance" by signing the Sino-North Korean Mutual Aid and Cooperation Friendship Treaty in 1961. The Treaty has two significant features. First, it has a tripwire clause. According to Article II,

> [T]he Contracting Parties undertake jointly to adopt all measures to prevent aggression against either of the Contracting Parties by any state. In the event of one of the Contracting Parties being subjected to the armed attack by any state or several states jointly and thus being involved in a state of war, the other Contracting Party shall immediately render military and other assistance by all means at its disposal.
>
> (Peking Review 1961, 5)

Second, it has no expiration. Article VII includes a provision that "[t]he present Treaty will remain in force until the Contracting Parties agree on its amendment or termination" (*Peking Review* 1961, 5).[29]

In sum, China had built a perceived identity of North Korea as a close friend, like blood brothers, from the very establishment of North Korea. It has treated North Korea according to this perceived identity. One example of their intimacy are songs sung together by the Chinese People's Liberation Army (PLA) and the North Korean People's Army (NKPA) during the Korean War. The songs were the military anthems of the PLA and the NKPA, composed by Chung Yul-song (Zheng Lucheng in Chinese). He was a Korean-born Chinese who had worked in China for the anti-Japanese movement and for Korea's independence during the 1930s and 1940s (Kim 2016b). Given the core status of the military in China and North Korea, the fact that their military anthems were composed by the same person indicates their very close relationship.

Oscillating but still friendly

In the 1960s, China and North Korea experienced deterioration in their relations because of different views on Brezhnev's Soviet Union, on Soviet assistance to Vietnam, and on the Cultural Revolution. China had a troubled relationship with the Soviet Union, while North Korea was gaining substantial material support from it. Moreover, China was opposed to participating in "united action" in the Vietnam War, whereas North Korea supported it openly. During the Cultural Revolution, the Red Guards in China targeted Kim Il-sung by criticizing North Korea's degeneration into a "revisionist country" (Chen 2003, 7; Cheng 2015, 129–130). However, the tense relations thawed following the Pueblo Incident in 1968 when North Korea seized a U.S. ship and its crew that was gathering intelligence. China announced that it firmly supported "the legitimate position of the North Korean government" (Cheng 2015, 131). Following this support, Chinese Premier Zhou Enlai paid an official visit to North Korea. In his speech at an official dinner, he stressed that "China and North Korea are neighbors connected by mountains and rivers, Chinese and North Korean have traditional friendship and very close relationship as if lips and teeth are mutually dependent" (Tianshanwang 2014).

In the 1970s, China changed its foreign policy to achieve rapprochement with the United States and opened its economic policy to limited market reforms. North Korea was unsatisfied with China's new policy orientation toward the Western world. Despite North Korea's dissatisfaction, however, China wanted to maintain friendly relations with Pyongyang – even if they were not as close as they used to be – because it did not want to be isolated from the communist bloc (Shen and Xia 2018, 227–228). Overall, the relations continued without serious problems until the 1980s, because China had to concentrate on its economic growth and North Korea had to prepare for the succession of power to Kim Jong-il. The most threatening crisis in Sino-North Korean relations popped up in the 1990s when China decided to normalize diplomatic relations with South Korea.

Nevertheless, these tensions did not affect the Chinese view of North Korea. From the North Korean perspective, this action was seen as a betrayal, but China still thought of North Korea as a friend. On August 25, 1992, the next day after normalization, an official stated that "China will continue to develop its relations of neighbor, friendship, and cooperation with North Korea. Any treaties between China and North Korea will never change" (Hiraiwa 2013, 321). Also, an editorial in the *People's Daily* on September 9, 1992, asserted that "the friendship between China and North Korea has been built on a solid foundation by revolutionists such as Mao Zedong, Zhou Enlai, and Kim Il-Sung" (Hiraiwa 2013, 329).

In short, from the 1970s to the 1990s, Sino-North Korean relations experienced some fluctuations, but continued to be friendly, as perceived by China at least. Given the fact that there was no mutual visit by top leaders of the two countries for almost seven years, North Korea likely felt some betrayal. Moreover, trade between the two countries continuously decreased to less than half its peak levels (Chen 2003, 9). So, the relationship between the two countries was not what it used to be.

Nevertheless, this does not mean that China's perception of North Korea as a friend changed. Even though there had been no meeting between top leaders of the two countries, China tried to continue the exchanges. For example, in 1993, Hu Jintao, then a member of the Politburo Standing Committee and secretary of the Secretariat of the Communist Party of China,

32 Identity and Chinese foreign policy

and who later became China's president following Jiang Zemin, visited Pyongyang with his delegation to celebrate the 40th anniversary of the end of the Korean War (Lim and Cha 2017).

Furthermore, China remained the largest outside supplier of food and oil to North Korea during this period (Chen 2003, 9). Therefore, China's perception of North Korea's identity changed from best friend in the 1970s to just friend in the 1990s. This identity was well expressed by President Jiang Zemin when he met the Japanese delegation led by Ishida Koshiro, chairman of Komeito (公明党), on October 8, 1991: "North Korea was a comrade in a past war. We maintain close ties, but it is not an ally" (Hiraiwa 2013, 312–313; Park and Kim 2014).

Strategic asset and liability

Since the mid-1990s, the Chinese perception of North Korea's identity started gradually changing once again. As the position of North Korea moved from best friend to friend, China began to analyze what the DPRK meant to the country as a friend; the friendship was shaped by notions of roles or functions of North Korea in relation to China. This change in friendship status was fueled by Pyongyang's obsession with developing nuclear weapons. According to Korean China expert Kim Heungkyu, three schools of thought emerged in China in the mid-1990s with differing ideas on how to approach North Korea's nuclear goals: the Traditional Geopolitics School, the Developing Country School, and the Rising Great Power Diplomacy School (Kim 2010). The Traditional Geopolitics School, which comprises a traditional geopolitics group and a socialist group, views North Korea as a special friend who can function as a buffer zone for China. Both the Developing Country Diplomacy School, which pursues China's continued economic growth, and the Rising Great Power Diplomacy School, which urges China to be more active while pursuing international affairs, regard North Korea as a burdensome friend (International Crisis Group 2009).

These two views have disintegrated into several positions in the era of President Xi Jinping: unconditional support for North Korea, abandonment of North Korea, maintenance of status quo, imposition of limited sanctions, imposition of strict sanctions, political realism, passive management, or indifference (Kim 2017c, 4). Nevertheless, these various positions can be largely converged into three arguments: abandoning, protecting, or persuading a friend. The extreme option to abandon North Korea is not realistic at this moment because it is so dramatic and unattractive to China. In fact, the Chinese People's Political Consultative Conference held in 2013 discussed this option at a session titled "Friendship with Foreign Countries" (Wang 2014a, 6). But this conference was more of a gesture to warn North Korea for its third nuclear test rather than serious policy debate over possible abandonment: the then Chinese Foreign Minister Yang Jiechi confirmed that there was no fundamental change in the Chinese policy toward

Identity and Chinese foreign policy 33

North Korea after the conference. Thus, Chinese policy toward North Korea moves between those two conflicting perceived identities of North Korea as either a useful friend or a troublemaker friend – but a friend nonetheless.

China's ambivalent attitudes toward North Korean nuclear issues are explained by how China sways between these two perceived identities of its friend. When the first North Korean nuclear crisis occurred in 1993, triggered by Pyongyang's withdrawal from the NPT, China abstained in the vote for the UNSC Resolution 825 that urged North Korea to reconsider its announcement to withdraw from the NPT and abide by its international obligations (UNSC 1993; UNBISNET Voting Record Search). This was the only abstinence made by a member of the UNSC on a total of 21 resolutions concerning North Korean nuclear and missile issues until 2018.[30] Previously, China had voted for all UNSC negative resolutions concerning North Korean nuclear and missile tests since 1993, in spite of these tests being coordinated in advance between China and North Korea.

In addition, contrary to its attitude in the first crisis, China took a more active role in addressing the second North Korean nuclear crisis in the early 2000s. When it comes to nuclear tests by North Korea, China's behavior has gradually changed since the first test in 2006. Even though China repeatedly expressed its resolute opposition to North Korean nuclear tests, it was reluctant to impose economic sanctions against North Korea. However, following the fourth test, China has changed its position to vote for economic sanctions, along with practically implementing them.[31]

China is in a relationship with North Korea where Beijing can show its discontentment or fury to Pyongyang but it cannot completely turn its back (*bianlianbufanlian*, 變臉不翻臉) (Park 2014a, 82). In other words, China has a mixed perception of North Korea's identity. On the one hand, North Korea is a strategic asset for China: the latter sees the former as a physical and psychological buffer zone in a possible conflict with the United States. On the other hand, North Korean actions create a strategic burden for China, in that China must shoulder pressure from the international community, including the United States, for North Korea's wrongdoings (Deng 2013). The perception of a troubled friendship with North Korea was reinforced after the Japanese Fukushima Nuclear Accident in 2011. The nuclear accident fundamentally changed Chinese awareness of North Korea's nuclear program from trouble to danger. Many Chinese scholars and government officials began to pay more attention to the reliability of North Korean nuclear technologies (Lee and Lee 2012). China realized that even if North Korean nuclear missiles would not aim at China, it could not be free from the effects of a possible nuclear accident because North Korean nuclear facilities are located near its border area, and nuclear tests can affect volcanic activities of Mt. Paektu (Cao and Yang 2016).

In short, China still perceives North Korea as a friend, useful but troublesome, and treats it as a friend, in a broader meaning of the word. Diplomatic ties and the Sino-North Korean Mutual Aid and Cooperation Friendship

34 *Identity and Chinese foreign policy*

Treaty demonstrate that the two countries have strong social bonds with each other. Meetings, including summits between top leaders and political elites from the two countries, show that China and North Korea have frequent and close social contacts. They also have various expressions of intimacy for each other. For instance, between 1971 and 2017, North Korea had the "most similar" voting pattern vis-à-vis China at the U.N. General Assembly: 92.16 percent in agreement with China (Fu 2018). Furthermore, the Ministry of Foreign Affairs of PRC generally takes charge of high-level meetings between states. In addition, the International Department of the Communist Party of China Central Committee (*Zhonggongzhongyangduiwailianluobu*, 中共中央对外联络部) organizes exchanges with North Korea, including every summit, because both China and North Korea are party-states governed by communist parties. As a result, China and North Korea are friends.

South Korea: from enemy to friend

A friend's enemy

The PRC and the DPRK were born to be friends, while the PRC and the ROK were born to be enemies. When the communist PRC established in mainland China in 1949, there was already the anti-communist ROK. Even though some South Koreans had personal relations with Sun Yat Sen, held in high respect by both the PRC and the Republic of China (ROC or Taiwan), it did not help in establishing relations between the PRC and South Korea, primarily because the two countries had different ideologies for their foundation of the state. There was no consideration of seeking common grounds while accepting differences (*qiucuntongyi*, 求存同異), which was the Chinese favored rhetoric for advancing practical interests. For example, when the *People's Daily* reported the establishment of the Korean government and the inauguration of President Rhee Syngman on August 12, 1948, it used unrefined words such as "imperialist," "treacherous guy," and "puppet" (*People's Daily* 1948). As a corollary, the two countries had no diplomatic ties. China recognized North Korea as the only legitimate regime on the Korean Peninsula, and South Korea recognized Taiwan as the sole legitimate government of China. This antagonistic relationship between China and South Korea was deepened by the Korean War. They became real enemies who fiercely fought each other on the battlefield. Additionally, undermining any potential of good relations, Mao Zedong's eldest son, Mao Anying, was killed in the Korea War by U.S. bombing (Roblin 2017).

These hostile relations between the two countries continued until the early 1970s. There had been encounters occasionally in the 1960s.[32] For example, sports teams from the two countries, such as ping-pong and volleyball teams, played against each other in international matches (*Kyunghyang Shinmun* 1965; 1969). In addition to the civilian-level encounters, there were

Identity and Chinese foreign policy 35

accidental contacts at the government level. For instance, people from the two countries had armistice meetings at the Panmunjom demilitarized area – two Chinese pilots even defected to South Korea by flying their aircraft there in 1961 (Chung 2007, 30). Both South Korea and China attended a non-nuclear states conference organized by the United Nations (*Kyunghyang Shinmun* 1968). But these contacts were not between friends, and for China, the perceived identity of South Korea from the 1940s to the 1960s, i.e., in Mao's era, was nothing more than an enemy.

Probable good neighbor

In the 1970s, as the world moved toward detente, China's view on South Korea changed gradually, albeit very slowly. For example, Chinese newspapers began to use a different language for South Korea: the *People's Daily* now called South Korean leaders "Park Chung Hee authorities (*Piao Zheng Xi dangju*, 朴正熙当局)," instead of labeling the government as the "Park Chung Hee puppet regime (*Piao Zheng Xi kuileidangu*, 朴正熙傀儡当局)" as in the 1960s (*People's Daily* Database).[33] However, it was South Korea that was most active in seeking improved relations. In 1971, South Korean Foreign Minister Kim Yong Sik said that the Korean government was examining expanding trade with the PRC in a feasible direction (*Kyunghyang Shinmun* 1971). In 1973, South Korea radically changed its foreign policy especially toward the communist bloc by abandoning the Hallstein Doctrine – a key tenet of West Germany's foreign policy, which stipulated that the country would not establish or maintain diplomatic relations with any state that recognized East Germany. Moreover, Seoul suggested directly to Beijing that the two countries should have negotiations for delineating the boundaries of the continental shelf between the two countries, and the following year, they lifted the ban on postal exchanges with communist countries including China (Chung 2007, 31).

However, China seemed to control the speed of exchanges with South Korea. After the normalization of relations with Japan and the United States in 1972 and 1979, respectively, China saw no reason to speed up normalization with South Korea. Furthermore, it could not help but pay careful attention to its friend North Korea. So, when Deng Xiaoping met with a Japanese press delegation in March 1980, he stressed that "it would not be in China's best interest to develop relations with South Korea" (Chung 2007, 57). Although some believe that Deng's words were only a diplomatic tactic to reassure North Korea (Chung 2007, 57), it was too early to judge whether the China's perception of South Korean identity had dramatically altered from enemy to potential partner. The Sino-South Korean relations during the period of the 1970s and the early 1980s can be summarized with then Chinese Foreign Minister Huang Hua's words that the "gate remained closed but not locked" (Chung 2007, 33; Ye 2017, 15).

36 Identity and Chinese foreign policy

The Chinese unlocked gate increasingly opened to South Korea since the 1980s. A historical incident occurred on May 5, 1983. A Chinese civilian aircraft headed from Shenyang to Shanghai, with 92 passengers and 5 crew members, was hijacked by 6 armed Chinese and landed at a U.S. Army base in Chunchon, South Korea (Haberman 1983). Before this incident, in 1982 and 1983, two Chinese Air Force pilots had defected to South Korea (Yu 1999, 205); China did not respond to either of these defections (Cho 2015). But with the hijacking incident, it was quite different: China immediately sent a telegram to Seoul saying that they would dispatch a delegation to resolve the matter (Chung 2007, 33). The incident was settled to the satisfaction of both the countries. All passengers and the aircraft crew returned to China, and the hijackers were sent to Taiwan as they wanted after temporary imprisonment (Chung 2007, 33).

The most significant result of this resolution was that it laid the groundwork for a normalization process between China and South Korea. First, this incident and the visit of the Chinese delegation to South Korea were the first official contact between the two countries since the end of the Korean War. Second, both used formal country names in communicating with or about each other. Before this incident, South Korea referred to China as Junggong (중공), which meant a Chinese communist country, instead of the PRC. In South Korea, at that time, the term "China" was only used to refer to the ROC (Taiwan). Similarly, China called South Korea *nanchaoxian* (南朝鮮), which indicated south of Chosun, instead of the ROK (Dae Han Min Guk), because it called North Korea Chosun. But in its telegram about the hijacking incident, China for the first time used its formal name, the ROK (Chung 2007, 33).

Furthermore, representatives from the two countries signed a memorandum of understanding by using their formal national names. Despite some conflict over using the official names on the document, they agreed to sign by removing the expression of "on behalf of the government" (Li 2009, 400; Fenghuangwang 2010). The process of negotiation provided the momentum that helped China change the perceived identity of South Korea from an enemy (or friend's enemy) to a good neighbor – and China subsequently incrementally expanded unofficial contact with South Korea (Liu 1991, 53; Li 2009, 401–404). Gong Ro-myung, then the head of the Korean representative and later foreign minister, believed that China understood South Korea's sincere intention that it did not want hostility anymore and wanted to establish a constructive relationship with China (Roh and Jung 2011).

Following these events, open trade between China and South Korea was initiated in 1979 (Liu 1991, 53). Although some trade had occurred, and was an open secret, before that time,[34] it was clandestine and indirect, via Singapore and Hong Kong, because both countries did not want to provoke their friends, North Korea and Taiwan (Chung 2007, 34–35). Nonetheless, the trade volume between the two countries dramatically increased by more than ten times during the 1980s (Chung 2007, 35–41; Snyder 2009, 40–42).

Identity and Chinese foreign policy 37

The prediction of Chinese leaders, including Deng Xiaoping, that normalization with South Korea would take some time was overturned thanks to the sharp increase in trade, which led to a closer economic relationship (Snyder 2009, 42). China was therefore ready to make friends with South Korea by the late 1980s.

Win-win friend

South Korea became a friend to China with the normalization of their diplomatic relations on August 24, 1992. Furthermore, their relations have been closer, politically and economically, since the normalization. According to a joint communique describing the normalization, the two countries had agreed to "develop durable good-neighborly relations of cooperation" (UPI 1992). The good-neighborly relations were confirmed when Chinese President Jiang Zemin first paid a state visit to Seoul. In their conversation about mutual concerns, the two leaders concluded that China and South Korea could be good neighbors against the bad neighbor Japan because of their common historical tragedy of Japanese colonial rule (Snyder 2009, 88).

The good-neighborly relations were upgraded to a "cooperative partnership for the twenty-first century" in November 1998 when South Korean President Kim Dae-jung visited Beijing (Lee 2010, 287). The cooperative partnership can be understood as a relationship between states that have no fundamental conflict of national interests and have mutual interests (Kim 2009, 294). Only two years later, the relationship between the two countries was elevated once again to "all round" cooperative partnership when Chinese Premier Zhu Rongji visited Seoul in October 2000. The use of the word "all round" indicated that China might have already had the intention to expand the area of cooperation into the political sector (Snyder 2009, 90). In fact, defense ministers of the two countries had begun to visit each other reciprocally around the time of Premier Zhu's visit. South Korean Defense Minister Cho Sung-tae went to China in 1999 for the first time after normalization and Defense Minister Kim Dong-shin visited Beijing in 2001, while Chinese Defense Minister Chi Haotian went to Seoul in 2000 (Lee 2012, 4; Jung 2015, 43).

Sino-South Korean relations continued to develop into closer strategic relations. In August 2003, the presidents of China and South Korea, Hu Jintao and Roh Moo-hyun, had a summit in Beijing and agreed to upgrade relations to a "comprehensive cooperative partnership" (Snyder 2009, 92; Lee 2010, 288). "All round" and "comprehensive" have no stark difference, but the latter involves more practical cooperation and the highest level of partnership, rather than a more limited strategic partnership (Kim 2009, 302; Lee 2010, 127). For example, the two countries agreed to set up a hotline for military communication, according to the comprehensive cooperative partnership, which was a step further than simply exchanges between top military personnel in joint meetings (Kim 2009, 302; Jung 2015, 46).

38 *Identity and Chinese foreign policy*

President Hu's address before the South Korean National Assembly on November 2005 describes the implications of China's changing perceived identity of South Korea. He asserted that relations between two countries had entered "the best stage in history," argued that they should politically "become a model of peaceful coexistence between countries that have different social systems," and celebrated that the two countries should culturally be "friends that can learn from and complement each other" (Du 2005). After South Korean President Lee Myung-bak took office in 2008, China and South Korea finally moved into a strategic level of relationship when President Lee visited China in May 2008. At the summit, President Hu defined China as "a close neighbor of the peninsula and a friend of the south and north of the Korean Peninsula" (Ministry of Foreign Affairs of China 2008). Furthermore, Hu answered in the affirmative when President Lee jokingly said, "I met President Hu Jintao for the first time today, and during the talks, I felt like a friend I had known for a long time. I'm not sure if President Hu thought so" (Song 2008).

These improvements in political relations, from good neighbor to strategic cooperative partner, were, arguably, overshadowed by the even more rapidly warming of economic relations between the two countries. For example, Sino-South Korean trade increased remarkably since the normalization of diplomatic ties in 1992, as seen in Figure 2.5. In 2018, South Korea was China's third largest trading partner, following the United States and Japan, excluding Hong Kong (Workman 2019). In addition to trade, the number of Chinese visitors to South Korea surged (see Figure 2.6).[35]

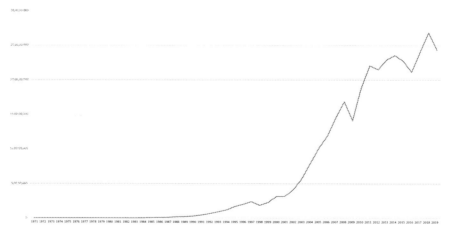

Figure 2.5 Trade Volume Between China and South Korea, 1979–2018 (US$ Millions).
Source: K-Start (http://stat.kita.net).

Identity and Chinese foreign policy 39

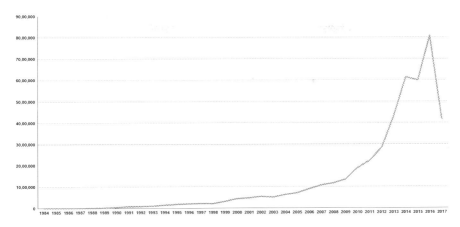

Figure 2.6 Chinese Visitors to South Korea, 1984–2017.
Source: Korea Tourism Statistics (kto.visitkorea.or.kr).

The above is evidence that the Chinese perception of South Korea's identity changed from enemy to friend post the normalization. Although there are conflicts between the two countries, such as over the Northeast Project,[36] China generally behaves like a friend to South Korea since that country's perceived identity has changed to friend. For instance, on the question of Japan's claim over the Dokdo Island (which the ROK has long claimed sovereignty over), Chinese Foreign Ministry Spokesperson Hua Chunying, in an unprecedented instance, said,

> China hopes that the ROK and Japan can appropriately settle relevant issues through dialogue and consultation. I must point out that territorial disputes between Japan and its neighbors all stem from Japanese militarism's wartime aggression and colonial rule. The Japanese side should deeply reflect on history and take real actions to win trust from its Asian neighbors.
>
> (Foreign Ministry of China 2014)

Moreover, China signed a currency swap agreement with South Korea in 2009 which was renewed in 2014 and 2017. The agreement contributed to maintaining the financial stability of South Korea in the face of the global financial crisis in 2008.

In short, China and South Korea are friends because of diplomatic ties (an evidence of social bonds); frequent meetings including summits, which demonstrate social contacts; and many expressions of intimacy, which are conveyed through their behavior and official statements. Therefore, for China, the perceived identity of South Korea is that of a friend.

40 *Identity and Chinese foreign policy*

Japan: from enemy to rival

Unforgettable history

Historically, China has been sometimes invaded and/or conquered by other nations. In the process, however, all nations who conquered China in the pre-modern era were eventually assimilated into the Chinese culture and political traditions over time, except imperial Japan. China suffered an unforgettable humiliation when it was partially occupied by a brutal Japan from the mid-1930s to the mid-1940s (which followed China's previous defeat by Japan in 1894–1895 in a conflict over supremacy on the Korean Peninsula). It was particularly humiliating for China, since Japan had long been placed at the bottom of the Asian hierarchy created by China during its own period of ascendancy in earlier eras. This experience of Japanese colonialism underlies China's continued long-term animosity toward Japan (He 2013, 223).

The animosity was not mitigated at all even after Japan's surrender in 1945 and the establishment of the PRC in 1949, because China and Japan were locked into opposing camps from the beginning of the Cold War: China in the communist bloc and Japan in the free world. As a result of these opposing views, then Japanese Prime Minister Yoshida Shigeru came up with a plan of "counter infiltration," which aimed to overthrow the communist regime in China by sending Japanese people into China through trade activities and encouraging anti-communist movements there (Inoue 2009). China also strengthened its hostility toward Japan. For example, the Sino-Soviet Treaty of Friendship, Alliance and Mutual Assistance, which was concluded in 1950, clearly stated that

> [t]wo Contracting Parties undertake to carry out jointly all necessary measures within their power to prevent a repetition of aggression and breach of the peace *by Japan* or any other State which might directly or indirectly join *with Japan* in acts of aggression [emphasis added].[37]

PARTNER *for economic growth*

Despite the lasting animosity, there were some efforts at exchanges and co-operation between the two countries in the economic sector. In 1960, Chinese Premier Zhou Enlai announced the concept of "friendship trade," which allowed business ties with certain Japanese companies that China recognized as "friendly." In addition to "friendship trade," he came up with the concept of "memorandum trade" in 1962, which aimed to increase the trade between China and Japan to US$100 million annually (Burns 2000, 39). However, these attempts failed to improve the relationship between the two countries, which continued to be hostile in accordance with China's negative view of Japan that was exacerbated by the anti-China stance of Sato Eisaku, a newly elected Japanese Prime Minister, and by the Cultural Revolution in China (Burns 2000, 39; Dreyer 2016, 115; Rose and Sýkora 2017, 108). During the era of Cultural Revolution, it was argued by the Chinese elite that if Japanese representatives wanted to negotiate for better trade with China, they should be required "to praise the Cultural Revolution, to study the little red book of Chairman Mao's quotations, and to listen to prolonged political lectures delivered by their Chinese counterparts" (Lee 1984, 7).

Still, there were episodes of warming of relations between the two countries. Spurred by the detente between the United States and China in the early 1970s, along with the end of the Cultural Revolution and the resignation of Japan's anti-Chinese Prime Minister Sato, China and Japan agreed to normalize their relations in 1972. The two countries finally signed a Treaty of Peace and Friendship in 1978. Japan also provided a loan to China when the latter started pursuing the policy of economic reform and opening up, and did not stop economic trade even when Western states cut off such exchanges due to the Tiananmen Square Massacre in 1989 (Kim 2016a, 35–36).

However, the warming of relations did not mean that China changed its perception of Japan fundamentally, as it did in its relationship with South Korea. Apart from economic exchanges, serious conflicts continued between Japan and the PRC over territorial as well as historical issues. In April 1978, dozens of Chinese fishing boats appeared around the waters of the Senkaku Islands/Daoyudao and some of them carried placards claiming China's sovereignty over the Islands (Cheng 1984/1985, 105). Moreover, Chinese Vice Premier Gu Mu stated unambiguously that the Islands belonged to China when he visited Japan to seek financial aid in August 1978 (Dreyer 2016, 168). Furthermore, political tensions between the two countries mounted over conflict over historical issues, such as conflict over the distortion of Japan's imperialist history in Japanese high school textbooks in 1982 and Prime Minister Nakasone Yasuhiro's official visit to the Yasukuni Shrine in 1985, where Class A Japanese war criminals are enshrined among the 2.5 million soldiers (Rose and Sýkora 2017, 111).

Although there were many mutual visits by top leaders from China and Japan in the 1990s, they could not change China's view of Japan. Most recently, China has been suspicious about Japan's move to send its peace-keeping troops overseas to cooperate with the United States on the missile defense and to increase its military spending (Burns 2000, 53).

Rival, close to enemy

In the 2000s, especially during the Koizumi Junichiro administration from 2001 to 2006, relations between Japan and China became worse because of Prime Minister Koizumi's visit to the Yasukuni Shrine (Tsunekawa 2009, 104–106; Chung 2012). Also, owing to China's rising power in the region, not only economically but also militarily, Japan began to see China as a potential threat. A drastic change occurred during the first term of Prime

42 *Identity and Chinese foreign policy*

Minister Abe Shinzo (2006–2007) when Prime Minister Abe upgraded the relations between Japan and China, seeking to build a strategic relationship of mutual benefit (Prime Minister of Japan and His Cabinet 2006; Jiang 2007). After reelection, during his second term that started in 2012, however, Prime Minister Abe and his administration regarded China as a direct security threat to Japan because of two cases of territorial dispute over the Senkaku Islands in 2010 and 2012 (Sakaki 2015; Hughes 2016; Lind 2016). In 2010, Japan detained the Chinese captain of a fishing boat on the charge of intruding in the waters off the Senkaku Islands, and China suddenly stopped its export of rare earth materials to Japan in retaliation. In 2012, the Governor of Tokyo Ishihara Shintaro ordered the Tokyo municipal government to nationalize three islets in the Senkaku Islands by purchasing them from a private Japanese owner, and later, the central government decided to nationalize them instead of relying on the local government. In response, China sent more than 1,000 fishing boats to the waters around the islets, claiming territorial sovereignty over them.

Having experienced these conflicts, the Abe administration eventually defined China as Japan's main national security threat in its defense white papers. For example, in the defense white paper of 2018, Japanese Defense Minister Onodera Itsunori states:

> China's recent activities, including its rapid military modernization and enhancement of operational capabilities, its unilateral escalation of actions in areas around Japan, and with the lack of transparency in the military build-up, present a strong security concern for the region including Japan and the international community.
>
> (Ministry of Defense of Japan 2018, i)

China similarly regards Japan as a rival that is very close to being an enemy. China has refused to recognize Japan's post-Second World War identity of a peaceful normal state (Gustafsson 2015, 129). Further, it is believed that China regards Japan as a security threat as well. For instance, China Central Television (CCTV) broadcast the military drill of the PLA Air Force that assumed Japan as a hypothetical enemy in 2014.[38] Moreover, according to a document written by strategists with the Chinese PLA, China posited Japan as number three among five potential threats including the United States, North Korea, the South China Sea dispute, and India.[39] Besides, Chinese President Xi Jinping had been reluctant to have a summit with Japanese Prime Minister Abe Shinzo for several years. In October 2018, these leaders had a summit in Beijing for the first time since 2012, which was their first time meeting in person except for a short meeting at the Asia-Pacific Economic Cooperation (APEC) summit in 2014.

Thus, in contrast to its ties with North Korea and South Korea, it is clear that China does not perceive Japan as a friend. Also, given China's proclaimed identity as a great power, it is inevitable for Sino-Japanese relations to experience heightened tensions, because both China and Japan seek supremacy in the region. And even though China and Japan have tried to improve their relations, especially after the normalization of diplomatic ties in 1978, economic interdependence has not led to political intimacy. China has refused to hold meetings between top leaders of the two countries despite Japan's repeated requests for several years. Besides, China has repeatedly denounced Japan for territorial and historical issues. Furthermore, it is hard to find enough social exchanges or expressions of intimacy to consider the two countries as friends.

Can the realist approach strike back?

Chinese foreign policy is shaped largely by its own proclaimed identity, and China's policies toward North Korea, South Korea, and Japan depend on their perceived identities. This argument accords with a key principle of constructivist social theory that "people act toward objects on the basis of the meaning that the objects have for them" (Wendt 1992, 396–397). In this sense, states are not alike because they can have different identities, differing perceived national interests, and differing meaning attached to events. However, some might not agree with this explanation. Perhaps, the refutation of the realist school of thought is the most important to consider. Both structural realists and neoclassical realists believe that states have similar objective interests with an anarchical international system. In that system the actual balance of power among states is very important in explaining unitary states' behavior to seek survival. A difference between these two realist schools of thought is that neoclassical realists take into serious consideration domestic factors that are neglected by structural realists (Viotti and Kauppi 2012, 43).

Structural realism

In the structural realists' view, especially the Waltzian view, the ordering principle of the international system is anarchy. Waltz argues that political structures can be defined by the organizing or ordering principle, the differentiation of units and the specification of their functions, and the distribution of capabilities (Waltz 1979). In regard to the ordering principle, international political systems are different from domestic political systems because domestic systems are centralized and hierarchical, whereas international systems are decentralized and anarchic (Waltz 1979, 88). In the arena of international politics, all states are equal because they each have their own sovereignty. Moreover, in IR, there is no entity that is able to monopolize the legitimate use of force as a government does. Of course, violence between sovereign states can be punished, such as the use of armed sanctions by the international community against Iraq's invasion into Kuwait in 1990. However, these armed punishments are uncommon. For example,

44 *Identity and Chinese foreign policy*

even though the then U.N. Secretary General Kofi Annan explicitly declared that the United States-led war on Iraq was illegal, no states were punished (Tyler 2004).

Because the international system is an anarchy, the absence of a world government leads states to the world of self-help (Waltz 1979, 104, 111). In addition, self-help in the international political system is "individualist in origin, spontaneously generated, and unintended" (Waltz 1979, 91). States act to ensure their security for themselves, and thus survival becomes their primary goal (Waltz 1979, 91–92, 105, 111). In the same vein, their preferences are also fixed (Legro and Moravcsik 1999, 12). Therefore, their functions are not differentiated, and they are all implied to have sameness as a unitary actor seeking survival, because states remain the same independent units as long as anarchy persists (Waltz 1979, 93, 104).

Moreover, anarchy is the permissive cause of war. Anarchy does not necessarily mean chaos, disorder, or conflict per se (Mearsheimer 1994, 10; 2001, 38). However, Waltz (1954; 1979) believes that anarchy is the cause of conflicts. Waltz (1954) divides the causes of war into three images: human nature (the first image), domestic system (the second image), and international anarchy (the third image). For him, the third image is the most important. He admits that the combination of the three images may enhance accurate understanding of IR because any one of the images is not sufficient (Waltz 1954, 14, 223). However, he thinks that the immediate causes of war, which are contained in the first and second images, are insignificant in many ways and cannot explain the recurrence of war (Waltz 1954, 232–235). This recurrence of war can be explained only by the third image that he wants to name a permissive or underlying cause of war (Waltz 1954, 232). After all, anarchy is a feature of the international system that makes states act uniformly to pursue self-help to survive. This self-help system prevents states from cooperating because of unequal distribution of gains, and due to fear of being subordinated to others (Waltz 1979, 105–107). Even though states can "form" the structure of international political systems by their interaction (Waltz 1979, 95), they cannot change key properties of the structure such as self-help. Therefore, this anarchy is likely to be violence-permissive and conflictual (Grieco 1997, 165).

Neoclassical realism

Neoclassical realism is worthy of consideration in foreign policy studies because scholars in this tradition look inside a state to explain its behavior. Even though Waltz (1979) strongly criticizes efforts to look into a state's domestic dynamics to explain its behavior as reductionism, many scholars, including neoclassical realists, pay attention to domestic politics for understanding world politics.

Like structural realism, neoclassical realism – a term coined by Gideon Rose (1998) – views the state as the most important actor in IR, and describes

Identity and Chinese foreign policy 45

state behavior as determined by anarchy and relative distribution of power. However, it is different from structural realism because it can provide the groundwork for a "general theory of foreign policy" by bridging the gap between structural realism and liberalism (Rose 1998, 145–148). It emphasizes "how systemic pressures are translated thorough unit-level intervening variables" (Rose 1998, 152). Neoclassical realists try to find these intervening variables by considering domestic politics, state power and processes, leaders' perceptions, and the impact of ideas to explain how states react to the international environment (Kitchen 2010, 118). For example, when it comes to explaining U.S. foreign policy, neoclassical realist Zakaria (1998) emphasizes how the power balance between the executive and the Congress shapes foreign policy, while Christensen (1996) pays attention to the role of public opinion.

Because domestic factors are an intervening variable, they have a limit in terms of their causal role. They do not determine state motives but "narrow down the range of acceptable policy options" (Dueck 2006, 25). This is well reflected in the discussion of Chinese nationalism and foreign policy. For example, the international behavior of contemporary China is far less puzzling when one considers China's search for positive collective self-esteem and its desire for great-power status, which can be managed domestically by political elites (Larson and Shevchenko 2014). Moreover, Chinese international behavior corresponds to relatively specific patterns of action inherited from exemplary episodes in that nation's history. The reenactment of such patterns allows Chinese foreign policy to be meaningful to the Chinese themselves (Shih 1993; Katzenstein 1997).

In addition to elite motivations, the masses who share the cultural understanding to which elites might appeal are influential (Grove 2010, 774). Some argue that Chinese nationalism would not make Chinese foreign policy assertive and offensive (Downs and Saunders 1998/1999; Zheng 1999; Zhao 2004a; Duan 2017), whereas others insist that Chinese nationalism can escalate to cause conflicts by being intertwined with China's grievances against the existing international order and its confidence due to its own growing economy (McCormick 2000). Meanwhile, the nature of Chinese nationalism can influence the overall character of its foreign policy, shaping it to be either offensive or defensive, and Chinese nationalism can also influence specific decisions in foreign policy by providing leverage to decision makers in terms of their consideration of domestic audience cost (Weiss 2014).

Unrealistic realism

Both structural realism and neoclassical realism are not persuasive in explaining China's inconsistent behaviors in the cases studied here. First of all, they are flawed in the theory itself. Waltz's explanation of anarchy as the ordering principle of the international system seems very simple, and overly parsimonious. It is true that anarchy is important to understand

46 *Identity and Chinese foreign policy*

international systems as well as causes of war. Nevertheless, the reality of international politics undermines his argument about how anarchy works. For example, Waltz repeatedly predicted the rise of a balance of powers against the United States after the end of the Cold War, because there was only a change in the ordering of national powers after the Cold War, not a change of the anarchical system itself, which endured and would endure (Waltz 1993, 2000). So far, however, we have not witnessed the balancing of powers against the United States. On the contrary, we have witnessed a burgeoning of global cooperation in many areas, from anti-terrorism to information communications and technology sharing.

Furthermore, the question of why some states such as Vietnam and Indonesia have less interest in strengthening their military capabilities, even under anarchy, cannot be answered by the realist approach. Besides, in this uncooperative and conflictual jungle, how can the world have seen more creation, than deaths, of states in recent years? Of course, these dynamics might occur not because of changing constructivist identity but because of the changing threats or distribution of power in the international system, as realists would argue. Or, they might be caused by changes in both identity and power, given the fact that explanations based on power and explanations based on identity are not mutually exclusive (Hudson 2014, 135).

However, this logic cannot be applied to explaining South Korean policy toward North Korea, as briefly discussed in Chapter 1. Despite no significant change in power and threat, South Korea has changed its North Korean policy according to its perceived identity of North Korea – swinging from a rival nation to defeat to being a potential friend and partner. Thus, it might be more plausible to posit that the changing perceived identity of other states can lead to the changing foreign policy of the state, more than changing nature of the international distribution of power.

Neoclassical realism is ideal to supplement the weaknesses of structural realism, due to its focus on how domestic politics shapes foreign policy and the international system. Domestic politics in this approach becomes an independent variable (or sometimes intervening variable) and foreign policy is the dependent variable. But this theorized consideration of how domestic politics interacts with realist assessments of the international balance of power in an anarchical system is too ideal. The approach often reduces the influence of domestic politics in any given case, in order not to abandon the conception of international pressure. But at the same time, international pressure such as the level of threat is hard to grasp and vague to define in terms of its influence on state behavior (Narizny 2017, 169). However, domestic factors are often more influential than neoclassical realists assume. For example, South Korea canceled its plan to establish the General Security of Military Information Agreement (GSOMIA) with Japan in 2012. The South Korean government tried to sign the Agreement with Japan in order to effectively counter security threats from North Korea, but it withdrew the

Identity and Chinese foreign policy 47

plan only because of South Korean's strong domestic opposition based on a nationalist domestic uprising, with strong anti-Japanese sentiment.

For these reasons, foreign policy studies on culture and identity can provide useful explanations that are often neglected by other approaches, particularly neorealism. For example, it is impossible to understand the reason why South Korea is unwilling to participate in the trilateral security cooperation with the United States and Japan to deter the North Korean threat without considering South Korea's strong anti-Japanese sentiment. From the realist view, South Korea should cooperate with Japan because the two countries have the same security goal to address the North Korean problem. Nevertheless, anti-Japanese sentiment in South Korea, which functions as a domestic factor, has not allowed South Korean leaders to cooperate with Japan. According to annual national surveys in South Korea, Japanese Prime Minister Abe has been always the most unpopular figure in South Korea among five leaders of Northeast Asian countries, including North Korean Leader Kim Jong-un. On a lighter note, South Koreans joke, though they widely accept it to be true, that the South Korean national soccer team can be defeated by any other national team, except the Japanese team – a point of unique cultural importance to the South Korean domestic public.

In addition to these flaws, structural realism and neoclassical realism are not appropriate to explain China's case. It is unrealistic that China should care about its survival today. Of course, it might be argued that China must worry about its survival because it was conquered and occupied by others in the past, including Japan. However, is it possible for present China to perish? It is too big to die, considering its large territory, huge population, strong military, and solid economy. Furthermore, as China always asserts, it puts emphasis on prosperity rather than survival. In addition, China has expressed different attitudes toward some interstate affairs covered in the study that cannot be explained by an appeal to realist state pursuit of self-interest and survival, which raised the initial research questions of this book. For example, the realist approach cannot well explain China's puzzling responses to similar actions by South Korea and Japan (i.e., the installation of military radar systems). Thus, this chapter proposes that identity plays the role of an independent variable in Chinese foreign policy, rather than being an intervening variable.

Neoclassical realism takes into account domestic factors as an intervening variable that influences the international system in shaping foreign policy. However, this study uses culture as a moderating variable that influences Chinese foreign policy. In addition, the direction is different. In neoclassical realism, the international system shapes the manner by which domestic factors (the second image) influence foreign policy, while this study takes the approach of focusing on domestic factors as independent and moderating variables, shaping foreign policy independently of the existing international system.

48 *Identity and Chinese foreign policy*

Nevertheless, two propositions from the realist view still need to be considered:

1 It might be true that international factors, including the Sino-U.S. relationship, affect the seemingly capricious attitudes of China.
2 National interests, or China's core interests, are more significant than any other factors in shaping China's relationship to the states investigated in this book.

However, the first proposition is not examined in the book because the U.S. factor is considered the control variable in the study of the effects of culture and identity on Sino-North Korean, Sino-South Korean, and Sino-Japanese relations. (If my arguments were to be rejected by the case studies, then the first proposition – that the Sino-U.S. relationship shapes China's responses to the case studies investigated here – could be considered.) Thus, only the second proposition is used to test the following null hypotheses:

H2: *Chinese foreign policy is influenced by Chinese core national interests.*
H2a: *Chinese inconsistent behaviors regarding North Korea are influenced by Chinese core interests.*
H2b: *Chinese inconsistent behaviors regarding South Korea are influenced by Chinese core interests.*
H2c: *Chinese inconsistent behaviors regarding Japan are influenced by Chinese core interests.*

Conclusion

Chinese foreign policy has been long influenced by its proclaimed identity as a great power and has recently been dependent on the proclaimed identity of a responsible great power. In practice, China has tried to behave as a responsible great power in both Sino-North Korean and Sino-South Korean relations. It actively moderated the SPT to tackle the North Korean nuclear issues with the self-consciousness of a responsible great power and sought to promote this image in IR.

Furthermore, China's behaviors vis-à-vis its relationship with North Korea, South Korea, and Japan are based on its perceptions of these countries' respective identities. It treated a friend as a friend and an enemy as an enemy. Though these arguments need to be elaborated by testing possible counterarguments by realists in the following chapters, both Chinese behaviors and statements found in the CFMSA and the *People's Daily* database sufficiently support them. For instance, China referred to South Korea 2,529 times and North Korea 5,527 times in the CFMSA database by using the word "friendly," whereas it mentioned Japan 5,916 times mainly using the less committal word "neighbor." In short, China and North Korea, as

Identity and Chinese foreign policy 49

well as China and South Korea, have social bonds, social contacts, and expressions of intimacy (through words and actions) just as friends do. However, despite social bonds of normalization between China and Japan, the two countries have had few social exchanges in times of conflicts and only rare expressions of intimacy via words and behaviors in their relations. Thus, North Korea and South Korea are perceived by China as friends, but Japan's perceived identity is not of a friend.

Notes

1 In this book, "identity" mainly indicates state identity because one of the goals of the study is to find the relationship between identity and a state's foreign policy in inter-state relations. Of course, it is not just state identity that is closely related to foreign policy. For instance, national identity can affect a state's foreign policy, especially at the domestic level. For details regarding national identity and foreign policy, see Prizel (1998).
2 The two identities here are not entirely new. Many scholars use a similar concept of identities. For example, even though Hoo (2018) uses the concept of global identity like Shambaugh (2013), he also used exactly the same term "proclaimed identity" in his dissertation that served as a springboard to his later book. Apart from this, the terms "imagined identity" and "self-identity", used by Lee (2018a), are very similar to proclaimed and perceived identities. However, *imagined identity* seems to have an implicit unreality because of the word imagined. Furthermore, Lee's notion of self-identity does not rely on the necessity of subjective proclamation by a state actor, and is based more on a concept of objective reality. Thus, my use of the terms proclaimed and perceived state identities is similar to, but still different from, these other scholars' use of these terms.
3 Mitzen (2006) named this kind of psychological security the ontological security, contrasting with physical security.
4 Maybe it was a mistake, but the U.S. government once recognized North Korea as a nuclear state in 2008. A report by the U.S. military claimed that the Asian continent had five nuclear powers: China, India, Pakistan, Russia, and North Korea (U.S. Joint Armed Forces Command 2008, 32).
5 According to Ichiro Ozawa, who was the former secretary-general of the Liberal Democratic Party in Japan and used this term first, "normal state" means a state that is willing to shoulder the responsibilities given by the international community and cooperates fully with other states in their efforts to build prosperous and stable lives for their people (Katahara 2007, 110). This definition is too ideal, however, given Japan's moves to be militarized as part of pursuit of "normal state" status.
6 North Korea recently often uses the term "strategic state" instead of referring to itself as a "nuclear state," but the conceptual meaning has no difference.
7 The so-called notion of "Mount Baekdu bloodline" has been used by the Kim family to legitimize its iron-fist rule in North Korea for the past seven decades. Mount Baekdu is the highest mountain on the Korean Peninsula, which people have considered as a sacred place from ancient times. It is also where North Korean founding leader Kim Il-sung is said to have fought against Japanese occupation forces, and where his son Kim Jong-il is said to have been born (Choon 2017).
8 The concept of reputation is also somewhat similar to Chinese face culture, which is discussed in detail in Chapter 4.

50 *Identity and Chinese foreign policy*

9 For the details about the formation of state identity, see Wendt (1994), Larson (2011), and Cho (2012).

10 Identity is relatively stable because it has some physical elements such as size or territory that are hard to change (Chafetz et al. 1998, 11–12).

11 Although President Roh was elected by direct presidential election after democratization movements in 1987, it is hard to describe his government as democratic because he was a military leader-turned politician and participated in an earlier military coup with his predecessor Chun.

12 For criticism on "sunshine policy," see Kim (2018).

13 Other than the presidents in Table 2.1, there were two other presidents who had no real power and several acting presidents in South Korea. All governments have a unification policy that is different from the NK policy. Only the four governments of Kim Dae-jung, Roh Moo-hyun, Lee Myung-bak, and Park Geun-hye named their NK policy.

14 "North Korea No. 2 Threat to Beijing after U.S., Chinese Military Strategists Say." *The Japan Times.* Retrieved from https://www.japantimes.co.jp/news/2017/01/31/asia-pacific/north-korea-no-2-threat-u-s-pla-strategists-say/#.XL_ftuhKi00

15 The Kim Dae-jung government that saw North Korea as the cooperative partner did not publish defense white papers from 2001 to 2003 to avoid the controversy over using the term of the enemy for North Korea.

16 Larry Kudlow, economic adviser to the U.S. President Trump, said "China is a first-world economy, behaving like a third-world economy" (Lester and Zhu 2018).

17 The discourse of the "Century of Humiliation" has been often used to promote Chinese nationalism with the notion of revival of Great China (Callahan 2010).

18 The translation is quoted from Shambaugh (2013). For this phrase and framework of a new type of great power relations, see the *People's Daily* news article by Chang et al. (2016).

19 In an address at the Central Conference on Work Relating to Foreign Affairs held in Beijing on June 2–23, 2018, President Xi called for efforts to break new ground in major country diplomacy with Chinese characteristics, with the guidance of the thought on the diplomacy of socialism with Chinese characteristics for a new era. He suggested ten points for foreign policy, and the second was to "advance major country diplomacy with Chinese characteristics to fulfill the mission of realizing national rejuvenation" (Yan 2018).

20 Other than China, the results show that China often uses the term to describe the United States, Russia, and India, while seldom uses it to describe other major powers such as Japan, France, or Germany.

21 Of the phrases containing *daguo*, "a new type of great power relations" is the most used in the press conferences of Ministry of Foreign Affairs of PRC, which recorded 100 uses of that term.

22 It is believed that Chinese scholar Wang Yizhou originated use of the term in China in his article "Chinese Diplomacy Oriented Toward the 21st Century" in 1999 (Shirk 2007, 107).

23 Deng opposes the notion that President Jiang is responsible for the origin of the responsible great power term. He argues that no national leaders contributed to the origin of the term (Deng 2015, 118).

24 Deng (2015) and Mao (2017) think Zoellick's remarks as the origin of the debate on the responsible great power.

25 Searching the phrase "blood alliance (*xuemeng*,血盟)" on the Database of People's Daily, China National Knowledge Infrastructure, and the website of Ministry of Foreign Affairs of PRC returns no results.

26 When Chinese President Xi Jinping first met with Korean President Moon Jae-in on the eve of G20 Summit in Berlin in 2017, the South Korean presidential

office, Chungwadae (Blue House), released to the press that Chinese President Xi mentioned "blood alliance" in talking about North Korean issue. The truth was that President Xi described the Sino-North Korean relations as "forged in blood" (*xianxueningcheng*, 鲜血凝成) in the past.

27 There are misunderstandings in South Korean media that the term "traditional friendship" emerged only after the normalization of China and South Korea relations in 1992. One alleged source for this misunderstanding is an article in the *People's Daily* in 1992 that used the expression. However, there are many articles on the *People's Daily* Database that used the term "traditional friendship" before 1992, tracing back to 1958.

28 There is also the opposite argument that the Sino-North Korean relations were not solid because they had different interests. For details of this argument, see Shen and Xia (2015; 2018).

29 Though the close relationship was deepened during the Korean War, there were some conflicts during the war between China and North Korea. Notable conflicts emerged over: (1) Kim Il-sung's insistence on advancing the PLA further to the South, (2) Kim's insistence on launching a counteroffensive against the U.S. troops, (3) Kim's endeavor to secure control over the railway system, (4) Kim's opposition to attacking the South before reaching an armistice (Shen 2013, 5; Shen and Xia 2018, 44–76).

30 It was surprisingly released by Chinese state media in 2011 that the treaty actually has an expiration every 20 years and was already renewed in 1981 and 2001 (Jeon 2018). So, the next renewal is due in 2021.

31 Along with China, Pakistan abstained from voting on Resolution 825.

32 In fact, China agreed to impose sanctions against North Korea before 2016, but was very passive in implementing them. For example, when the United States wanted to blacklist more than four North Korean companies, China agreed to list only three of them (Glaser and Billingsley 2012, 9–11).

33 Although there were very few direct exchanges between China and South Korea, it does not mean that they had no interest in each other. Media search results from the *People's Daily* and the Naver News Library show that newspapers in each country reported on each other almost every day.

34 Although he did not explicitly explain it, Chung (2007) stated that the first time the term "Park Chung Hee authorities" was used in the *People's Daily* was on January 27, 1979. This is not the case because there were many articles that referred to the South Korean government as "Park Chung Hee authorities" before 1979.

35 For instance, the Soviet Union during this time accused China of increasing trade with and showing goodwill to South Korea (*Kyunghyang Shinmun* 1981).

36 The number of visitors plummeted in 2017. This sharp decline is discussed in Chapter 6.

37 China's Northeast Project involves a territorial dispute between South Korea and China over a region that has historically belonged to both China and Korea, and that continues to be a source of diplomatic conflict.

38 Ministry of Foreign Affairs of China. "Conclusion of the 'Sino-Soviet Treaty of Friendship, Alliance and Mutual Assistance'." https://www.fmprc.gov.cn/mfa_eng/ziliao_665539/3602_665543/3604_665547/t18011.shtml

39 "*kongjunshoubaoguangjiaxiangdiri* F-2 (空軍首曝光假想敵日F-2)" *MingPao*. Retrieved from https://news.mingpao.com/pns/%E4%B8%AD%E5%9C%8B/article/20141209/s00013/1418061741675/%E7%A9%BA%E8%BB%8D%E9%A6%96%E6%9B%9D%E5%85%89%E5%81%87%E6%83%B3%E6%95%B5%E6%97%A5f-2

3 Chinese face culture and foreign policy

Culture and identity are not identical, but they are inseparable because they are formed and influenced by each other. For example, identity, particularly collective identity, depends on cultural difference or culturally sanctioned/promoted thinking and behavior. Culture has a great impact on human action and also on state behavior through the following factors, or any combination of them: (1) when it takes the form of worldviews, (2) when it provides criteria for distinguishing right from wrong and just from unjust, and (3) when it explains cause-effect based on shared belief in authority derived from experience and the consensus of recognized elites (Goldstein and Keohane 1993, 8–10).

China is no exception. Rather, it is one of the most prominent examples of states that have a culture-influenced foreign policy. This chapter explores Chinese traditional culture and its influence on foreign policy. Among many features of Chinese culture, this book specifically delves into the Chinese culture of saving face (*mianzi*, 面子), because it is expected to be able to explain China's conflicting behaviors toward perceived friends North and South Korea and perceived potential adversary Japan.

Culture and foreign policy

Culture in foreign policy analysis

The discussion of culture in social science can be traced back to its founding fathers – Karl Marx, Max Weber, and Emile Durkheim – and even to the ancient Greek philosophers, namely, Aristotle, Plato, and Socrates (Wiarda 2014). In the modern development of political science, it was Almond and Verba's *The Civic Culture* (1965) which heralded studies on political culture. It had a very sophisticated theoretical statement about democracy and how it is created and sustained according to various types of political culture: parochial, subject, and civic. Pye (1965) argued that political culture provides structure and meaning in the political sphere in the same manner that culture, in general, gives coherence and integration to social life. Despite its

Chinese face culture and foreign policy 53

relative decline in the 1970s, mainly due to criticism by structuralism and institutionalism, political culture began to make a comeback in the late 1980s to early 1990s (Chilcote 1981; Inglehart 1988; Munck 2007; Wiarda 2014, 105–106). Nationalism has been one of the most preferred topics of a cultural approach, but it has also been used to explain many other phenomena, such as modernization, inter-ethnic violence, and authoritarianism (Gellner 1983; Anderson 1991; Greenfeld and Eastwood 2007; Varshney 2007).

The attention to culture, similar to identity, among IR scholars has notably increased since the collapse of the Soviet Union, because mainstream IR theories failed to foreshadow or properly interpret the aftermath of this event (Katzenstein 1996, 2–4). Following the fall of the Soviet Union, states seemed less likely to ask each other "whose side are you on?" but rather began to ask "who are you?" because the world was no longer dominated by two superpowers, namely, the United States and the Soviet Union (Huntington 1993).

Especially in the post-Cold War era, national identity and nationalism have been examined as a source of international conflicts. Some argue that war can result from surges of nationalism following revolutions (Mansfield and Snyder 1995) and that charismatic leaders who can manipulate national sentiments make conflict more likely (Byman and Pollack 2001), while others maintain that nationalism itself is not a sufficient factor to cause conflict (Posen 1993; Laitin 2007). In these kinds of scholarly debates, culture (i.e., political culture) is essential to the study of politics, including the FPA, because it provides a framework for organizing people's daily worlds by locating the self and making sense of the actions and interpreting the motives of others. It also offers a framework for grounding an analysis of interests, for linking identities to political action, and for predisposing states toward some actions and away from others (Ross 2009, 134).

Influence of culture on foreign policy

Like identity, culture, too, is hard to define. Given various aspects of culture in the study of social science, Hudson suggests one conception that "political culture is all the discourses, values, and implicit rules that express and shape political action and intentions, determine the claims groups may and may not make upon one another, and ultimately provide a logic of political action" (Hudson 2014, 126). One of the significant features of culture, particularly political culture, is that culture influences behavior and interpretations of behavior (Helen Spencer-Oatey 2012, 4). So, culture can be a useful concept for the FPA.[1]

There are some critics who claim that culture affects foreign policy (Welch 2003; Sharp 2004; Breuning 2007). However, culture does matter. Culture frames the context in which politics occurs, links individual and collective identities, and provides a framework for interpreting the actions and motives

54 *Chinese face culture and foreign policy*

of others (Ross 2009, 139–140). In so doing, culture influences the structures and processes of decision-making by shaping perception, cognition, and reasoning (Vlahos 1991; Hudson 1997; Grove 2010). The perception, cognition, and reasoning of national leaders are shaped by internal and external forces. For example, the culture of liberal democracy explains the democratic peace thesis that there is no war between democracies because of their cultural preference for negotiation and dialogue to solve a conflict. Also, the sociocultural similarity between democracies at the international level can play a role in preventing conflicts between them (Geva and Hanson 1999).

Another example is the debate over Chinese strategic culture between Johnston (1995) and Feng (2007). Although strategic culture is related to military strategy rather than foreign policy, cultural influence on foreign policy can be sufficiently inferred from this debate because military strategy is heavily dependent on a state's foreign policy direction. According to Johnston (1995), the long-standing Chinese strategic culture explains Chinese assertive behavior in foreign policy crises during 1949–1985. Relying on his research into Chinese history in *Seven Military Classics*, he argues that China's strategic culture has been offensive despite its weak material capability. His finding refutes the conventional notion of Chinese strategic culture as a product of the Confucian-Mencian paradigm and that thereby understands Chinese strategic culture as peaceful and harmonious.

On the contrary, Feng (2007) notes that Johnston's approach to China's "offensive realism" misses the fact that leaders' beliefs may shift with context. By using a research design that ranks strategic preferences only for "self" and not providing for interactions with the "other," or for changes in the strategic environment, Johnston misses the dynamic relationship between culture and decision-making (Feng 2007). By using the Verb in Context System (VICS) to analyze the relationship between leaders' beliefs as influenced by strategic culture, Feng introduces more rigorous methodological tools to bring the measurement of cultural variables closer to the individuals making the decisions. For example, Feng investigates Mao Zedong's public speeches during the Korean, Sino-Indian, and Sino-Vietnamese wars to see whether Mao's belief system better reflects an offensive or defensive strategic culture.

In sum, the effect of culture on foreign policy is (1) to influence the perception of individuals and groups, and thus to influence the behavior of a state, (2) to shape diplomatic activities through social interaction and language that reflect culture, and (3) to gain domestic support for foreign policy (Zhang 2017, 43–49). Culture provides a tool to understand others and guide behavior because it is the crystallization of the long accumulation of experience and interaction. Furthermore, culture often functions as a diplomatic skill. For example, when they meet, leaders of China, Japan, and South Korea usually use quotes from old Confucian classics, Buddhist texts, or poems that are representative of Asian culture.

Chinese face culture

Face culture means the cultural predisposition to protect one's prestige, honor, or reputation. This face culture is not unique to China but is universal because people are human (Hu 1944; Goffman 1955; Jarvie and Agassi 1969). Although the existence of face culture is universal, the degree to which people take it seriously and the level of its influence on society are not universal. For example, the Japanese are very sensitive to losing face (Pharr 1990), even more than Americans (Kirchner et al. 2017). Furthermore, the Chinese are more concerned about face than Americans at the international level, despite no significant difference at the individual level (Gries 2010; Gries et al. 2011). In China, almost everyone experiences face-related issues in their daily life (Li and Su 2006, 239). So, it is not surprising that 83.2 percent of the respondents of an online survey in 1998 considered face to be very important, whereas only 2.7 percent responded that it was not important (Chan 2006).

Though China, Japan, and South Korea share similar cultural features and relatively emphasize face in their culture, these countries have different attitudes toward face. Concerning the three factors of self-face, other-face, and mutual face, Chinese people place the greatest value on self-face, while South Koreans and Japanese consider mutual face to be the most important (Lee 2015c).[2] This pattern suggests that the Chinese might show aggressive response when they lose their face because self-esteem and humiliation are related to aggression, anger, and violence (Websdale 2010; Walker and Knauer 2011).

How to define face in Chinese culture

Defining an invisible but definitely existing thing is extremely difficult. Although the face is a part of the body, face in cultural meaning is not tangible at all. At the universal level, across cultures, face can be defined as "the positive social value a person effectively claims for himself by the line others assume he has taken during a particular contact," and, thus, as "an image of self-delineated in terms of approved social attributes" (Goffman 1955, 213). More simply, it can be defined as "the public self-image that every member wants to claim for himself," consisting of the negative face and the positive face (Brown and Levinson 1987, 61). Another definition, in a universal sense, is to define face as "the public image which a person claims for himself/ herself and is also recognized by others" (Zhang 2017, 88). Although it has universal character to some degree, face in Chinese culture is very peculiar in that it has practical power in Chinese society. For example, in his book *My Country and My People*, the distinguished Chinese modern thinker Lin Yutang wrote that the "three Muses ruling over China" were "Face, Fate and Favour," and not political leaders (Lin 1936, 186). This notion of face is not physiological but psychological, which can be "granted, and lost and

56 *Chinese face culture and foreign policy*

fought for and presented as a gift" (Lin 1936, 190). In addition, Chinese novelist Lu Xun picked *mianzi* ("face") as "the most complex and potent key to understanding Chinese national character and national spirit" (Hinze 2012, 16). He wrote in an essay:

> Tradition has it that in the Qing Dynasty some foreigner[s] went to the Zhongli Yamen [the Foreign Ministry of imperial China] to make certain demands, and so frightened the mandarins by his threats that they agreed to everything; but when he left he was shown out through a side door. Denial to the main gate meant that he had lost face. If he lost face that meant that China gained face and came off the victor.
>
> (Foster 2006, 157)

Face, as a translation of *mianzi* (面子) or *lian* (脸), is a very significant concept in Chinese society that dominates social interactions through which the Chinese establish and maintain social relations (Jiang 2009). It was Hu Hsien Chin who first introduced Chinese face culture into the academic arena. In her seminal work "The Chinese Concept of 'Face,'" she defined *mianzi* as "a reputation achieved through getting on in life, through success and ostentation," and distinguished it from another notion of face, *lian*, which was "the respect of the group for a man with a good moral reputation" (Hu 1944, 45). In other words, *mianzi* involves the social prestige and reputation of a person, while *lian* indicates a person's moral character and honor (Ju 2016, 280).

In this same vein, a survey analysis showed that citizens of Wuhan city responded by classifying *mianzi* as applicable to social situations with others and *lian* as applicable to moral situations by answering that "adultery revealed" fell under *lian* and "sending a gift declined by receiver" came under *mianzi* (Zuo 1997).[3]

However, the distinction between *mianzi* and *lian* is opposed by the argument that not every Chinese person speaks Mandarin, since a variety of dialects are spoken in China depending on the region. Since China is a big country with many mountains that make it difficult to travel to other regions, people in some regions do not use Mandarin that has both *mianzi* and *lian* in the vocabulary, but speak their own dialects that only have *mianzi* (King and Myers 1977). Nevertheless, according to an empirical study of face, there are correlations between "which places" and the notion of social face, and between "with whom" and the notion of moral face (Ju 2016).

Definition of the universal meaning of face is not very useful for understanding Chinese face culture because there are some essential differences between universally defined face and face with Chinese characteristics.[4] For example, having been greatly influenced by Confucianism, Chinese face culture is strongly intertwined with hierarchical and close relations and the principle of reciprocity (Ho 1976). Of course, it is undesirable to maintain that Chinese face should be distinguished from a universal one, in that it

Chinese face culture and foreign policy 57

can be unsatisfying to argue that "[t]he Chinese act that way because that is the Chinese way" (Pye 1988, 6). Given that differences surely exist between Chinese face and universal face, however, it is more appropriate to use the definition of Chinese face culture, rather than universal face culture, to explain Chinese actions. On the other hand, the distinction between *mianzi* and *lian* has no practical advantage when we discuss Chinese face culture. In fact, Koreans and Japanese use the same word with Chinese characters to express the meaning of face. It is 体面, which literally means body and face, and is pronounced as *chemyeon* in Korean and *taimen* in Japanese. This term includes both social prestige and moral reputation in a single word, similar to how non-mandarin speakers in China use *mianzi* to express two slightly different meanings. In this context, face in English can cover both attributes of Chinese face culture: the moral-oriented face and the social-oriented face. So, I use the singular term face or Chinese face rather than *mianzi* or *lian* in this book, except for situations where clear distinction is needed or the original Chinese wording itself is necessary to be used.[5] For these reasons, Chinese face culture, in this book, is simply defined as a psychologically valuable notion that should not be lost, but saved, and is based on the expected protocol of mutual respect and deference between people, regardless of whether people are Chinese or not. This concept of Chinese face culture also applies to the behavior of states.

The dynamics of Chinese face culture

Seeking face

The concept of face in Chinese culture works in three ways: seeking face (active meaning), saving face (passive meaning), and losing face (negative meaning).[6] Seeking face is very similar to offering a proclaimed identity (for details, see Chapter 2), in that one tries to make one's own image as one wants. Seeking face is "a dynamic and continual life-long process rather than a one-time occurrence" (Zhang 2017, 89). Seeking face is pursued by a person who wants to establish a face before another person makes the first move. A person with a face has good social status, and can enjoy many a good relationship (*guanxi*, 关系) – an indispensable notion in Chinese society (Tsang 2016). Such persons are also sought as mediators in dealings with people because it is expected that they understand and respect the meaning of *face* for all concerned (Solomon 1971, 127–128). In so doing, i.e., establishing more relationships, they make their faces "bigger." It is a virtuous cycle to upgrade the social status.

In this context, it is reasonable for Chinese people to seek face actively. For example,

> [w]hen a Chinese is arrested, perhaps wrongly, the natural tendency of his relatives is not to seek legal protection and fight it out in a law court,

58 *Chinese face culture and foreign policy*

> but to find someone who knows the magistrate personally and intercede for his *favour*. With the high regard for personal relationships and the importance attached to *face* in China, the man who intercedes is always successful if his *face is big enough* [emphasis added].
>
> (Lin 1936, 187)

Seeking face is closely related to seeking self-esteem, self-satisfaction, and showing-off. Although Chinese face itself has features of self-esteem and self-satisfaction, seeking face ensures these characteristics, while saving face and losing face involve maintaining and protecting them. A series of studies on the consumption of luxury goods in China show well this aspect of seeking face. For example, despite their relatively low level of income, Chinese people prefer to purchase expensive luxury goods because they want to improve their face by not lagging behind others who have luxury goods and who may feel superior to those who do not have them (Li and Su 2007; Lee 2015c). Consumers who seek face are more willing to pay a premium price (Siu et al. 2016).

One good example of seeking face is the tributary trade in Chinese history. The tribute system was a twofold ritual: the exchanges of diplomatic delegation and the trading of goods. In terms of trade, the tribute system was not profitable at all to China because it usually gave a large amount of largesse in return for gifts from a tribute state. It was China that shouldered the financial burden in the tribute trade with the Chosun dynasty in Korea (Pratt 2006; Hamashita 2008, 99). For Ryukyu, now Okinawa in Japan, the tribute trade was so profitable that maintaining it was a matter of survival (Smits 1999, 34). Matteo Ricci, an Italian Jesuit who worked for the Ming court, derided this situation by writing that

> the Chinese themselves (who are by no means ignorant of the deception) delude their king, fawning with devotion as if truly the whole world paid taxes to the Chinese kingdom, whereas on the contrary tribute is more truly paid to those kingdoms by China.
>
> (…, as cited in Fletcher 1968, 208)

Other than financial loss, another burden for China in the tribute trade system was to assure the security of tribute states in exchange for their tributary compliance (Wang 2013, 213). The Ming dynasty could not but engage in the war to assist Chosun when Japan invaded Chosun in 1592, because it had the responsibility to protect its tribute Chosun. The Ming rapidly declined because of this military support to the tributes and were eventually conquered by the Qing. Despite these burdens, Chinese emperors were satisfied with the system because they and their country gained prestige from the tribute trade system (Fairbank 1942, 135). When the delegation from a tribute state met the emperor, they had to show their respect to him. Furthermore, the fact that they came to the capital of China and had an audience with the emperor indicated that the tribute state from which they came recognized that the ruler of China had the mandate of Heaven to rule all mankind and its countries. Chinese emperors and China as a whole therefore sought face by using the tribute system that could give China a superior position in relation to its neighbors (Zhou 2011).

However, the seeking of face entails a risk of losing face when it fails. Thus, seeking face should be conducted cautiously, and it should not be attempted when it is likely to be declined by others. This is the reason why Qing did not force the Western countries to conform to the tribute trade system.

Saving face

While seeking face shows the active dimension of the dynamics of Chinese face culture, saving face indicates its relatively passive dimension. If there were no face to be saved because a nation or person were in the process of seeking face, saving face would not be necessary. Moreover, if one already lost one's face, it would be too late to try to save it. Thus, saving face is typically, albeit not always, located between seeking face and losing face. Because the threat of losing face usually takes place in negative, rather than positive, social situations, the dynamic of saving face also works in negative situations (Han 2016).

The dynamic of saving face operates in three different ways: saving one's face, saving another's face, or both.[7] Given the protocol of reciprocity in Chinese face culture, a good way to save one's own face is to save another person's face first, or at the same time. The better is to make others gain face or at least help others not to lose face.

Another good way to save one's face is to offer a sacrifice, keep a low profile, and be humble. In this context, some researchers argue that saving face is the driving force behind politeness and conformity in Chinese society (Brown and Levinson 1987; Pye 1988, 31; Tao 2017). Making a sacrifice ultimately helps save a person's face in its entirety. Additionally, keeping a low profile helps one prevent losing face when events or matters go in a different way than one had hoped (Ho 1976). Sacrificing oneself may not always be good in terms of utilitarian, practical benefits, because it often requires a person to relinquish or concede something in return for saving face. An extreme example is Xiang Yu, who was a competent Chinese general and leader of the rebel forces that overthrew the Qin dynasty. He was defeated by his competitor Liu Bang and left with only a few soldiers. He could have returned to his stronghold and prepared to strike back, but instead he decided to kill himself because he was humiliated and could not have saved face had he appeared before his people in the stronghold (Loewenberg 2011, 692).

One episode about the Qing dynasty also reflects a creative way of saving face. When any delegation had an audience with the Chinese emperor, the

60   *Chinese face culture and foreign policy*

members had to kneel three times and knock their head to the floor nine times in supplication, as a ritual to express respect for the emperor. However, the Tongzhi Emperor (late Qing) was not sure whether the Western delegates would kowtow when they met him: for if they didn't, he would lose not only his but also China's face. So, a clever courtier, Wu Kedu, advised the Emperor to circumvent this situation and save face by not demanding the ceremonial kowtow from foreigners. The Emperor, thus, ordered envoys to be exempted from the ritual, reasoning to the courtiers that they were undereducated and did not understand correct ethical behavior (Topping 2013, 62–63).[8]

Yet another way to save face is to neglect or avoid the difficult (negative) situation – perhaps, by undertaking a (nonsensical) strategy of self-comfort and distorting the actual cowardice by insisting otherwise. An episode that highlights such a pattern concerns the Guangxu Emperor, the successor of the Tongzhi Emperor. In 1900, the Boxer Rebellion – a peasant uprising that was aimed at driving all Westerners from China as a result of their privileged position in the empire – was at its peak. The Boxers were encouraged in this endeavor by the Guangxu Emperor and Cixi, the ruling empress dowager. In response, an international force was organized by the Western powers, which captured Beijing in the summer of 1900 (*Encyclopaedia Britannica* 2019). The loss of Beijing meant a loss of face for the Guangxu Emperor, Cixi, and China as a whole. So, instead of accepting the humiliating defeat terms, the rulers went westward to Xi'an for a hunting trip (Guangxu 1901). They believed that they could save their face because they did not flee the Western occupation, but had only gone hunting to protect people's security.

Losing face

The worst face dynamic a Chinese person can experience is losing one's face. Richard Wilhelm, German missionary and Sinologist, observed Chinese society in late Qing China and described "the strict injunction to avoid causing the feeling of shame to another and that one should not 'lose one's face' oneself" (Wilhelm 1928, 360). Two points are important to understand in this context: one is what causes a person to lose face, and the other is how one responds after losing face.

First, the cause that makes an individual feel a loss of face can be internal and/or external. Internally, one might lose face when an embarrassing or shameful feeling arises from "unintentional and undesired social predicaments or transgressions" (Schlenker and Leary 1982) or due to disappointment by failing to meet one's social expectations (Modigliani 1971). To be specific, this feeling emerges when there is a public violation of widely accepted social norms, and someone else witnesses the violation, even if the norms were violated unintentionally (Edelmann 1985). Externally, people feel humiliated when they are rejected or treated disgracefully by others (Ho 1976; Scheff 1988), or when they fail to meet others' expectations (Ho 1976).

Chinese face culture and foreign policy 61

Second, one can resolve the feeling of humiliation internally or externally. Internally, people who lose their face may try to restore face by rebuilding a good face with favorable self-image (Kim and Nam 1998, 523–524). Externally, those who lose face may wish to retaliate to regain their face. Some studies argue that strategies like retaliation and aggression are unhelpful as a cooperative effort to recreate a good image (Ho 1976; Oetzel and Ting-Toomey 2003). However, more research points out that there are strong correlations between retaliation and losing face (McKee 2008; Hui and Bond 2009; Chen 2015; McCauley 2017). When someone loses their face, they are less generous and more aggressive to others. According to studies on humiliation, which can be translated into *losing face* here, humiliation can cause a variety of violent responses in terms of retaliation, including violent crime, terrorism, war, mass-killing, and genocide (McCauley 2017, 225–256, 260).

In *Collective Biographies of the Records of the Grand Historian of China* (*Shijiliezhuan*, 史记列传), there are many episodes about losing face and its remedies. Among a total of 70 biographies, 31 are related to the dynamics of face, and 22 of those 31 have stories about losing face and overcoming the situation. More interestingly, only two biographies deal with recovery vis-à-vis loss of face through internal strategies, while people from seven stories overcame their lost face by retaliation against others (Lim 2012, 298–299).[9] For example, General Li Guang fought well against the Northern barbarian Xiongnu, but was expelled from the military with unjustified accusations, and he retired to a rural area. One day, a drunk local official stopped him while he was returning from a hunting trip; this was a loss of face for him. So, when he was reinstated in the military, he asked the emperor to arrange for the local official to be placed under his authority and then killed him (Lim 2012, 311–312).

Figure 3.1 depicts the three face dynamics discussed below.

In sum, although it has some similarities to universal face culture, Chinese face culture is uniquely influential in Chinese society and strongly governs Chinese behaviors. The aforementioned three dynamics of this face culture

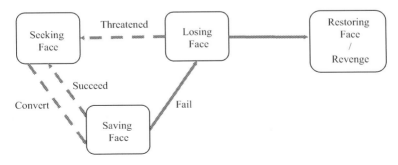

Figure 3.1 Relationship Between Dynamics of Chinese Face Culture.

62 *Chinese face culture and foreign policy*

are closely intertwined. Saving face is often located between seeking face and losing face, which often occur in chronological order. To save face, one can make sacrifices or escape from the negative situation. Once face is lost, one tries to regain face again or to retaliate to overcome the feeling of shame and humiliation. Even though those dynamics work at the individual level, they can be applied to the collective face of the state or other collective entities, because face has a social context and is formed in social relations and interactions (Qi 2017). Collective face is particularly important in China because Chinese people equate themselves with the group or the state to which they belong (Zhu 2016). Losing face can affect the family's face, the group's face, and the state's face.

Effect of face culture on Chinese foreign policy

What effect does it have?

In Chinese tradition, an individual's face is closely related to a group's face to which the former belongs. Thus, China's state reputation is intertwined with (is often the same as) its *face*, and the state's face is directly linked to its leader's face. Against this background, clearly, face culture is bound to influence China's policymaking (as also discussed earlier in this chapter).

Arguments for cultural influences on Chinese foreign policy are nothing new. Other than research on Chinese strategic culture, many studies find Confucian features are useful in understanding in Chinese foreign policy. For example, Qin (2011) argues that four key elements of contextuality, correlativity, complementarity, and changeability have played a significant role in China's foreign policymaking. Zhao (2018) believes that the Chinese Communist Party (CCP) has employed Confucianism to promote nationalist sentiments among the Chinese people and, thus, Confucianism has served as the underlying ideology to secure the CCP's political legitimacy and to enhance a more assertive foreign policy. Zhang (2015) asserts that Confucianism lays the groundwork for China's grand strategy of inclusive relationalism due to its inclusive humanism.

Evidence of cultural effects on Chinese foreign policy is found in the language of Chinese leaders and elites. Although it might be only rhetoric, Chinese leaders and political elites often invoke meaningful words and phrases from Chinese classics to convey their will or thinking in a more elegant manner. For example, President Xi Jinping likes to use words from Chinese classics. In Xi's recent speech at the 18th Meeting of the Council of Heads of Member States of the Shanghai Cooperation Organization (SCO) on June 10, 2018, he started by quoting Confucius' second sentence in *Analects*, "What a joy to have friends coming from afar!" He also quoted Mencius's remarks to explain international issues of hegemony and power politics, traditional and non-traditional threats, trade protectionism, and the clash of civilizations (Xi 2018c).

The relations between culture and foreign policy are also clearly explained by Chinese Foreign Minister Wang Yi. He described China's new foreign policy of Major-Country Diplomacy with Chinese Characteristics as follows:

> The unique features of China's diplomacy originate from the rich and profound Chinese civilization. In its five thousand-year history, the Chinese nation has developed the human-oriented concept of loving all creatures as if they are your kind and all people as if they are your brothers, the political philosophy of valuing virtue and balance, the peaceful approach of love, non-offense and good-neighborliness, the idea of peace being of paramount importance and harmony without uniformity as well as the personal conduct of treating others in a way that you would like to be treated and helping others succeed if you want to succeed yourself. These traditional values with a unique oriental touch provide an endless source of invaluable cultural asset for China's diplomacy…Over 2,000 years ago, China's great philosopher Confucius said, 'the virtue of the sage will last long and the cause of the sage will thrive'. To promote peace and development of mankind is just such a lofty and everlasting cause. We will actively explore major-country diplomacy with Chinese characteristics, make joint efforts with people of other countries and work for the establishment of a harmonious world of lasting peace and common prosperity.
>
> (Wang 2013)

In line with influence of culture on Chinese foreign policy, Chinese face culture has played a role in foreign policy. However, the levels of their effects are different. Chinese traditional culture such as Confucianism has influenced overall Chinese foreign policy at the macro level, while China's face culture has more influence on specific incidents at the micro level. In this context, the working of face culture is similar to the discourse of reputation in IR theory. Reputation in IR theory came out of research on deterrence in terms of the problem of credibility. In that sense, it is a "belief based on an actor's past behavior that informs predictions about his or her future behavior" (Renshon et al. 2018, 327). Reputation is formed when an observer explains an actor's behavior as dispositional rather than situational and uses the past to predict similar behavior in the future (Mercer 1996, 7). For example, the United States should always respond vigorously to any Soviet Union move to test the waters, so as to keep a reputation of resolve (Schelling 1966).

Chinese face culture and the discourse of reputation are also similar in that influential leaders are very important in presenting face and forming reputation (Renshon et al. 2018). In Chinese history, China's face was the emperor's face because he was the most powerful person in his country, even when he had no real power because the fate of the court was shared by the emperor. Furthermore, both face and reputation occasionally are

64 *Chinese face culture and foreign policy*

not accurate representations of the truth. For example, even though there were air battles between the Soviet Union and the United States during the Korean War, they were covert and caused no damage to the reputation of either side (Carson 2016). In so avoiding reputational harm by publicizing the results of air battles, both states could prevent the unintended escalation of conflict to total war between them. In the same manner, China named its troops as the People's Volunteer Army. By putting "Volunteer" on the name, China was prepared just in case it experienced the negative situation of losing face, i.e., if this army lost important battles. Lastly, Chinese face culture and reputation have common attributes, as both put more emphasis on face and reputation than on actual gains and losses. For instance, the United States and the United Nations arguably participated in the Korean War and faced numerous casualties not to save South Korea for South Koreans but to save their face in the international arena (Schelling 1966, 124–125).

However, Chinese face culture and reputation are not the same. First, all leaders of China have been bound by face culture because they are Chinese, and Chinese culture is strongly influenced by it. But not all leaders, even in the same country, value reputation highly. For example, some leaders are more willing to use military force to defend their reputation than others, if they are more sensitive to self-monitoring their foreign policy behaviors (Keren 2018).

Second, face dynamics are not so much about whether a person has a good face or not (in fact, the very notion of face implies only good and honorable behavior), but on whether a leader or a state saves or loses face. On the contrary, reputation can be good or bad. In other words, a leader or a state can develop a good reputation or a bad reputation but they cannot have bad faces. So, reputation is usually combined with a value judgment as to whether an actor is good or bad, while the concept of face in Chinese culture is not as concerned with valuation.

Third, related to the previous point, a leader or state might have multiple reputations depending on the issue at hand, whereas face does not vary as easily. For example, Singapore has a good reputation for its political stability and transparency, but simultaneously a bad reputation regarding human rights and political freedom. It has been always in the top ten of the most transparent countries among 180 countries and territories in the world by executing strong anti-corruption measures including high salaries and harsh punishment for corruption (Quah 2007; Transparency International 2018). At the same time, Singapore is well known for the poor political rights of citizens and atrophied civil liberties (Reyes 2015).

In addition to being similar (though still different) to notions of reputation, Chinese face culture also has similarities to the dynamics of naming and shaming, as introduced in studies on international human rights. "Naming and shaming" is one of the most preferred strategies in the human rights field to force states to comply with international norms, including human rights norms (Hafner-Burton 2008, 689). The strategy involves public pressure and condemnation of states that violate international rules and norms by calling out the names and behaviors of these states officially (Friman 2015, 3–5; Koliev and Lebovic 2018, 439). One interesting example of naming and shaming is the renaming of a street by the United States to shame the Soviet Union: in 1984, the U.S. Congress changed the name of the 16th street in front of the (then) Soviet embassy in Washington, DC, to "No. 1 Andrei Sakharov Plaza," in honor of the anti-Soviet dissident and Nobel peace laureate (1975) who was exiled four years before the renaming. As a result, the Soviets could not help but mention, and see, his name whenever they used the address of their embassy. Two years later, Sakharov was allowed to go back home (Pizano 2014; Abrams 2016). More recently, invoking the Soviet renaming, U.S. Senator Ted Cruz began a campaign in 2014 to rename the street on which the Chinese embassy is situated after Liu Xiaobo, the world-renowned Chinese dissident and Nobel peace laureate (2010), who died in prison in 2017 after years of captivity; Senator Cruz and Representative Mark Meadows have repeatedly introduced this bill in the Congress (Newman 2017).

However, the difference between the naming and shaming strategy and the Chinese face culture is that the dynamic of the former involving external actors is not as influential as the organic force of Chinese face culture. For example, even though people in the state, named and shamed by the international community, are negatively affected by the same (Ausderan 2013), it does not mean much to the governments that are named and shamed, given their unchanged attitudes (Hafner-Burton 2008).

How does it work?

Chinese face culture influences state behavior through the dynamics of seeking, saving, and losing face. First, seeking face is deeply reflected in the current Chinese foreign policy of President Xi Jinping, who is pursuing his "Chinese Dream" (Zhongguomeng, 中国梦), which is to construct a New Type of Great Power Relations and Major Country Diplomacy with Chinese Characteristics. As discussed in Chapter 2, Chinese moves to become a responsible great power clearly correspond with Chinese efforts to seek face in the world. One striking example is the nature of China's public diplomacy. Although Chinese public diplomacy has recently received more attention under President Xi, the CCP had long ago launched a kind of public diplomacy as a part of its communist propaganda. For example, it encouraged Chinese organizations in the United States to publish newspapers promoting the CCP's position and highlighting imperial Japan's cruelty. *Vanguard Weekly* (*Xianfeng Zhoukan*, 先锋周刊) and *Chinese Vanguard* were first published by the Zhongguo Gong-Nong Gemin Datongmeng (Grand Revolutionary Alliance of Chinese Workers and Peasants) at the end of 1927 and April 1928, respectively (Lai 2010, 71–72).[10] Furthermore, the CCP started publishing the *Voice of China* magazine in the 1930s

66 *Chinese face culture and foreign policy*

in Shanghai and *China Digest* in the late 1940s in Hong Kong, again, for propaganda (Aoyama 2007a, 159).[11] In addition, the CCP began publishing *People's China* (English version) in 1950 and *Beijing Review* in 1958 (Aoyama 2007b, 3). Public diplomacy in this era was conducted through "regular publications, leaking the favorable information to the chosen foreign journalists, and foreign language broadcasting" (Aoyama 2007b, 4), and it aimed to seek face with clearly defined characteristics: peace-loving, victimized by foreign invasion, anti-hegemonic, communist, and a developing country (Wang 2003).

After reform and opening up in 1978, and the end of the Cold War, Chinese propaganda gradually transformed into public diplomacy, which means transformation from a simple tool of promotion to a strategy in advancing foreign policy. As China became more intertwined in international affairs in 1980, it became more sensitive to national image abroad; and publicity to the outside world it became more important in foreign policy (Shambaugh 2007, 47). Against this backdrop, the CCP renamed the Department of Propaganda to the Department of Publicity in the late 1990s, despite no change in the Chinese title (Hartig 2016, 85). Under Presidents Jiang Zemin and Hu Jintao from the 1990s to the 2010s, public diplomacy accelerated to improve China's global image by focusing on Chinese economic development, in the era of Jiang, and on China's peaceful rise in the era of Hu (Cho and Jeong 2008, 459; Brady 2015, 54–55). In particular, President Hu was the first Chinese leader who announced that public diplomacy was one of the essential goals for Chinese foreign policy, by advocating for "an objective and friendly publicity environment" in the speech at the Tenth Conference of Chinese Diplomatic Envoys Stationed Abroad on August 30, 2004 (Wang 2008, 263–264). A prominent action plan was to establish the Confucius Institute (*Kongzi Xueyuan*), which now has 548 institutes around the world.

Chinese public diplomacy mainly based on advancing China's cultural heritage has continued and been strengthened by President Xi Jinping. In his speech at a conference on how to enhance China's cultural soft power on December 30, 2013, he asserted:

> To strengthen China's soft power, the country needs to build its capacity in international communication, construct a communication system, better use the new media and increase the creativity, appeal and credibility of China's publicity...The stories of China should be well told, voices of China well spread, and characteristics of China well explained.
>
> (Xi 2014a)

President Xi's public diplomacy is not just words: he has pushed ahead with the ambitious One Belt, One Road (*Yidai Yilu*, 一带一路) program – officially renamed the Belt and Road Initiative – which aims to improve China's image in the process of integrating the economy and the transportation network of approximately 50 countries, while also spreading Chinese culture to them (Li 2018; Sterling 2018).

Chinese face culture and foreign policy 67

While the above dynamics refer to China's efforts in seeking face, saving face was pervasive in Chinese leader Deng Xiaoping's foreign policy. Deng's guiding principles in Chinese foreign policy can be summarized through 28 Chinese characters:

Lengjingguancha, Wenzhuzhenjiao, Chenzhuoyingfu, Taoguangyanghui, Shanyushouzhuo, Juebudangtou, Yousuozuowei (冷静观察，稳住阵脚，沉着应付，韬光养晦，善于守拙，决不当头，有所作为).

(People's Daily 2012)

These can be translated into "be calm and observe the situation; hold our ground; hide our strengths and bide our time; be good at keeping a low profile; don't take the lead; do what you can" (Brady 2017, xvi–xvii). Although he did not use the exact 28 characters, Deng first mentioned the first three phrases of these guiding principles in 1989 when China faced domestic difficulties and international pressure due to the Tiananmen incident in 1989 (Chen and Wang 2011, 197; Vogel 2011, 657–659). He told his colleagues,

When it comes to the international situation, three sentences can summarize it. First, we should observe calmly. Second, we should secure our position. Third, we should cope with affairs calmly. We need to be calm, calm, and calm; we should focus on our own job and do it well.

(Deng 1994)

Regarding the most famous term *Taoguangyanghui*, it is known that he used the term only once in 1992, when he was discussing the problems of development in China. He claimed, "We will only become a big political power if we keep a low profile [*Taoguangyanghui*] and work hard for some years; and we will then have more weight in international affairs" (Chen and Wang 2011, 197).

These principles have since then served as the overarching strategy of China's foreign policy. President Jiang Zemin repeatedly asserted that Deng's principles were China's foreign policy principles, and the same was true of Jiang's successor, Hu Jintao (Chen and Wang 2011). Some viewed his foreign policy as more focused on "do what you can or get some things done (*yousuozhuowei*)," which is rather assertive, compared to "hide your strength and bide your time (*Taoguangyanghui*)" (Cabestan 2010; Johnston 2013; Amako 2014, 15–16; Doshi 2019). While the principle of "hide strength and bide time" seemed to apply during the peaceful rise proposed by President Hu, controversy emerged over an increased focus on "do what you can or get some things done (*yousuozhuowei*)," when President Xi Jinping suggested a more resolute direction of foreign policy.

In fact, the exact meaning of these terms and their status are controversial. For example, *Taoguanfyanghui*, the key term, can have various meanings: "1. suffer a lot and wait for revenge; 2. hide somebody's capabilities and avoid leadership; 3. keep a low profile and bide one's time" (Mierzejewski

68 *Chinese face culture and foreign policy*

2012, 80, endnote 31). Furthermore, it is ambiguous whether these 28 characters represent a Chinese grand strategy or simply tactics (Chen and Wang 2011, 196–197). Nevertheless, the important point is that they are firmly related to Chinese saving-face culture. In particular, hiding strength and keeping a low profile is exactly the same dynamic of saving face by being humble and, if necessary, sacrificing what one has. Furthermore, unwillingness to take on leadership is another way of attempting to save face by avoiding the negative situation, because undertaking the leadership role would entail China shouldering more of the burden while engaging with international issues that have the potential to go poorly, thus undermining China's efforts to save face.

Moreover, the dynamics of losing face are more related to Chinese action rather than to its words. As explored in Chapter 2, Chairman Mao Zedong declared that the Chinese people had stood up through their revolutionary efforts. Mao was describing Chinese state-building in this way as a grand effort of seeking face following the loss of face during the Century of Humiliation. Mao's comments describe a way to recover from lost face by gaining a new face. All efforts after the formation of the PRC, from Mao's tenure to current President Xi's tenure, have been geared toward this recovery from China's lost face. For instance, President Xi has repeatedly proclaimed and promised the realization of the Chinese Dream of the "great rejuvenation of the Chinese nation" as well as promised to restore China's status as a rightful great power in the world (Doshi 2017).

One action of China to restore its lost face was the long quest for permanent membership in the UNSC. Although the CCP kicked the KMT out of mainland China, it was the KMT-ruled ROC that had been a member of the United Nations and a permanent member at the UNSC because it was a charter member. Even though the ROC had been expelled from power, the UNSC seat was not transferred to the newly empowered PRC because the United States did not want to expel the ROC from the seat, despite many debates over the representation of China at the United Nations General Assembly throughout the 1950s and the 1960s (Cheung 2015). Many countries including the United Kingdom and France recognized the PRC and voted for "restoring" its seat: the PRC finally joined the United Nations and took permanent membership by replacing the ROC in 1971 (Cheung 2015).

The United Nations General Assembly Resolution 2758, titled "Restoration of the lawful rights of the People's Republic of China in the United Nations," recognized that

> the representatives of the Government of the People's Republic of China are the only lawful representatives of China to the United Nations and that the People's Republic of China is one of the five permanent members of the Security Council.
>
> (U.N. 1971)

Chinese face culture and foreign policy   69

The joint effort by the United States and Japan to achieve dual U.N. representation for the PRC and Taiwan failed. Following this episode, the Ministry of Foreign Affairs of China celebrated what they called "a major victory won on this issue through protracted struggle by China and many justices upholding third world countries and other countries" (Ministry of Foreign Affairs of PRC, 2004).[12]

China does not try restoring its face only by gaining face where it previously lost face. The other way to restore face following national humiliation is to retaliate. An excellent example of this method is China's military attack on Vietnam in 1979. As is true for any war, the Sino-Vietnamese War, too, has varied, complicated causes, such as Deng Xiaoping's negative perception of Vietnam (Zhang 2010), Chinese political elites' negative perception of Vietnam (Vogel 2011), and Vietnam's alliance with the Soviet Union (Ross 1988). From the perspective of losing face, however, China's decision to go to war with Vietnam was a retaliation against Vietnam for causing China to lose face.

In the Sino-Soviet conflict, Vietnam had allied with the Soviet Union, not with China (Ross 1988); and it had even signed a Treaty of Friendship and Cooperation with the Soviet Union in 1978, which expressed full support for each other (Soon 1980, 56–57). Given the friendly relationship between China and Vietnam in the early 1970s, China felt Vietnam's dramatic leaning toward the Soviets was a loss of face. This is the reason why China pointed out Vietnam's intimacy to the Soviets as one reason to attack it, and used the term "punishment" in a statement in *People' Daily* on December 25, 1978 (Zhang 2010, 3). Although it did not actually win the war (Joffe 1987; O'Dowd 2007), China unexpectedly declared withdrawal from Vietnam on the grounds that the "lesson" that it wanted to teach Vietnam was fully completed (Quang 2017). After all, China launched the Sino-Vietnamese War to "punish" Vietnam (Amako 2014, 6) and to restore its "psychological equation" (Kissinger 2011, 133).

Simply put, Chinese face culture is reflected in Chinese foreign policy, as summarized in Table 3.1. In particular, words and behaviors in Chinese foreign policy are explained well by the three dynamics of Chinese face culture: seeking face, saving face, and losing face. At the same time, no use of *mianzi*

Table 3.1 Examples of Chinese Face Culture in Chinese Foreign Policy

Types of Dynamics	Examples
Seeking face	• Chinese dream
	• Public diplomacy
Saving face	Principle of hide the strength and bide the time
Losing face	• Restoring the position in the United Nations
	• Sino-Vietnamese War (retaliation)

70   *Chinese face culture and foreign policy*

or *mian* referring to *face* is found in the CFMSA database. Of course, the reason for this absence might be that *mianzi* is not an appropriate word in a diplomatic and official language. When a spokesperson refers to *mianzi*, it might entail losing face itself, given the features of Chinese face culture. Let us assume that a person requests someone for something. Accepting the request would give face to the requestor, who therefore saves face. If the request is declined, however, the requestor loses face. If someone else reads the requestor's mind before the request is even made, and does a favor in advance, then the requestor gains a big face.

However, *lian* is found four times on the CFMSA database. The first usage is found in the regular conference on February 3, 2016, regarding North Korea's ballistic missile launch. Spokesperson Lu Kang said,

> During the stalemate of the Six-Party Talks, in response to relevant countries' constant outcry for pressure and sanctions, the DPRK started a nuclear test and conducted it over and over again. In this sense, the DPRK did *slap* the relevant country across *the face*. As for *whose face* did the DPRK *slap*, the country itself knows well [emphasis added].
>
> (CFMSA 2016)

The second usage of *lian* offered a similar expression as the first one. At the press conference on August 24, 2017, reacting to a report in the Indian media about India's road construction plans in a disputed area of the China-India boundary, Chinese Foreign Ministry Spokesperson Hua Chunying said, "[The] report makes me feel that India is slapping its own face" (CFMSA 2017).

The third usage of the term was on May 30, 2018, regarding the U.S. tariff on Chinese goods. Spokesperson Hua Chunying said,

> I believe that we all share the same feeling that when it comes to international relations, each and every flip-flop [*bianlian*, 变脸] will only lead to further depletion and *squandering of a country's credibility and reputation* [emphasis added].
>
> (CFMSA 2018)

The last usage, on December 17, 2018, referred to a *slap in the face*. Answering a question about U.S. National Security Adviser John Bolton's argument against China's plan to take over Zambia's national power and utility company, Spokesperson Hua said, "You may share the same feeling with me that this is not the first time for US officials to be *slapped in the face* on such kind of issues" (CFMSA 2018).

Although the uses of *lian* in all four examples above do not exactly match with the Chinese face culture features, still, they clearly evoke the Chinese concept of losing face. Face in all three examples is used to criticize the other party: accusing the other party of losing face due to inappropriate

Chinese face culture and foreign policy 71

Table 3.2 Mianzi/Lian in CFMSA Database

	Date	*Usage*
Mianzi/Mian	February 3, 2016	A slap in the face
Lian	August 24, 2017	A slap in the face
	May 30, 2018	Flip-flop/squandering of credibility and reputation
	December 17, 2018	A slap in the face

words or behaviors. Although the Chinese spokespersons use variants of the expression a slap in the face, they use the same to describe what happens to others but never to describe China. Table 3.2 lists these uses.

In short, Chinese face culture is an active force that shapes Chinese foreign policy. Given *Taoguangyanghui*, Chinese face culture itself might be seen as a primary force driving foreign policy at the level of national strategy. However, there are questions as to what extent guiding principles such as *Taoguangyanghui* actually direct foreign policy. Considering the many examples mentioned earlier, it is most likely that Chinese face culture actively functions only when events that directly catalyze face culture occur. Therefore, as described in Hypothesis 3, face culture is likely to moderate Chinese foreign policy rather than directly make it:

H3: *China's foreign policy is moderated by Chinese face culture.*

Observations regarding the relations between China and the two Koreas

Chapter 2 discusses China behavior toward North Korea and South Korea according to two types of identities: the proclaimed identity of one's own self and the perceived identity of others. China treats a friend as a friend and an enemy as an enemy. It is undeniable that every relationship has its ups and downs. China's relations with both North Korea and South Korea are no exception. That being said, fluctuations within an understandable range are not the subject of discussion in this book.[13] The study focuses on some abnormal cases in which China did not treat a friend as a friend but as a non-friend. They are beyond normal fluctuations in relationships because they oscillate too far from the boundary line of "friend" and move too close to the boundary line of "enemy." In these cases, China treated a friend as non-friend and vice versa, which runs counter to the argument that China acts by virtue of identity. Is the argument flawed from the very beginning? Or is there any other factor to consider that influences Chinese behavior? Observations on two important incidents attempt to address these questions: the Garlic War between China and South Korea and North Korea's second nuclear crisis. In these incidents, China took different and

72　*Chinese face culture and foreign policy*

unexpected stances toward the two Koreas.[14] Thus, these observations also provide clues to understanding China's puzzling behaviors – the core subject of this book.

The Garlic War

Background

The Garlic War, a trade dispute between China and South Korea over Chinese garlic from 1999 to 2000, was the first official conflict between the two countries after normalization in 1992. It originated following the price crash of garlic in South Korea in the late 1990s. South Korea was the largest per capita consumer of garlic in the world in 2018 (Baek 2018) and was a top five global garlic producer in 2016 (Ham 2018). In 2018, garlic consumption per capita was 6.7 kg, while it was 9.2 kg in 2000 during the Garlic War (Choi et al. 2019, 707). After normalization, South Korea's garlic imports from China had been on the increase. For example, garlic imports tripled in the three years from 1996 to 1999, before the Garlic War erupted (Ministry of Foreign Affairs of the Republic of Korea 2000). In addition, domestic production of garlic had been increasing from 1997 to 1999 (Chung 2003/4, 556).

Developments

Against this backdrop, the garlic price in South Korea suddenly and sharply decreased in 1999. For example, the farm sale price of garlic nosedived by 44 percent from ₩2,719 per kilogram in 1998 to ₩1,520 in 1999, and the wholesale price dropped from ₩3,097 per kilogram to ₩1,859 in the same period (Chung 2003/4, 555). As the garlic price rapidly decreased and concerns over the increasing import of Chinese garlic among Korean garlic farmers were growing, the National Agricultural Cooperatives Federation (NACF or *Nonghyup* in Korean), which is the biggest farmers' association in South Korea, filed a request with the Korea Trade Commission (KTC) on September 30, 1999, to investigate damages caused by Chinese garlic to Korean farmers (National Archives of Korea 2006). On October 27, the KTC recommended a provisional safeguard measure to the Ministry of Finance and Economy (MOFE) and the MOFE imposed a provisional tariff on Chinese garlic for 200 days, increasing the tariff from 30 to 315 percent during the period (Yonhap News Agency 2000). Following this measure, the KTC adopted a positive judgment on imposing tariffs on the import of Chinese garlic on February 2, 2000, with MOFE determined to officialize the imposition on March 17, 2000 (Yonhap News Agency 2000). Having had two working-level negotiations before the deadline of adopting the provisional safeguard, the South Korean government decided to take the safeguard measure by applying a tariff of 315 percent on frozen and pickled garlic and a tariff of 436 percent on peeled garlic from China for the next three years, effective beginning June 1, 2000 (Choi 2000, 86–87; Chung 2003/4, 553).

Chinese face culture and foreign policy 73

China's retaliation began immediately. On June 7, 2000, China's Ministry of Commerce decided to impose a ban on the imports of South Korean cell phones and polyethylene (Snyder 2009, 66; Ye 2017, 94, note 2), which was already hinted at in mid-March (Chung 2003/4, 554). But China's revenge was excessive given the comparative trade volume of Chinese garlic and South Korean cell phones and polyethylene. In 1999, South Korea's import of Chinese garlic amounted to $8.98 million while China's imports of cell phones and polyethylene from South Korea were valued at $41.40 million and $470.13 million, respectively (Kim 2001, 83).

Surprised by China's strong countermeasure, the South Korean government had a third negotiation with China in Beijing on June 29, 2000, and the two countries reached an agreement on July 31, 2000 (Choi 2000, 88; Ministry of Foreign Affairs of Republic of Korea 2000). As a result, South Korea decided to lower tariffs and ensure an import quota of Chinese garlic instead of imposing a dramatic tariff or outright abolition on Chinese garlic. In return, China lifted the ban on the imports of Korean mobile phones and polyethylene, which became effective on August 2, 2000 (Ministry of Foreign Affairs of the Republic of Korea 2000).

However, it was not the end of the war. In April of 2001, Chine alluded to resuming its ban on Korean goods on the grounds that South Korea did not import the agreed quota of Chinese garlic (National Archive of Korea 2006). So, South Korea satisfied China's demand by expanding its garlic imports from China. In 2002, the conflict was about to reoccur when the NACF asked the South Korean government to extend the safeguards against Chinese garlic with four more years of restrictions, lasting until 2006. But this proposal did not escalate into a conflict between South Korea and China because the South Korean government promised financial support to their garlic farmers, rather than seeking to restrict Chinese imports (National Archive of Korea 2006).

China's strange behavior

China's sever retaliation surprised South Korea more, because the two countries had enjoyed a good relationship as friends after normalization; China's response is hard to understand in many ways. First, China had several opportunities to resolve the dispute before imposing a total ban on Korean goods. Second, it declined the suggestion from South Korea for an increase in the imports of other Chinese goods such as corn and sesame (National Archive of Korea 2006). Third, the retaliation was disproportionate. China's ban on South Korean mobile phones and polyethylene restricted 52 times more trading value than the amount of Chinese garlic affected by South Korea's safeguard. Last, China outright banned South Korean imports instead of stepping up measures such as imposing tariffs or quotas.

One possible explanation is that China felt it had lost face due to the actions of a friend. Given the complicated causes of the garlic price crash in

74 *Chinese face culture and foreign policy*

South Korea, and South Korea's large trade surplus to China at that time, China might have believed that South Korea provoked it without any good reason.[15] This presumption is substantiated by Chung (2003/4, 557–558): "China side regarded South Korea's safeguard measures as ungrounded and discriminatory, which undermined its 'face' in the eyes of the international community."

The second nuclear crisis of North Korea

Background

The first North Korean nuclear crisis occurred in 1993, provoked by North Korea's withdrawal from the NPT, and ended with the Agreed Framework between the United States and the DPRK in 1994 (Cotton 2003, 262; National Archive of Korea 2017). Almost ten years later, the second nuclear crisis of North Korea took place in 2002 when North Korea allegedly admitted the existence of a nuclear program with highly enriched uranium to the Assistant U.S. Secretary of State for East Asian and Pacific Affairs James Kelley during his visit to Pyongyang on October 3–5, 2000 (Kwak and Joo 2007, 1). North Korea's First Vice Foreign Minister Kang Sok-ju defended their nuclear program to Kelley, claiming that North Korea had no choice but to develop the program as it felt threatened by the United States, which had included North Korea in the "axis of evil" (Cotton 2003, 271; Funabashi 2007, 125; Pritchard 2007, 37). Nonetheless, North Korea's nuclear program was clearly in violation of the 1994 Agreement that required the country to freeze its development of nuclear weapons.

Developments

The United States responded to this admission and the breach of the 1994 Agreement quickly. On November 14, the Bush administration announced that the United States was no longer bound by the 1994 Agreement and suspended oil supply to North Korea (Harrison 2005). On December 27, North Korea retaliated by unfreezing its nuclear program, which was on hold as per the 1994 Agreement, and expelling the IAEA inspectors who had been monitoring the freeze. This was followed by North Korea's decision to withdraw from the NPT on January 10, 2003, along with the restarting of the Yongbyon nuclear facilities (Pritchard 2007, 43).[16]

As tensions between North Korea and the United States grew, North Korea constantly asked for bilateral dialogues, but the latter refused (Pritchard 2007, 57). Washington was strongly opposed to bilateral negotiations with Pyongyang as a matter of policy (Funabashi 2007, 158). To break this stalemate, China was willing to take the role of an honest broker (Khan 2003). It was unexpected because China was reluctant to engage in the first

North Korean nuclear crisis, when China remained a bystander (Lee and Kim 2017, 30).

To persuade North Korea into sitting at the table, China raised the stakes to shut down the oil pipeline to North Korea for three days in early March 2003, on the pretext of maintenance (Funabashi 2007, 323–324; Shirk 2007, 124–125). The action was very effective. Consequently, Three-Party Talks were held among Beijing, Pyongyang, and Washington on April 23–25, 2003, and this was followed by the SPT in which South Korea, Japan, and Russia participated as well (Pritchard 2007, 85–86).

China's strange behavior

It was not strange that China changed its stance toward North Korea in the intervening years between the first and second crises, from being a bystander to being an intermediary in the negotiations. What piques my curiosity is China's decision to cut off oil supply to North Korea. Given the importance of oil to North Korea, and especially under the condition of suspended oil supply by the United States, China's decision to close the oil pipeline is not easy to understand. If they were friends, it would be more normal to persuade North Korea with words, not with punishment. One assumption is that China felt that it had lost its face due to the actions by North Korea. It tried to mediate between North Korea and the United States by seating them at the negotiation table using its "big face," but this effort was declined by North Korea.

However, apparently, some in the Chinese camp, too, opposed the decision to cut off North Korea's oil supply, at least according to one memoir. Lee Soo-Hyuk, who was the South Korean representative for the SPT, wrote in his memoir that "I asked Chinese representative Wang Yi for this matter. He said China as a big state did not treat a small neighbor, North Korea, like that" (Lee 2011). Wang Yi's disagreement above, too, can be explained by Chinese face culture. The strong punishment also involves a loss of face for China because, as the Chinese representative mentioned himself, exacting this kind of punishment rather than engaging in dialogue is not the mark of a great power.

The hypothesis

The two episodes discussed above provide various face culture cues to help interpret China's behaviors. I hypothesize that the dynamics of Chinese face culture can explain China's assertive foreign policy responses to the actions of North Korea and South Korea:

H3a: *Chinese face culture leads to assertive Chinese foreign policy when China loses its face.*

Conclusion

Culture is essential to understanding China. The Confucian culture, in particular, is a very widespread, though ambiguous, influence in China. Chinese face culture in comparison is a more precise and direct cultural force that regulates people's behavior. And though it does not mean that culture is everything, it is a significant consideration.

Even in FPA, the influence of culture is evident, despite its difficulty to be measured – the unseen does not mean the unimportant. Culture, especially Chinese face culture, is blended into Chinese foreign policy. More precisely, it influences Chinese foreign policy through the three dynamics of seeking face, saving face, and losing face. Sometimes these dynamics shape diplomatic strategies, while also shaping guiding principles that underlie overall Chinese foreign policy, such as national security strategies.

China's behavior in the aftermath of the Garlic War and the second North Korean nuclear crisis can also be explained through the Chinese face culture dynamics. Both the Sino-North Korean and the Sino-South Korean relationships have had their share of ups and downs. For example, there have been periods of no exchanges between leaders of China and North Korea. There have been conflicts over Kimchi, over the historical memory of events, and over the so-called Northeast Project between China and South Korea, too. The fluctuation in relations over conflicts is common in any relationship. But in the aforementioned incidents, China behaved as though it did not identify the two Korea as friends, and punished them both rather harshly. It is likely that the discrepancy between identity and behavior in these cases might have stemmed from China's feeling of a loss of face, owing to the actions of friends. Nonetheless, a question that arises is: did China respond vigorously to undesirable actions of North and South Korea because of the exceptional loss of face caused by the action of perceived friends?

Notes

1 Hudson suggests the goals for a research agenda of the FPA as determining (1) the extent to which cultural factors affect any given foreign policy, (2) how cultural differences lead to predictable patterns of interaction and under what conditions we expect culture to be more important in foreign policy, and (3) how we recognize and evaluate change in culture. For these goals, she asserts that the FPA should include comparative analysis (uncovering the differences in culture), subnational analysis (looking at power nodes within the society which link to culture), discourse analysis (tracing the discourse between power nodes), horizon analysis (what becomes possible and not possible from each competing story), and interaction analysis (when two countries have different stories/definitions of the situation that are ascendant, how do they interact) (Hudson 2014, 136–137).
2 The three factors of self-face, other-face, and mutual face are developed by Ting-Toomey and Oetzel (2001).
3 To interpret the data for cluster analysis, he came up with four clusters of behavior that are not in accord with proper morality: incompetent behavior, bad habits, and private matters being disclosed (Zuo 1997, 36).

Chinese face culture and foreign policy 77

4 On the contrary, Gries (2005) examines Chinese nationalism by using the word *face* as a cultural universal that can be applied to all humans, because he believes humans cannot exist by themselves without any relations with others (Gries 2005, 23). But this approach fades out the unique characteristic of Chinese face.

5 Face sometimes can also be the translation of *mianmao* (面貌). For example, at the roundtable to honor the 120th anniversary of Mao's birthday in 2013, President Xi said, "Mao is a great figure who changed the *face* of the nation and led the Chinese people to a new destiny [emphasis added]" (Zhao 2016, 86). The use of face in his remarks was a translation of *mianmao*, not *mianzi* or *lian*.

6 Brown and Levinson (1987, 61) divided face into two related aspects of negative and positive face. The former describes "the basic claim to territories, personal preserves, rights to non-distraction," and the latter describes "the positive consistent self-image or personality claimed by interactants." This conception can be also applied to Chinese face culture. But it is insufficient to achieve the purpose of this study because it does not explain how this face culture works to shape foreign policy.

7 The dynamics of Chinese face work not only at the individual level but also at the collective level. So, "[the] uniqueness of Chinese face is that an individual would take actions not only for the face of oneself but also for the face of the greater self" (Wu 2013, 156).

8 In Chinese history, there are many examples of face-saving excuses. One example is the Ming's withdrawal from Vietnam after their victory over the Ming–Hồ War. Despite its victory, the Ming court realized that ruling Vietnam was a very stressful thing, so they wanted to withdraw. But they could not find any justification until a Vietnamese rebel leader gave an excuse to save Ming's face (Wang 2011, 154–156).

9 The remaining 13 stories tell of solutions for both regaining face and exacting revenge.

10 *Xianfeng* magazine is translated as *The Pioneer* in some documents instead of *Vanguard*.

11 The *Voice of China* is different from the *Voice of Free China* that was run by the ROC from 1949 to 1988.

12 The title of the commentary statement is, "Struggle to restore China's lawful seat in the United Nations."

13 Chung (2007) and Ye (2017), following him, describe these kinds of conflicts over "low politics" between China and South Korea as "soft" clashes.

14 Another observation is the so-called 2010 Senkaku Boat Collision Incident between China and Japan, which led to China's unexpected retaliation of banning the export of rare earth metals to Japan. However, this incident is not discussed in this chapter, but briefly in Chapter 4.

15 In fact, some argue that the reduction in garlic prices was attributed more to domestic production than to the import of Chinese garlic (Chung 2003/4).

16 After walking out of the NPT, Pyongyang declared that the withdrawal was effective immediately (Cotton 2003, 274).

Although Article X of the NPT requires that a country give three months' notice in advance of withdrawing, North Korea argues that it has satisfied that requirement because it originally announced its decision to withdraw March 12, 1993, and suspended the decision one day before it was to become legally binding.

(Arms Control Association 2019)

4 Case study
Japan's THAAD radar deployment

Japan has two THAAD-linked Army Navy/Transportable Radar Surveillance (AN/TPY-2) systems: one at the Shariki base installed in 2006 and the other at Kyogamisaki in 2014. This deployment is a natural extension of the Japan-U.S. alliance – the two have been working closely to develop a missile defense system for years.

As noted in earlier chapters, China did not take harsh action against Japan despite these installations – a sharp contrast to the South Korean case. Although Japan normalized its diplomatic relations with China 20 years earlier than South Korea did, Japan is still a non-friend to China. In fact, as briefly discussed in Chapter 2, China and Japan are more like rivals or potential adversaries. Against this backdrop, a few questions arise (in the context of this study's main enquiry, namely, China's behavior): why is China silent about Japan's radar installations? Does China actually think of Japan as a valuable friend, and was not bothered when Japan introduced the radars? Does China believe that the THAAD radars in Japan can cause no harm to Chinese national interests? Or, was China not angry because it knew that there was nothing better to expect from Japan, since Japan was not a friend to China?

This chapter explores the background and development of the Japanese deployment of THAAD radars to find a good answer to the above questions. This Japanese case has a knotted skein that is hard to unravel, including issues such as North Korea's missile capabilities, the U.S. grand strategy, and Japan's domestic politics. For the purpose of this book, however, this chapter focuses on the AN/TPY-2 as closely as possible to test several hypotheses.

Background

Along with the United States, which intended to build the missile defense system, Japan had joined the development of the system from the beginning.[1] Two years after the United States, during the Reagan administration, revealed the Strategic Defense Initiative (SDI) in 1985, the Japanese government signed an Agreement Concerning Japanese Participation in Research for the SDI (Kaneda et al. 2007, 51). However, Japan's participation was

Japan's THAAD radar deployment 79

Table 4.1 Japan's Description of North Korean Missile Threat in the Defense White Papers

Year	North Korea's Action	Japan's Response
1993	Launch of a Nodong-1 missile to East Sea	North Korea's Nodong missile is described for the first time as a threat to Japan's security
1994–1997	–	North Korea's nuclear and missile programs pose a threat to Japan
1999	Launch of Taepodong-1 missile in 1998	Japan expressed its concerns for North Korea's long-range missile
2001	–	Japan expressed its concerns for North Korea's missiles and actual deployment of missiles
2004	–	Japan expressed its concerns for North Korea's development and deployment of missiles that could reach all of Japan
2005	–	Japan expressed concerned about North Korea's missiles mounted with biochemical weapons

Source: Nam and Lee 2010, 70–71.

not necessarily driven by a sense of the practical usefulness of the system for military use, but was a tool to strengthen the U.S.-Japan alliance for political purposes (Jimbo 2002, 57; Kaneda et al. 2007, 53–54). So, there was no significant progress for the missile defense system in Japan immediately after the U.S.-Japan SDI initiative was signed in 1985.

In the 1990s, however, Japan changed this view and began to see the missile defense system as having a possible security purpose, because of Chinese military exercises in March 1996, which included the firing of a bunch of short-range ballistic missiles, and North Korea's missile test of Taepodong-1 in August 1998 (Swaine et al. 2001, 11–17; Jimbo 2002, 56). In particular, North Korea's Taepodong -1 missile, which had flown over Japan's territory, greatly influenced Japan's reassessment of threats by missiles because North Korean missiles allegedly had a long enough range to reach Japan (Kaneda et al. 2007, 55; Takahashi 2012, 10). As seen in Table 4.1, Japan even mentioned the threat from North Korean long-range missiles such as the Taepodong-1 in its annual defense white paper of 1999 for the first time (Nam and Lee 2010, 71).

Developments

The first radar at Shariki

In December 2003, Japan's Cabinet and Security Council decided to deploy the Patriot Advanced Capability (PAC)-3 and the Standard Missile

80 Japan's THAAD radar deployment

(SM)-3 (Block I-A) to counter ballistic missile threats. Japan issued a document titled "On Introduction of Ballistic Missile Defense System and Other Measures," which covered the lower-tier Ballistic Missile Defense (BMD) with a surface-to-air system and the upper-tier with a sea-based system (Toki 2009; Takahashi 2012, 10). To implement the plan, the Japanese government revised its Self-Defense Forces Law to legalize possible interceptions of ballistic missiles.

Against this backdrop, in July 2005, the Japanese and the U.S. governments began considering the possibility of deploying an X-band radar in Japan, which was the newest type of surveillance system of the United States, in order to strengthen the joint response capability of the missile defense system by linking the radar to Japan's established radar net (Mulgan 2005, 65, footnote 15). This consideration was officialized in a document describing the U.S.-Japan alliance – "Transformation and Realignment for the Future" – signed on October 29, 2005, by the U.S. Secretary of State Condoleezza Rice and Secretary of Defense Donald Rumsfeld, as well as their Japanese counterparts, Minister of Foreign Affairs Machimura Nobutaka and Minister of State for Defense Ohno Yoshinori. The document stated:

> [T]he optimum site for deployment in Japan of a new U.S. X-Band radar system will be examined. Through timely information sharing, this radar will support capabilities to intercept missiles directed at Japan and capabilities for Japan's civil defense and consequence management. In addition, as appropriate, the U.S. will deploy active defenses, such as Patriot PAC-3 and Standard Missile (SM-3) to support U.S. treaty commitments.
>
> (Ministry of Foreign Affairs of Japan 2005)

In November 2005, the United States and Japan agreed to deploy a mobile X-band radar system to more effectively detect cruise and ballistic missiles with advanced targeting discrimination technology (Pekkanen and Paul 2010, 183).

In 2006, the discussion over the deployment of an X-band radar accelerated. On February 6, in the press briefing about the fiscal 2007 defense budget, a senior U.S. Missile Defense Agency official said that the United States hoped to have the deployment of the X-band radar in Japan within the next six months (Igarashi 2006). On May 1, the U.S. and the Japanese governments agreed to the realignment of the U.S. Forces in Japan. In the agreement, titled "United States–Japan Roadmap for Realignment Implementation," the X-band radar was described as ready to deploy at the Air Self-Defense Force Shariki Base in the summer. According to an official report,

> The optimum site for deployment of a new U.S. X-Band radar system has been designated as Air SDF Shariki Base. Necessary arrangements

Japan's THAAD radar deployment 81

and facility modifications, funded by the USG [the U.S. government], will be made before the radar becomes operational in summer 2006. The USG will share X-Band radar data with the GOJ [government of Japan].

(Ministry of Foreign Affairs of Japan 2006b)

Despite the two governments' argument that the radar system was directed at North Korea's missile threat, it implicitly had an intention to monitor China's missile sites, given common concerns about China's military build-up. For example, Japanese Defense Minister Nugata outrightly said at the news conference to announce the above agreement that "China's military spending is increasing in line with its economic development, and China needs to make it transparent for its neighboring nations to feel at ease" (Tang 2006).

The X-band radar system – the AN/TPY-2 – was temporarily moved to Misawa Air Base and then set up at the Shariki base in June 2006 (Svan 2006). The AN/TPY-2 can operate in two modes: forward-based and terminal. The forward-based mode can monitor up to 1,800–2,000 km, with boost-phase surveillance, while the terminal mode can monitor up to 600–900 km, with terminal phase surveillance. The radar at Shariki operates in the forward-based mode (Park 2015).

The second radar at Kyogamisaki

Right after the deployment of the first X-band radar in Japan, the United States considered deploying another radar system in the western Pacific region somewhere in Guam, South Korea, or Japan, namely, Kyushu or Okinawa (Park 2006). In December 2006, the United States asked Japan to allow it to deploy its second radar in the south of Japan for monitoring North Korea's Taepodong-2 launch site (Shin 2006b).

In 2012, the plan to deploy the radar, which had been dormant for a while, resurfaced. In August, the U.S. Department of Defense discussed the additional deployment of the radar in southern Japan to supplement the X-band radar positioned in northern Japan. Compared to the first deployment that put emphasis on North Korea's missile threat, the United States revealed that its real target was China. For example, a U.S. missile defense expert said, "The focus of our rhetoric is North Korea. [But] the reality is that we're also looking longer term at the elephant in the room, which is China" (Entous and Barnes 2012).

On September 17, 2012, during his visit to Tokyo, U.S. Defense Secretary Leon Panetta announced that Japan had agreed to deploy another AN/TPY-2 to defend against ballistic missiles. Panetta noted that the radars did not aim at China but were solely designed to counter North Korea (Barnes 2012). On February 22, 2013, U.S. President Barack Obama and Japanese Prime Minister Abe Shinzo confirmed in their meeting in Washington that

82 *Japan's THAAD radar deployment*

they had agreed to deploy another early-warning radar system. The Kyogamisaki base in Kyotango, located on the East Sea near Kyoto, was selected as the place to host the second radar (Kyodo News 2013). On April 29, 2013, U.S. Defense Secretary Chuck Hagel said that he and his Japanese counterpart, Onodera Itsunori, had made progress on plans to deploy another X-band radar system in Japan (Azuma 2013).

On June 11, 2014, having had several repeated confirmations of the deployment by defense ministers from the United States and Japan for almost two years, the U.S. Department of Defense finally said that it expected to complete the deployment of the second AN/TPY-2 radar in Kyogamisaki in southern Japan by the end of 2014 (Syring 2014). On December 26, the U.S. Department of Defense and the Japanese Ministry of Defense jointly announced the deployment of a second AN/TPY-2 radar at Kyogamisaki in Japan to enhance sensor coverage for BMD and to augment an existing radar at Shariki (U.S. Department of Defense 2014). Just like the radar at Shariki, the AN/TPY-2 at Kyogamisaki is run in the forward-based mode that has a longer range than the terminal mode.

China's response

It was evident that the two X-band radars in Japan were not limited to detecting missile threats by North Korea. Their ultimate target was indisputably China. This claim was substantiated by remarks from both U.S. and Japanese officials who expressed their concerns about China. For example, as earlier mentioned, Japanese Defense Minister Nugata and U.S. Defense Secretary Rumsfeld expressed similar views on China's increased military spending during their talks in May 2006 (Tang 2006).

Nevertheless, China's response to the Japanese THAAD radars was relatively lukewarm, compared to its harsh reaction against South Korea later. China has, of course, consistently opposed the development of missile defense by the United States, mainly, for two reasons: (1) the U.S. missile defense would lead to a vicious cycle of an arms race; (2) it would neutralize China's efforts to maintain a viable strategic deterrent and ultimately pose a threat to the survival of China (Romberg and McDevitt 2003; Yuan 2003; Roberts 2004).

In line with this position, China has not concealed its discontent over the deployment of radars in Japan. For instance, Chinese Foreign Ministry spokespersons explained China's view on Japan's X-band radars twice at press conferences. On September 23, 2013, when Japan decided to deploy the second X-band radar around Kyoto, Chinese Spokesperson Hong Lei said:

> We have noted relevant reports and are concerned about that. China believes that some individual country or bloc of countries' unilateral deployment of anti-missile system or engagement in bloc cooperation

under the pretext of guarding against the nuclear and missile 'threat' from the DPRK will make no contribution to regional non-proliferation, nor will it be conducive to peace and stability of the Asia-Pacific, rather, it may produce *a severe and negative impact on global strategic stability*. We maintain that political and diplomatic means should be adopted in dealing with the issue of missile proliferation, so as to fully accommodate different countries' legitimate concerns over the anti-missile issue and safeguard global strategic stability [emphasis added].

(CFMSA 2013)

Although he asserted China's opposition to the deployment of the radar system in Japan, the Chinese spokesperson did not explicitly express that the radar could pose a threat to China's security. Instead, he indirectly expressed the same by mentioning the threat to global stability. By using the word "pretext" for the justification of the radar deployment, he indicated that China believed that the radar was ultimately targeted at China. For instance, Li Qinggong, deputy secretary of the China Council for National Security Policy Studies, said, "It will be like killing a fly with a bazooka if it is used to contain Pyongyang. I believe it is mainly aimed at detecting China's missiles" (Weitz 2012b, 13).

The X-band radar was mentioned again on October 23, 2014, when the second radar in Japan was almost completely installed. Chinese Spokesperson Hua Chunying answered a question regarding the radar as follows:

The anti-missile deployment in the Asia-Pacific by a certain country in the pursuit of unilateral security goes against *regional strategic stability* and mutual trust, as well as *peace and stability in Northeast Asia*. Such an action is particularly concerning when the situation in the region is complex and sensitive. The Chinese side believes that the relevant country should proceed from regional peace and stability, stay committed to maintaining regional security through political and diplomatic means, *and shall not infringe upon other countries' security interests* under the pretext of aforementioned action [emphasis added].

(CFMSA 2014)

This expression of opposition was slightly different from the 2013 one. The goal of global strategic stability was reduced to a regional goal, and then to a more local Northeast Asian goal. Furthermore, Spokesperson Hua Chunying asserted security interests directly despite the fact that the subjects of these security interests were "other countries," not China directly. However, it was unambiguous that her remarks admitted China's view on the radar system as a security threat.

Other than spokespersons' remarks, there were some other timid complaints from the Chinese side. For instance, when Chinese Defense Minister Liang Guanglie met his U.S. counterpart, Panetta, who came to China right

84 Japan's THAAD radar deployment

after visiting Japan to announce the deployment of the second X-band radar on September 19, 2012, Liang asked Panetta, "Isn't the base in Aomori prefecture...enough?" (Weitz 2012b, 11).

However, China did not go further. It is noteworthy that additional opposing remarks by Chinese top leaders are hard to find. No harsh response can be found regarding the first X-band radar in Japan. No exceptionally harsh expression in diplomatic rhetoric can be found either. Furthermore, no action was taken by China against Japan's decision to deploy the X-band radars.

Analysis

Japan's identity to China

As discussed in Chapter 2, China does not identify Japan as a friend, not in the least, despite the close relationship in trade between the two countries. Although China perceives Japan as one of its most important economic partners, it sees Japan as a potential adversary at the same time, partly due to continuing conflict over territorial issues and partly due to Japan's atrocities in China during the Second World War era, without any repentance even to this day.

Around the times when Japan deployed radars in 2006 and 2014, Sino-Japanese relations were at their lowest level. Sino-Japanese relations had been getting worse for several years when the deployment of the first X-band radar began to be discussed by Japan and the United States. These poor relations were caused not by the radar but by other historical issues. One historical issue was Japanese Prime Minister Koizumi Junichiro's visit in 2006 to the Yasukuni Shrine that honors about 2.5 million Japanese war dead – including 14 class-A war criminals from the Second World War. Thus, the prime minister's prayer visit to the shrine signaled to China that Japan does not regret its wrongdoings during the war.

This shrine visit has been a very sensitive issue for China, and it was mentioned 429 times in Chinese press conferences for the past 18 years – always strongly opposing these visits by Japanese leaders (CFMSA). For example, Foreign Ministry Spokesperson Zhang Qiyue said on July 6, 2004, when Prime Minister Koizumi vowed an annual homage to the shrine:

> China is *firmly opposed* to homage paid by Japanese leaders to the Yasukuni Shrine. We express our *dissatisfaction* and regret about the provocative remarks continuously made by Japanese leaders in *defiance* of the just appeal of the victimized peoples [emphasis added].
>
> (CFMSA 2004)

The content in Japanese history textbooks is another issue that has affected the Sino-Japanese relations. Time and again, history textbooks in Japan

Japan's THAAD radar deployment 85

have stoked controversy in Asian countries that have shared the tragic experience of Japanese colonial rule. However, the history textbook by Fusosha Publishing, which seemed to justify Japan's atrocities during the Pacific War, precipitated unprecedented mass protests in China and South Korea when the Japanese Ministry of Education approved it for a junior high school (Inuzuka 2013). The protests in China continued for weeks, condemning Japan for distorting history and boycotting Japanese products (Zhao and Hoge 2006, 424). China's Foreign Ministry summoned Japan's ambassador to China to voice its disapproval and released a statement that said, "[T]he Chinese government expresses indignation toward the Japanese government for approving the revised textbook in spite of China's strong representations on many occasions" (Hu and Song 2005).

The divisions between China and Japan became further aggravated around the period when Japan was considering deploying the second AN-TPY-2 system. The main reason for the worsening relations between the two countries was the territorial dispute over the Senkaku Islands/Diaoyudao. On September 7, 2010, there was a collision between a Chinese trawler and Japanese Coast Guard's patrol boats, which occurred in the process of chasing and fleeing. On September 8, Japan arrested and detained a Chinese captain of the fishing boat on charges of intruding and illegally fishing in the waters of the Senkaku Islands. China demanded the release of the captain immediately, but Japan declined. In retaliation for the detention, China suddenly stopped its export of earth rare materials to Japan, which were indispensable to Japan's high-tech industry (Green et al. 2017, 66–94).

This was not the end of story. In 2012, the Governor of Tokyo, Ishihara Shintaro, ordered the Tokyo municipal government to nationalize three islets in the Senkaku Islands by purchasing them from a private Japanese owner. To prevent this nationalist governor from purchasing them and, in turn, doing harm to relations with China, the Japanese central government decided to intervene in the matter and to nationalize them instead of allowing a purchase by local government. Contrary to Japan's expectation that its action would calm tensions, China sent more than 1,000 fishing boats to the waters around the islets claiming territorial sovereignty over them (Green et al. 2017, 128–145). In addition to this action, the Chinese Foreign Ministry released a statement, saying:

> [T]he Chinese government solemnly states that the Japanese government's so-called 'purchase' of the Diaoyu Island is totally illegal and invalid. It does not change, not even in the slightest way, the historical fact of Japan's occupation of Chinese territory, nor will it alter China's territorial sovereignty over the Diaoyu Island and its affiliated islands.
> (Ministry of Foreign Affairs of PRC 2012)

Furthermore, the Chinese State Council published a white paper on Diaoyu Dao, claiming it as an "inherent territory" of China.

86 *Japan's THAAD radar deployment*

Although the treaty for diplomatic ties between China and Japan remained valid during these periods, exchanges between the two countries stopped. Because of the worsening of relations from mid-2000s to mid-2010s, there was no visit by a Japanese prime minister to China for seven years (2011–2018), no visit by a Chinese foreign minister to Japan for eight years (2010–2018), no high-ranking economy dialogue for eight years (2011–2019), and no exchange between military leaders for six years (2012–2018). Further, there were no expressions of intimacy. For example, on September 30, 2012, Chinese Foreign Ministry spokesperson said, "[T]he Japanese government has *brazenly* made the wrong decision to 'purchase' the Diaoyu Islands [emphasis added]" (CFMSA 2012). The word "brazenly" is the translation of Chinese word *Hanran*, which is a very inappropriate word in diplomatic rhetoric given its meaning.[2] Therefore, it is plausible to conclude that Japan's perceived identity by China was not that of a friend during the period.

Did China lose face?

There was no evidence to demonstrate that any dynamics of Chinese face culture worked in the process of Japan's deployment of two X-band radars. Although China expressed its opposition to the deployment, it did not demand a strong action such as the withdrawal of the radar system. In other words, from the start, in this case, China did not expect mutual deference that has been essential in relations where Chinese face culture works. Therefore, it might be true that China did not retaliate against Japan for its deployment of the THAAD radars because it never lost its face. And China did not lose its face because the dynamics of Chinese face culture themselves had no chance to work.[3]

Chinese core national interests

According to a remark by Chinese Foreign Ministry spokesperson, China believed that X-band radars in Japan were a potential threat to the security and stability in the region. However, as mentioned above, China did not explicitly assert that the deployment of X-band radars in Japan is matter of Chinese core national interests. In contrast, in the South Korean case, described in Chapter 5, China reiterated that South Korea's decision to deploy the THAAD system is a grave infringement on Chinese core national interests of security.

Is there any difference between the THAAD radars in South Korea and in Japan? If yes, then China's no retaliation policy toward Japan might have had a point. However, the two radar systems are the same model of AN/TPY-2 that are technically identical. The only difference is that the radar in South Korea is run on the terminal mode and the radars in Japan are operating on the forward-based mode. Essentially, radars in Japan have a longer range of 2,000 km. It means that China's argument is not adequate at all.

In short, if China's core national interests are affected due to the THAAD radar in South Korea, they should be affected by the radars in Japan as well. By that reasoning alone, China's retaliation against both Japan and South Korea should be the same.

Conclusion

Any specific link between the proclaimed identity of China as a responsible great power and China's behavior toward Japan after the deployment of X-band radars is not found. However, as China perceived Japan as a quasi-adversary, it behaved according to this perceived identity. Since there was no retaliation by China against Japan after its deployment of radars, China's behavior was not influenced by its core national interests (as also mentioned earlier). Even if no retaliation can be assumed as an inconsistent behavior given Japan's perceived identity of enemy, Chinese core national interests cannot explain the reason why China did not retaliate. Thus, the hypothesis that inconsistent behavior by China is influenced by national interests can be rejected. In addition, it is hard to test Chinese face culture as a moderating factor. Although in this case, as mentioned above, there was no question of China losing face because Chinese face culture did not work in this scenario, however, it does not necessarily mean that no retaliation can be explained by no loss of face. This is the fallacy of denying the antecedent. Nonetheless, the hypothesis cannot be rejected either.

In short, the Japanese case supports the hypothesis of perceived identity (H1f), whereas it strongly rejects the hypothesis of national interests (H2c). For other hypotheses, the case cannot determine the results.

Notes

1 The missile defense system includes the previous Theater Missile Defense (TMD) and National Missile Defense (NMD), both of which fell under the Ballistic Missile Defense. The TMD systems aim to defend against short-range and theater-range ballistic missiles usually up to 3,500 km by being deployed in a military theater of operations, while the NMD systems were intended to defend the territory of the United States against intercontinental ballistic missiles (Cronin 2002, 3).
2 For the context of using *Hanran*, see Chapter 5.
3 In the case of the visit by Japanese leaders to the Yasukuni Shrine, the Chinese face culture works as follows: when China demanded the Japanese leaders not to visit the shrine, they temporarily stopped visiting for a number of years. So, in this context, China saved its face.

5 Case study
South Korea's THAAD system deployment

Since the normalization of Sino-South Korean relations in 1992, relations between the two countries have developed remarkably. The relationship has dramatically upgraded from good-neighborly cooperation to cooperative partnership for the 21st century, comprehensive cooperative partnership, and strategic cooperative partnership. It took only 16 years, from 1992 to 2008, for the two countries to develop the highest level of relationship.

However, there have been frictions such as the dispute over Kimchi trade, the historical issue of the Northeast Project, and illegal fishing in the West Sea by Chinese fishermen. But these are usual and acceptable conflicts between friends to some extent, except perhaps for the Garlic War (briefly discussed in Chapter 3). Even the Garlic War might be seen as a quarrel between friends who had yet to become close and were in the course of gradually coming to know each other, because the war occurred only eight years after their normalization of diplomatic ties. Furthermore, it was resolved in a relatively short period of time, without escalation to a highly unraveled political issue.

However, the recent conflict due to the THAAD deployment in South Korea cannot be blamed on an immature friendship, because it occurred between friends in a strategic cooperative relationship, who had developed relations of friendship for more than two decades after normalization. When South Korean President Park Geun-hye attended the China Victory Day parade in September 2015, which was held to celebrate the 70th anniversary of victory over Japan in the Second World War, she was seated close to President Xi – to the immediate left of his wife, Peng Liyuan. (Russian President Vladimir Putin was seated to President Xi's immediate right.) In contrast, when newly elected South Korean President Moon Jae-in and his wife visited Beijing in December 2017, Chinese leaders gave the couple the cold shoulder by inviting them to only one banquet and one luncheon over four days. The only reason for this dramatic change in China's attitude in two years was South Korea's deployment of the THAAD system. In addition to the cold-shoulder diplomacy, Beijing launched massive economic retaliation against Seoul, which was an immoderate action against a friend.

Why did ROK's deployment of THAAD make China so angry? Does China believe that South Korea should not be a friend anymore? Is it really because the radar system is a substantial challenge to Chinese national interests? Or, does this case support the hypothesis of China responding due to a loss of face, as observed in Chapter 3? To find answers to these questions, this chapter examines detailed developments in South Korean THAAD deployment.[1] In fact, the THAAD issue is very complicated because it is intertwined with many critical problems that can be mainly divided into three axes: domestic politics of South Korea, U.S. grand strategy, and nuclear and missile capabilities of North Korea.

Background

The best relationship in history

Although the Sino-South Korean relationship has been greatly influenced by North Korean issues and the U.S. position on the same, bilateral exchanges between China and the ROK have become increasingly robust since normalization.[2] As briefly discussed in Chapter 2, trade volume and mutual visitors between the two countries have remarkably increased, by more than 100 or 1,000 times. The Sino-South Korean relationship developed into a strategic cooperative partnership in May 2008 when South Korean President Lee Myung-bak paid a visit to Beijing in the first year of his term. Despite his five visits to China and 11 summits with Chinese President Hu Jintao, however, there was no further development in positive relations between the two countries because the conservative Lee government had strong pro-American proclivity.[3] The Lee government believed that the U.S.-South Korean relationship was the most important and that this important relationship was gravely undermined during the period of his predecessor, President Roh Moo-hyun (Kim 2008; Konish and Manyin 2009; Ma 2011). Moreover, North Korea's provocation of the Cheonan sinking and the shelling of Yeonpyeong Island in 2010 also contributed to the status quo in the Sino-South Korean relationship.

As both countries coincidentally experienced leadership changes in March 2013, however, expectations for the development of improved bilateral relations between South Korea and China increased. Korean President Park Geun-hye and Chinese President Xi Jinping met these expectations in the beginning. When she was just president-elect, President Park selected China as the destination of her first special envoy, who usually has a mission to promote the new president and explain his or her foreign policy (Kim 2013). Chinese expert Ruan Zongze, vice president of China Institute of International Studies, said that it was a sign that President-elect Park would have a more balanced foreign policy toward neighboring countries, especially China (Liu and Zhang 2013). Until then, it had been customary for South Korean presidents to visit the United States, Japan, China, and

90 *South Korea's THAAD system deployment*

Russia, in that order, after they were inaugurated. President Park broke the practice by paying a state visit to China on June 27, 2013, after a visit to the United States in May 2013. At the summit, Presidents Park and Xi adopted the Korea-China Joint Statement on Future Vision, in which the two leaders agreed to

> [m]ake concerted efforts to further enrich the 'strategic cooperative partnership' in all related areas, including detailed implementation strategies such as strengthening strategic communications in political and security affairs, expanding cooperation in economic and social spheres, and expediting diverse channels of people-to-people exchange.[4]
>
> (Ministry of Foreign Affairs of the Republic of Korea 2014, 85)

Improved relations between South Korea and China became more prominent when President Xi visited Seoul on July 3–4, 2014. It was the only time a new Chinese president paid a visit to South Korea first, before visiting North Korea (Byun 2017, 99–100). The Chinese side began to acclaim Sino-South Korean relations as the best period in history, with President Xi's visit to Seoul.[5] Similarly, at the reception by the Chinese embassy in Seoul in May 2004, Chinese Foreign Minister Wang Yi said that Sino-South Korean relations were experiencing the best period in history, thanks to the efforts made by the people from the two countries (Wang 2014c). Moreover, the Chinese Ambassador to South Korea, Qiu Guohong, wrote in the *People's Daily* on July 3, "At present, China-ROK relations have never been better" (Qiu 2014). On July 4, the second day of his visit to Seoul, President Xi himself delivered a speech at Seoul National University, which has been the cradle of South Korean elite, saying that "now the two nations clearly have a strategic cooperative partnership and the relationship is better than ever before" (Xi 2014b).

The peak of the "best period" relationship between the two countries was President Park's participation in China's military parade marking the 70th anniversary of the victory over Japan in the Second World War on September 3, 2015. She was the only national leader from among countries allied with the United States to attend this event. Many experts explained Seoul's tilt to China as based on strategic thinking that a close relationship with China could be helpful for reunification and, at least, for checking North Korea (Draudt 2015; Wang 2015).[6]

This "best relationship" period continued until the end of 2015. There was progress on two issues, which had long been challenging the Sino-South Korean relations. On December 20, 2015, the Korea-China Free Trade Agreement (FTA) finally came into effect. Discussions regarding the Korea-China FTA first kicked off in September 2004 when South Korean President Roh Moo-hyun and Chinese President Hu Jintao agreed to jointly start a feasibility study. However, there had been slow progress because of concerns about practical benefits in South Korea, contrary to China's proactive interests in moving the FTA forward. It gained momentum, however, after the Park government took office. Finally, the FTA was officially signed by the two governments on June 1, 2015, after 14 rounds of negotiations at the working level. President Xi called the FTA a "monumental event" that would "realize a new leap and bring more tangible benefits to the peoples of the two countries" (China FTA Network 2015; Tiezzi 2015).

In addition to the enactment of the Korea-China FTA, defense ministries of the two countries opened a hotline at the end of 2015. On December 31, China's Defense Ministry Spokesperson Yang Yujun said in a press conference that General Chang Wanquan, state councilor and minister of National Defense of the PRC, reported:

> The Chinese side was happy to see that China-ROK relations in various fields had witnessed comprehensive development in recent years, and bilateral cooperation had continued to deepen. The Chinese side will continue to implement the consensus reached between President Xi Jinping and President Park Geun-hye, strengthen the military-to-military exchange and cooperation, push forward sustained development of the mil-to-mil relationship, and jointly maintain regional peace, stability and prosperity.
>
> (Ministry of National Defense of PRC 2015)

Back to normal

The "best period," however, soon came to an end. All along, the THAAD issue – their unresolved source of conflict – had been simmering. First, the relations went back to normal, and later worsened.

The THAAD deployment became the focus of attention after June 3, 2014, when General Curtis M. Scaparrotti, commander of United States Forces Korea (USFK) and head of the U.N. Command, made remarks about the system at a breakfast meeting of the National Defense Forum, organized by the Korea Institute for Defense Analyses (KIDA), which is the only security think tank under the Ministry of National Defense of the ROK. General Scaparrotti said, "I recommended the deployment of the THAAD missiles to South Korea," adding, "unlike recent media reports claiming that a preliminary study is currently underway, it would be more accurate to say that an initial review is being conducted" (Park 2014b).

Although it was the first time the U.S. military had publicly announced that it was considering deploying the THAAD system in South Korea, the issue was raised a few years ago during the nomination hearings of two predecessors of General Scaparrotti. In 2008, at his nomination hearing, the USFK Commander nominee General Walter L. Sharp suggested that the development of THAAD could be crucial "to provide the layered, systematic missile defense capability required to protect critical United States facilities in the Republic of Korea" (Sankaran and Fearey 2017, 325). Following General Sharp, General James D. Thurman at his nomination hearing in 2011 as USFK Commander testified that "a THAAD system could

92 *South Korea's THAAD system deployment*

be used to provide layered defense and also improve early warning for the Korean Peninsula as well as enhance BMD early warning in the region" (Sankaran and Fearey 2017, 325).

However, THAAD had not been seriously discussed until the Park government took power, because South Korea had been building its own missile defense system, known as Korea Air and Missile Defense (KAMD).[7] But the THAAD issue resurfaced due to North Korea's missile provocations. As North Korea advanced its missile and nuclear capabilities, concerns began to grow that the KAMD could not effectively defend South Korea. For example, on June 20, 2014, South Korean Defense Ministry Spokesperson Kim Min-seok said in a press briefing that "the current Patriot missile defense system (PAC-3) in Korea is incapable of intercepting the improved version of North Korea's Rodong missile, which flew at an altitude of about 160 km in a recent drill" (Hwang 2014).

Developments

Strong opposition from China

China has opposed the expansion of the U.S. anti-missile system to other regions, especially Asia, since the late 1980s (Teng 2015). Beijing has long felt besieged by the U.S. missile defense system. For instance, on August 12, 2009, Foreign Minister Yang Jiechi asserted at the Conference on Disarmament in Geneva that "the missile defense program by some countries in the Asia-Pacific region would do no good to regional peace and stability" (Teng 2015). Moreover, Luo Zhaohui, director-general of the Department of Asian Affairs with the Foreign Ministry, said in April 2012 that "building a missile defense system in the Asia-Pacific region will have negative effects on global and regional strategic stability, and go against the security needs of the countries in the Asia-Pacific region" (Weitz 2012a).

Negative remarks regarding THAAD began to emerge from China in 2014. Although he did not directly mention THAAD because a decision was yet to be made on its deployment, Chinese President Xi was said to have expressed his concerns to President Park during a South Korea-China summit in July 2014. Xi noted that the U.S. missile defense system would not be helpful to Chinese security interests and asked for South Korea's consideration (Seong 2014). On September 30, 2014, the U.S. Deputy Secretary of Defense Robert O. Work admitted that the United States and South Korea were working toward the deployment of THAAD.

> We are considering very carefully whether or not to put a THAAD in South Korea. We're doing site surveys. We're working with the government of South Korea now to determine if that is the right thing to do. We've emphasized to both China and to Russia that these are not strategic anti-ballistic missiles.
>
> (Work 2014)

China was not pleased with these developments. On October 23, 2014, Foreign Ministry Spokesperson Hua Chunying answered a question about the U.S. delivery of the X-band radar system to Kyogamisaki sub-base in Kyoto, Japan:

> The anti-missile deployment in the Asia-Pacific by a certain country in the pursuit of unilateral security goes against regional strategic stability and mutual trust, as well as peace and stability in Northeast Asia. Such an action is particularly concerning when the situation in the region is complex and sensitive.
>
> (CFMSA 2014)

From late 2014, China began to raise the tone of its opposition. For example, on November 27, 2014, the Chinese Ambassador to South Korea, Qiu Guohong, warned that if South Korea allowed the U.S. military to deploy the THAAD system in its territory, it would hurt Sino-South Korean relations (Yonhap News Agency 2015). Chinese high-ranking officials also joined in voicing their opposition to THAAD. On February 4, 2015, Chinese Defense Minister Chang Wanquan conveyed China's concerns about THAAD to his counterpart, Korean Defense Minister Han Min-gu, when he visited Seoul. Following Defense Minister Chang's remarks, Chinese Assistant Minister of Foreign Affairs Liu Jianchao came to South Korea on March 16 and reiterated China's concern regarding the possible deployment of the THAAD system in South Korea: "We would appreciate it if South Korea could consider China's interest and concerns as important.... We hope that the U.S. and South Korea make a reasonable decision on the THAAD issue" (Yu 2015). Three months later, on May 31, 2015, Sun Jianguo, the admiral of the PLA Navy and deputy chief of staff for the PLA General Staff Department, met with Korean Defense Minister Han and expressed China's concern about THAAD at the Shangri-La Dialogue in 2015 (Lee 2015a).

It was in January 2016 that the controversy that had subsided for a while returned with force. In response to North Korea's fourth nuclear test on January 6, 2016, South Korean President Park Geun-hye left open the possibility of the THAAD system deployment by saying that the government would consider such action in accord with South Korea's national security and national interests, during an official statement and subsequent press conference on January 13, 2016 (Park 2016). Park's remarks led to a series of statements from the Chinese side. On the same day as Park's remarks, Chinese Foreign Ministry Spokesperson Hong Lei said at a press conference:

> China holds a consistent and clear position on anti-missile issues. It is our belief that every country should keep in mind *other countries' security interests* and regional peace and stability while pursuing its own security interests. The situation on the Korean Peninsula is highly sensitive. It is hoped that relevant countries can bear in mind the larger

94   *South Korea's THAAD system deployment*

picture of regional peace and stability and cautiously and properly deal with the relevant issue [emphasis added].

(CFMSA 2016)

Moreover, on January 27, *Global Times* (*Huanqiu Shibao*, 环球时报), the sister newspaper of the *People's Daily* that is the mouthpiece of the CCP, carried an editorial arguing that:[8]

South Korea should avoid using the THAAD missile system as leverage against China. The system will pose a threat to China's security. If Seoul does so, it will severely hurt mutual trust between China and South Korea. [It should be prepared to pay the penalty for this decision.]
(Global Times 2016)

On February 7, Yoo Jeh-Seung, the South Korean deputy defense minister for policy, formalized discussion of THAAD by saying, "It has been decided to formally start talks on the possibility of deploying the THAAD system to South Korea as part of steps to bolster the missile defense of the Korea-U.S. alliance" (VOA 2016). On February 12, during his interview with Reuters, Chinese Foreign Minister Wang Yi argued that the detection range of the X-band radar, a component of THAAD, would go beyond the Korean Peninsula and into China's territory, causing direct harm to Chinese strategic security.[9] He described the situation by quoting two Chinese ancient episodes: "When Xiang Yu's nephew Xiang Zhuang dances the dance of swords, what he really means to do is to kill Liu Bang" (*xiangzhuangwujian yizaipeigong* 項莊舞劍 意在沛公) and "Everyone knows what Sima Zhao's ambitions are" (*simazhaozhixin lurenjiezhi* 司馬昭之心 路人皆知) (Seong 2016). On February 22, Chinese Ambassador Qiu Guohong said,

China vehemently opposes the THAAD deployment…Much effort has been made to develop bilateral ties to today's level, but these efforts could be destroyed in an instant with a single problem. [Once destroyed, it] could take a long time to recover.
(Tiezzi 2016; Yonhap News Agency 2016)

In March, many Chinese diplomats, including Minister Wang Yi, Vice Minister Wu Dawei, and China's Permanent Representative to the United Nations Liu Jeiyi, continuously expressed China's opposition to THAAD deployment in South Korea. Finally, Chinese President Xi Jinping himself joined the fray. According to Zheng Zeguang, Vice Minister of Foreign Affairs, during the U.S.-China summit held on March 31, President Xi told U.S. President Barack Obama that China was "firmly opposed" to U.S. plans to deploy the THAAD system in South Korea (Brunnstrom and Wroughton 2016). Furthermore, President Xi, jointly with Russian President Putin, announced two joint statements in three days at the summit of the Shanghai

Cooperation Organisation (SCO) on June 23–24 and at the summit between China and Russia in Beijing on June 25, both of which expressed opposition to THAAD (Ye 2016). Once again, President Xi expressed his opposition to THAAD when he met with South Korean Prime Minister Hwang Kyo-ahn on June 29, 2016. President Xi demanded that South Korea should pay attention to "China's reasonable security concern, and prudently and properly deal with the possible deployment of the THAAD missile defense system in South Korea by the U.S." (Ministry of Foreign Affairs of PRC 2016).

China's retaliation

Despite China's strong opposition, the South Korean government decided to deploy the THAAD battery. On July 8, 2016, South Korean Deputy Defense Minister for Policy Yoo Jeh-Seung announced that South Korea and the United States had agreed to deploy THAAD to better protect South Korea and the U.S. military in the region from North Korea's growing nuclear and ballistic missile capabilities (Choe 2016). On the same day, Chinese Foreign Ministry Spokesperson Hong Lei said, "China has expressed strong dissatisfaction with and firm opposition to the decision, and has summoned the ambassadors of the US and the ROK to lodge our representations" (CFMSA).

When it comes to China's anger over the decision, one noteworthy response was an exceptionally written four-part series of articles in the *People's Daily* from July 29 to August 4, by the pseudonymous writer Zhong Sheng (Swaine 2017, 6). The name Zhong Sheng literally means "the sound of a bell," but it is translated into "China Voice" in the English version of the *People's Daily* because *Zhong* is the same sound as the first letter of *China* in Chinese. This four-part series be understood as a way of expressing China's attack on a country; China had earlier used the same strategy to criticize Soviet party leaders by publishing a series of nine open letters in the *People's Daily* from September 6, 1963, to July 14, 1964 (Li 1995, 92).

Strangely, the South Korean government had dismissed the possibility of retaliation by China from the beginning, despite Korean China watchers' warning. For example, Yoo Il-ho, deputy prime minister and finance minister, said that China was a member of the World Trade Organization (WTO), and it was unreasonable for China to engage in economic retaliation for a political issue. Prime Minister Hwang Kyo-ahn said that Korea did not have to worry about China's economic retaliation because of high interdependence between South Korea and China (Chun 2017).

However, although Chinese Foreign Ministry Spokesperson Hong Lei avoided an answer to the question of countermeasures by China on July 8, 2016, Spokesperson Lu Kang confirmed that China would take corresponding measures to safeguard its interests (CFMSA). In line with this Foreign Ministry statement, Chinese Defense Ministry Spokesperson Senior Colonel Yang Yujun said, "We will pay close attention to relevant actions of the

96 *South Korea's THAAD system deployment*

U.S. and the ROK and will take necessary measures to maintain national strategic security as well as regional strategic equilibrium" (Ministry of National Defense of PRC 2016).

China's retaliation began ambiguously, compared to China's previously direct retaliations, such as the explicit ban on imports or exports during the Garlic War. These ambiguous retaliations may be based on characteristics of Asian culture. One example is the Japanese culture of *sontaku*, which requires people to surmise or conjecture a superior's feelings or wishes and to act on them without explicit directions. Although the practice is unofficial and has no legal binding, *sontaku* regulates people's behaviors. The mechanism is similar to administrative guidance in law, which is a non-binding recommendation but has practical force in China, South Korea, and Japan. The Chinese version of *sontaku* is *Chuaimoshangyi* (揣摩上意), which describes the expectation that lower-level actors should read the minds of leaders beforehand and take appropriate measures.

China's initial retaliation against South Korea seems to be based on this type of administrative guidance, which is an oral directive that is hard to be officially identified in most cases (Yoo 2017).[10] For example, Qian Hongshan, assistant minister of Foreign Affairs, said that although negative consequences were not intended by China, the THAAD issue negatively affected the exchanges in many areas between China and South Korea, which was a natural response from ordinary Chinese people (Zhao 2016). Furthermore, when it came to questions about growing restrictions against South Korean pop stars in China, Chinese Foreign Ministry Spokesperson Geng Shuang said,

> First and foremost; I have never heard about any restriction on the ROK. Second, the Chinese side is always positive to people-to-people and cultural exchanges with the ROK. However, I believe you can all understand that such kind of exchanges should be based on public support. Third, the Chinese side's steadfast opposition to the deployment of the THAAD system by the US in the ROK is well known to all. The Chinese public has voiced their dissatisfaction as well. Relevant parties must have taken note of that.
>
> (CFMSA)

Under this covert retaliation, South Korea experienced substantial damages and harassment by China in many sectors. According to the Bank of Korea, one year of retaliation was expected to reduce South Korea's economic growth by 0.4 percent while many economic experts estimated that economic damage by Chinese retaliation could be almost 1 percent of GDP in 2017 (Lee 2017a; Park 2017b). Chinese retaliation against South Korea's THAAD deployment comprised both economic and non-economic retaliations. Economic retaliation was all-round and persisted for a considerable period of time. First, normal administrative processes including visa issuance and customs clearance by China were delayed. For example, the China's embassy in South Korea suspended issuance of multiple-entry business visas. Despite denial by the Chinese Foreign Ministry, South Korean businesspeople felt that the suspension was due to the extreme strengthening of the requisites and the screening process (Yoo 2016). Customs clearance also took more time to be completed than before. If one typo was found on a document, Chinese customs requested the Korea Customs Service to verify that the document was not a forgery (Son et al. 2016).

Second, a regulation that bans Korean culture in China, the so-called *Xianhanling* (限韩令), became operative. No Korean stars could get approved for their entertainment activities by Chinese authorities, and some events featuring Korean music and TV stars were canceled (Qin and Choe 2016; Meick and Salidjanova 2017, 7; Park 2017). South Korean trade surplus related to culture and entertainment was recorded at US$66.6 million in June 2016, but it decreased to just US$2.2 million in October 2017 due to China's restrictions on Korean cultural activities (Lee 2018c).

Third, restrictions on group tours to South Korea were imposed. On March 3, 2017, the China National Tourism Administration ordered travel agencies in China to stop selling either group or individual tour packages for Chinese citizens wishing to travel to South Korea (Meick and Salidjanova 2017, 7; Kim 2017g). Due to this order, Chinese tourists to South Korea decreased by 63.6 percent in April 2017, compared to the same period in the previous year (Choi 2017). As seen in Figure 5.1, Chinese tourists to South Korea had sharply increased in the so-called "the best period in history" from 2013 to 2016. However, tourism nosedived in 2017 post the THAAD deployment in mid-2016.

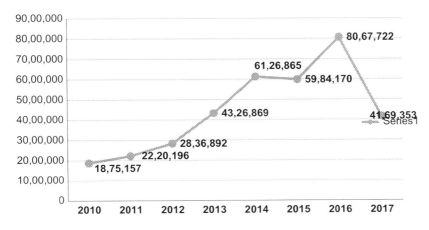

Figure 5.1 Chinese Tourists to South Korea (2010–2017).
Source: Korea Tourism Organization (2018).

98 *South Korea's THAAD system deployment*

Fourth, South Korean companies suffered at various levels. A few examples are as follows: investment by Chinese companies in South Korean companies was canceled. A Korean company, Lotte, had an unexpected tax investigation by Chinese authorities in 2016. Electric cars and trucks that installed Korean batteries were excluded from Chinese government subsidies. Korean cosmetics were not approved for import into China by the Chinese government (Meick and Salidjanova 2017, 7; Park 2017).

Other than economic retaliation, China also carried out low-intensity military and political retaliatory measures. In February 2016, a Chinese expert on missile defense, Wu Riqiang, warned that "if a limited war were to occur between the U.S. and South Korea, the THAAD system in South Korea should be naturally the primary target of the People's Liberation Army" (Cho 2016). The Chinese military did not conceal its will to retaliate against the deployment of THAAD. Senior Colonel Wu Qian, the spokesperson for China's Ministry of National Defense, said at a press conference on March 31, 2017, that "the Chinese military's opposition to the deployment of the THAAD system will definitely not stay on words only" (Panda 2017). For instance, Chinese military aircraft have repeatedly entered South Korea's Air Defense Identification Zone (KADIZ) without advance notification since THAAD deployment, and the number of trespassing cases has increased over the past several years (Noh 2018). However, Chinese Defense Ministry Spokesman Ren Quoqiang said, "The exercise in question is part of an annual training of the Chinese Air Force, and conforms to international laws and customs. We hope the South Korean side will not be startled by such an insignificant event" (Shim 2018b).

One form of political retaliation by China was that China gave South Korean politicians the cold shoulder when they visited Beijing. When South Korean President Moon Jae-in sent two special envoys to China, Lee Hae-Chan and Chung Eui-yong, on May 19, 2017, and March 12, 2018, respectively, to meet the Chinese president, President Xi sat alone at a head table, while the Korean envoys were seated below him at a different table in both the meetings. In the past, the South Korean special envoys, sent by Presidents Lee Myung-bak and Park Geun-hye, were seated side by side at one table with the Chinese president (Lee 2017d). Although China explained it was a new diplomatic practice, it did not apply this new practice to other countries (Lee 2018b).

Even President Moon was not granted an exemption from this Chinese diplomatic discourtesy. When he arrived at the Beijing airport, he was greeted by Kong Xuanyou, the deputy foreign minister, despite this being a formal state visit. In contrast, Philippine President Rodrigo Duterte was greeted by Foreign Minister Wang Yi and U.S. President Donald Trump was greeted by State Councilor Yang Jiechi at the airport (Oh and Park 2017; Volodzko 2017b). Furthermore, President Moon only had one official lunch and dinner with Chinese leaders during his stay for four days, which is obviously intentional mistreatment given the Chinese culture of

"Fanju (饭局)" that puts emphasis on having meals together with others (You 2017). Meanwhile, there was an incident in which two Korean reporters were severely beaten by Chinese guards while trying to cover an event involving their president in Beijing; and the Chinese government declined their request for an apology (Gao 2017).

Analysis

South Korea's identity to China

Although identity can change, it takes a certain amount of time for that to happen – especially perceived identity, because it is socially constructed by interactions with others over time, and changes must be perceived and confirmed by repeated interactions. Words and behaviors provide a litmus test that can investigate whether there is a change in the perceived identity of South Korea for China. In fact, it is hard to find any fundamental change in how China refers to South Korea. As mentioned earlier, China referred to Sino-South Korean relations as "best period in history" in 2014 and 2015. Although the term was not used anymore after the THAAD deployment, China did not blame South Korea overtly. Instead, strong language was reserved for criticizing the deployment of the THAAD system itself, rather than criticizing South Korea.[11] Table 5.1 shows that there was no change in China's perception of South Korean identity as a friend during 2016–2017. Although the two friends experienced conflict over THAAD, and thus their relationship was not as good as it was in the past few years, the relationship could be still regarded as friendly, even while the THAAD conflict was ongoing.

In addition to these friendly wordings, Chinese actions could be interpreted as behaviors toward a friend, except for the excessive retaliation against the specific issue of THAAD. Of course, post-THAAD deployment, Chinese behaviors were not as intimate as in the past, especially during their "best period in history." But even then, national leadership exchanges between the two countries never really stopped.

An example that reflects friendly undertones at the national leadership level is President Xi Jinping sending birthday wishes, a handwritten note at that, on February 1, 2016, to President Park Geun-hye, who was celebrating her 64th birthday on February 2 – even after she had left open the possibility of the deployment of the THAAD system in January (Wang 2016). Another example is the gift that South Korean President Moon Jae-in received from President Xi during his visit to Beijing. Although President Moon was shown diplomatic discourtesy, the gift of a go board and go stones, both made of jade, was meaningful because jade was the gift from former President Park to President Xi on her first visit to China in 2013.

The annual fishery negotiations between South Korea and China, which took place even after the radar deployment in 2016 and produced favorable

100 *South Korea's THAAD system deployment*

Table 5.1 China's Official Statements on South Korea as a Friend (2016–2017)

Year	Date	Statements by Chinese Foreign Ministry Spokespersons (Excerpts)
2016	February 29	China and South Korea jointly try to preserve peace and stability on the Korean Peninsula and commit to developing the China-ROK strategic partnership
	August 23	South Korea is our important neighbor
	November 21	China has always held a positive attitude toward the cultural exchanges between China and South Korea
2017	January 3	China has always held a positive attitude toward economic and cultural exchanges between China and South Korea
	March 10	China and South Korea are important neighbors to each other
	March 31	The Chinese government attaches importance to economic and trade cooperation between China and South Korea
	April 17	In fact, before the South Korean government made this decision [to deploy THAAD system], China-South Korean relations have reached the highest level in history
	May 11	China and South Korea are close neighbors
	June 20	China and South Korea are important neighbors to each other. China has always attached importance to developing China-South Korean relations
	November 23	China and South Korea are neighbors who cannot move away
	December 12	China and South Korea are close neighbors and important partners to cooperate
	December 14	Both China and South Korea are victims of the Second World War

Source: CFMSA.

results for South Korea, also provide a glimpse into the continued positive relations between the two sides. Illegal fishing by Chinese fishermen in the West Sea located between South Korea and China has been a thorny issue between the two countries because armed conflicts between the South Korean coast guard and Chinese fishermen often occur when Korean military officials crack down on the fishermen (Kim 2019). Against this backdrop, the two countries have agreed to reduce the amount of fishing by Chinese fishermen in the restricted waters for three consecutive years since 2016 (Ministry of Oceans and Fisheries of ROK 2018).

Further, the Lee Myung-bak government (2008.2–2013.2), which was known for pro-American propensity, had more meetings with China than were held during the first half of Park Geun-hye's presidency (20013.2–2017.3), as seen in Table 5.2. More interestingly, the year 2015, which is often seen as the best year in Sino-South Korean relations, recorded the lowest number of meetings between the two countries. Given this discrepancy, the number of meetings is insignificant to understanding the nature of the

South Korea's THAAD system deployment   101

Table 5.2 High-Level Meetings Between China and South Korea (2008–2017)

Year	Leader	Ministerial/Vice-Ministerial Level	Total
2008	4	22	26
2009	4	26	30
2010	5	29	34
2011	2	24	26
2012	5	29	34
2013	2	19	21
2014	4	15	19
2015	3	12	15
2016	2	17	19
2017	4	20	24

Source: Diplomatic White Papers of ROK, 2009–2018.

two countries' relationship. However, the continuation of exchanges (especially through summits), rather than the raw number, is more important and reflects an unbroken relationship, wherein intimacy can be disregarded. Furthermore, there is no remarkable difference in the number of meetings, including summits, during the post-THAAD era vis-à-vis the pre-THAAD era comprising the years 2011, 2013, and 2014. In this sense, the perceived identity of South Korea has not essentially changed for the period under consideration.

In sum, the perceived identity of South Korea as friend to China has not fundamentally changed, despite the conflict over the deployment of the THAAD system. As seen in Table 5.2, social contacts between the two countries have continued, and the number of summits has been stable. Furthermore, a CFMSA search shows that statements used to describe South Korea and Sino-South Korean relations have continued to adhere to the identity of South Korea as friend. Most importantly, the symbol of the social bond between the two states, namely, joint communiques to establish diplomatic relations, has never been abrogated. Thus, China and South Korea are still friends.

China's losing face

China, however, reacted angrily to the THAAD deployment despite continuing to perceive South Korea as a friend. China's reaction can certainly be considered excessive because it lasted for more than two years. Given the case of China's ban on exports of rare earth metals to Japan in 2010, which had previously been the most powerful retaliation measures taken by China, the retaliation for such a considerable period of time against South Korea seemed to cross the line between treating South Korea as a friend and a non-friend. Similar to the North Korean case, discussed in Chapter 4, there is a good explanation for this behavior offered by Chinese face culture.

102 *South Korea's THAAD system deployment*

China failed to save its face after the South Korean deployment of THAAD, and retaliated when it felt it had lost face.

Failure to save face

At first glance, China did not seem to seek face during the THAAD issue, because it had no direct, proactive role to play in the deployment of THAAD, which was basically a matter between the United States and South Korea – the former had the system and sought to deploy it, and the latter had to approve the deployment and provide the site. So, it may seem that the dynamic of Chinese face culture applicable was that of saving face, rather than seeking face. However, this is not the case. The main reason for the THAAD system deployment was to enhance South Korea's security against North Korea's advanced missile and nuclear capabilities (Klingner 2015). South Korea's changed views in accepting THAAD were directly caused by North Korea's provocations, given that President Park mentioned the possibility of its deployment right after North Korea's fourth nuclear test. These provocations by North Korea should have been tackled in the framework of the SPT, to which China was devoted as a responsible great power. So, South Korea's agreement to deploy the THAAD system had an adverse effect on China's efforts to seek face as a responsible great power. In this context, the United States maintained that China should turn its anger away from South Korea and toward North Korea, whose actions provided the impetus for the radar deployment (Kim 2017f). Nonetheless, China should have prevented the deployment of the THAAD system to save its face without creating a negative situation. Therefore, South Korea's decision to deploy it was a failure of saving face from the Chinese perspective.

In addition to losing face due to the failure of the SPT to restrain North Korean provocations (thus leading to the THAAD deployment), it is apparent that China lost face because it was ignored by South Korea. South Korea did what China repeatedly asked the country not to do, despite China's requests for mutual deference. Chinese President Xi Jinping personally had asked South Korea to consider, or respect, China's interests at least three times over several years when he met with South Korean President Park Geun-hye and Prime Minister Hwang Kyo-ahn. Each time, however, South Korea invoked the so-called "three no's principle" regarding THAAD: "No request had been made by Washington, no discussions had taken place, and no decision had been made" (Park and Choi 2016).

The critical event was President Xi's meeting with Prime Minister Hwang Kyo-ahn on June 29, 2016. Before the meeting, Prime Minister Hwang met with Premier Li Keqiang on June 28. Even though Prime Minister Hwang met both the Chinese leaders in two consecutive days, he did not notify either of them about the THAAD deployment. However, only a week later, on July 8, the South Korean government announced its decision to deploy the

South Korea's THAAD system deployment 103

THAAD system. China might have, reasonably enough, felt completely ignored by South Korea. In fact, a year later, Chinese Foreign Minister Wang Yi told this story, which had embarrassed the Chinese diplomats, to the Korean special envoy of President Moon Jae-in:

> When Hwang traveled to China in late June, Chinese President Xi Jinping proposed having discussions through various channels on the THAAD issue in a way that wouldn't harm either side's interests. Shortly after that, [South Korea and the United States] announced the THAAD deployment without any explanation to China ahead of time.
>
> (Kim 2017e)

Beyond being disrespected due to South Korea not informing China of upcoming actions, China believed that South Korea was disloyal to China as a friend. When President Xi Jinping delivered a speech before college students at Seoul National University on July 4, 2014, he put emphasis on loyalty while speaking about the future of Sino-Korean relations. He noted that Chinese people historically have argued that loyalty and righteousness are the nature of a "gentleman" (Xi 2014b). Furthermore, President Xi quoted the Chinese traditional idiom *Yin Shui Si Yuan* (饮水思源) when he met President Park on September 5, 2016. The idiom can be literally translated into "when you have water, don't forget where it comes from," which means, "don't forget who made you who you are." President Xi mentioned this idiom in relationship to South Korea's anti-Japan movements, reminding President Park of China's support in the past, and that the country should not betray China in the present (Jo 2016). But the THAAD system was deployed after all; as a result, China felt it was betrayed by South Korea and thereby lost face.

Restoring lost face

When it came to restoring its humiliated face, China used the option of seeking retaliation. As examined earlier in the chapter, China's retaliation has been twofold: economic and non-economic. China employed the two methods together, which highlights that China's fury against South Korea stemmed from losing face. Despite the fury, the two countries agreed to recover bilateral relations on October 31, 2017 (Glaser and Collins 2017). Further, in an attempt to thaw the ties and rebuild the Sino-South Korean relationship, the South Korean government officially came out with strategies to appease China in November 2017, for example, the "three no's principle," which means "no further anti-ballistic missile systems in Korea, no joining of a region-wide US missile defense system and no military alliance involving Korea, the US and Japan" (Volodzko 2017a). Nonetheless, China has to date shown no tangible signs of having been placated.

Chinese core national interests

It seems plausible that China treated a friend almost as a non-friend because it was a matter of protecting China's core national interests given the inseparable relationship between missile defense and the national security of a state. Some researchers believe that China's retaliation against the deployment of THAAD system is identical to other cases where China believed its national interests were being infringed, including the Norwegian and the French cases briefly touched upon in Chapter 1 (Meick and Salidjanova 2017, 8). However, I believe the South Korean case is different from these cases because the pathway to retaliation was greatly influenced by Chinese face culture. Nevertheless, the argument for national interests being a driving factor in China's response deserves a closer examination because China itself argued that the THAAD system would cause major damage to Chinese national interests.

As seen in Table 5.3, a variety of core national interests appeared in the *People's Daily* news articles between 2008 and 2018. They can be largely divided into three categories: state unity, national security, and development interests of China. The state unity category includes core interests that are necessary for maintaining the entity of China, which include issues of Taiwan, Xinjiang, Tibet, Hong Kong, the Diaoyu Islands, sovereignty, national unification, ethnic unity, and so on. The category of national security includes maritime interests and security, airspace security, border areas, the South China Sea, and so on. The development category includes issues related to supporting China's continuous growth, including people's welfare, science and technology innovation, and securing developmental profits. The Korean Peninsula falls under the category of national security. China's concern is related to insuring stability on the Korean Peninsula. In fact, Chinese scholars have emphasized stability and development on the Korean Peninsula, and include the North Korean issue when they refer to the Korean Peninsula as relating to China's core national interests (Zeng et al. 2015, 261).

The THAAD issue clearly could fall under the national security category. In fact, China officially argues that the deployment of THAAD infringes on China's security interest. For example, Chinese Foreign Minister Wang Yi said that "[o]bviously it will undermine *the strategic security interests of China*" [emphasis added]. He more specifically explained,

> The coverage of the THAAD missile defense system, especially the monitoring scope of its X-Band radar, goes far beyond the defense need of the Korean Peninsula. It will reach deep into the hinterland of Asia, which will not only directly damage *China's strategic security interests*, but also do harm to the security interests of other countries in this region [emphasis added].
>
> (Swaine 2017, 3)

Table 5.3 Chinese Core National Interests Appearing in the *People's Daily* (2008–2018)

Year	Chinese Core National Interests	
	Existing	*Newly Added*
2008	Taiwan, state sovereignty	National security, Tibet, development profit
2009	Taiwan, state sovereignty, territorial integration, Tibet	National unification, Macao, Xinjiang, ethnic unity
2010	Taiwan, state sovereignty, territorial integration, Tibet, national unification	Diaoyu Islands, core values, pop culture
2011	State sovereignty, territorial integration, Tibet, national security, Tibet, development profit, national unification, ethnic unity	National dignity, overall stability of political system and society, stability of social harmony, airspace security, territory
2012	State sovereignty, territorial integration, national unification, Diaoyu Islands, national security, development profit, Macao	maritime interests, Hong Kong
2013	Taiwan, state sovereignty, territorial integration, national unification, Diaoyu Islands, national security, development profit, overall stability of political system and society, maritime interests	Ideology, core business secrets of medium and large state-owned enterprises
2014	Taiwan, state sovereignty, territorial integration, Tibet, core values, national security, development profit, national dignity, Xinjiang, maritime interests	Independence, data sovereignty, Falungong, information territory, basic system, South China Sea
2015	Taiwan, state sovereignty, national security, Tibet, Macao, Xinjiang, Hong Kong, ideology	People's welfare, national modernization, state peace, science and technology innovation
2016	Taiwan, state sovereignty, territorial integration, Tibet, national unification, national security, development profit, national dignity, maritime interests, Macao, Xinjiang, Hong Kong, independence, people's welfare, South China Sea	East China Sea, state regime, border interests, Korean Peninsula
2017	Taiwan, state sovereignty, territorial integration, Tibet, national security, development profit, maritime interests, Xinjiang, independence, South China Sea	Maritime security, territorial sovereignty
2018	Taiwan, state sovereignty, territorial integration, national security, development profit, territorial sovereignty	

Source: Lee (2017b, 51); *People's Daily* Database.

106 *South Korea's THAAD system deployment*

Wang's conception of the THAAD system as affecting Chinese security interests is also found in remarks by Chinese Foreign Ministry spokespersons at various press conferences. As seen in Table 5.4, THAAD has been mentioned in terms of Chinese strategic security interests and security interests multiple times from 2015 to 2018. The word THAAD (萨德) first appeared on February 5, 2015, and was mentioned a total of 347 times at subsequent press conferences (CFMSA). But it is noteworthy that the term THAAD suddenly disappeared from press conferences in 2018.

Judging from statements by China, it might be plausible to argue that China's coercive retaliation against South Korea was due to China's concern about THAAD threatening to undermine China's strategic security interest and core national interests. And as a *People's Daily* commentary put it, in matters related to its national interests, "China has not given in, is not giving in, and will never give in" (Galbraith 2019). The controversy over the technical capacity of the THAAD system, and whether it can monitor China's Intercontinental Ballistic Missile (ICBM), and thus emasculate China's deterrence, is a matter of technical truth and beyond the scope of this book. The point is that China believes and argues that this is the case. And for this reason, China retaliated against its friend for deploying THAAD.

Nevertheless, there are still some questions. First, if China was really concerned about its national security interests, shouldn't China have retaliated against the United States rather than South Korea? Although South Korea agreed to provide the site for the THAAD battery, the system is operated by and belongs to the U.S. military. China has strongly opposed THAAD because it allows the United States to directly monitor China's missiles. President Xi Jinping expressed such Chinese concerns to the U.S. President Obama at the summit. Foreign Minister Wang Yi, too, said that one who has insight could rightly determine the intention of the United States in deploying the THAAD system in South Korea. But if these intentions were clear, and if they were a threat to China's core national interests, then China should have expressed its fury against the United States and should directly demand its removal.

Second, if reactions are driven by national security interests, shouldn't China have strongly retaliated against Japan, too, for deploying a radar similar to the South Korean THAAD system? China expressed its grave

Table 5.4 Types of Chinese National Interests Relating to THAAD (2015–2018)

Types	Frequency
Strategic security interests	39
Security interests	33
Strategic interests	1

Source: CFMSA; Lee (2017e).

concerns for Japan's THAAD radar system, which can also reach Chinese territory, only two times at a Foreign Ministry press conference, compared to more than 300 times for the South Korean THAAD issue.[12]

Third, if national security interests were paramount, shouldn't Russia have retaliated against South Korea, because it is also affected by the THAAD system? In fact, Russia closely cooperated with China including issuing joint statements to oppose the deployment (Rinna 2018). But Russia has not employed any retaliatory measures against South Korea. Is it just because the THAAD system poses a threat to China while only causing low-level anxiety to Russia? (Sinha 2018)

Lastly, why has China's retaliation become lukewarm after South Korea helped it to regain face? Although until 2018 there was no clear evidence of full recovery of Sino-South Korean relations, there were declaratory remarks suggesting the end of retaliation; and THAAD was not mentioned in Chinese Foreign Ministry press conferences in 2018. This thawing in ties was a result of South Korea's efforts to give face to China (e.g., South Korean President Moon putting up with China's humiliation during his state visit; concessions including the "three no's principle" mentioned above).

In short, it is hard to jump to the conclusion that China's severe retaliation against South Korea is caused by a threat to Chinese core national interests. By taking the above questions into consideration, China's argument for strategic security interests looks like an excuse to retaliate against South Korea's action that caused China to lose face.

Conclusion

The Sino-South Korean relationship has continuously improved since the normalization of diplomatic relations in 1992. Despite some ups and downs in their relations, the relationship reached a peak in 2014 and 2015, the so-called best period in history. However, things completely changed in 2016. As the South Korean government announced the possibility of deploying the U.S. THAAD system and later formalized the deployment on its territory, China severely resented South Korea's "betrayal." China's resentment was caused by what it considered a loss of face. Furthermore, this resentment against the actions of a friend (South Korea) led to excessive retaliation against Seoul.

This case supports the hypothesis that China behavior toward the ROK is dependent on its perceived identity of South Korea. However, even the THAAD conflict does not seem to have changed the perceived identity of South Korea as a friend, as can be seen by examining China's words and behaviors. The case also strongly supports the hypothesis that Chinese face culture leads to assertive Chinese foreign policy when China loses its face. China lost its face in the process of opposing the deployment of the THAAD system in South Korea. To recover from humiliation due to the actions of a friend, China chose to take economic as well as non-economic

108 *South Korea's THAAD system deployment*

retaliatory measures. However, China's argument for its strategic security interests slightly supports the hypothesis that Chinese inconsistent behavior on South Korea is influenced by Chinese core national interests. However, there is also good evidence that China only uses its argument for core interests as an excuse for retaliation due to a loss of face. Thus, findings from this case do not weaken the hypothesis regarding the effect of Chinese face culture. Meanwhile, China has hardly behaved as a responsible great power in the South Korean case – neither through words nor through behaviors. As a result, the South Korean THAAD case strongly supports Hypotheses H1d and H3a, while offering only slight support for H2b. As concerns H1b (*China's proclaimed identity of a responsible great power influences its policy toward South Korea*), the effect of this proclaimed identity is unknown.

Notes

1 Because the THAAD case is a relatively recent event, there are no documents to reveal its inside story, when compared to the North Korean case examined in Chapter 4. So, the analysis here is heavily dependent on news articles in constructing developments.
2 Since China has been a good friend of North Korea and South Korea has been a good friend of the United States, the Sino-South Korean relationship is unlikely to be completely independent of the Sino-U.S. relationship and the inter-Korean relationship. However, the United States and inter-Korean relations are controlled to simplify the discussion, as suggested in Chapter 1.
3 In fact, President Lee had the same number of summits (11) with the U.S. and Chinese counterparts during his term from 2008 to 2013. When meetings with Chinese Premier Wen Jiabao were included, President Lee had a total of 16 summits with Chinese leaders.
4 To be specific, Seoul and Beijing agreed to promote close communications between the two leaders, as well as set up four channels of strategic dialogues:

> [D]ialogue between the Korean Director of National Security Office and the Chinese State Councilor; foreign policy and security dialogue; policy dialogue among parties; and a joint strategic dialogue between national research institutes. The two countries also agreed to hold the Vice Foreign Ministerial Strategic Dialogue twice a year.
> (Ministry of Foreign Affairs of ROK 2014, 85)

5 There was an unfortunate incident regarding dissemination of the expression "best period in history," later in 2015 when President Park visited Beijing. The Presidential Office, Blue House, released a press release in which President Xi was quoted as saying, "The Sino-South Korea relationship developed into the best period in history because of cooperation by President Park and me." But they canceled this release because it was mistranslated by an intern.
6 President Park's personal preference for China might be more important than strategic considerations in guiding her actions, judging from her unconventional way of ruling, revealed through her impeachment trial. She was the most popular Korean politician in China because the Chinese had a good regard for her due to her apparent fluency in Chinese and her understanding of Chinese culture.
7 On March 9, 2016, quoting the interview report by the Voice of America (VOA) Korea, the Korean news agency Yonhap reported former Secretary of Defense

Leon Panetta saying that he discussed the THAAD system with South Korea during the Lee Myung-bak presidency. However, his remarks cannot be found in the VOA interview report on March 3, 2016, neither in the English version nor in the Korean version.

8 In the English version, the phrase "paying the penalty" was removed; the equivalent phrase was retained in the Chinese original. It must be noted here that the identity of *Global Times* is controversial: it is considered the voice of the CCP, and sometimes also seen to engage in a form of yellow journalism.

9 Wang Yi's argument was repeated as such on February 15 by Foreign Ministry Spokesperson Hong Lei.

10 In this context, the South Korean government was unwilling to file a lawsuit with the WTO against China, where the two countries are members.

11 There were some criticisms of President Park after the THAAD issue in Chinese media, but these criticisms used quotations from South Korean's own media that criticized President Park, rather than offering independent criticism. This is typical of China's tactics when it wants to criticize somebody. One uncommon case is the criticism of President Park's incapacity by Chinese Korea specialist Li Dunqiu (2017). *Global Times* carried his contribution titled "President Park Completely Put South Korea into Chaos" in a 2017 issue.

12 This is explored in Chapter 7.

6 Case study

North Korea's Taepodong-2 launch and the first nuclear test

North Korea's provocations against the international community have long been a big headache, specifically its development of a nuclear program and a missile program as a possible vehicle for a nuclear bomb. Despite 20 UNSC resolutions to prevent North Korea's nuclear ambitions, the international community has failed to tackle this issue, and Pyongyang has increasingly developed their nuclear and missile capabilities for the past several decades. Finally, North Korea declared on February 10, 2005, that it had nuclear weapons, and stipulated its status as a nuclear power in the national constitution on April 2012.

Many states, especially the United States, have ascribed the failure to prevent North Korea's nuclear development to China's lack of action (and will) on the issue. Thus, the United States has pushed China to exert its influence on North Korea, so that North Korea would refrain from any further provocations and comply with the UNSC resolutions. But China has been reluctant to accept the U.S. request and has not exerted vigorous pressure on North Korea. Rather, it has supported North Korea, albeit implicitly, and still treated its neighbor as a friend.

However, this has not always been the case. As discussed in Chapter 3, China treated North Korea as a non-friend by closing the oil pipeline to North Korea in 2003, in an action more dramatic than a simple quarrel between friends.[1] In 2006, there was one more shutdown of the pipeline (Khan 2006). Did this shutdown mean a change in China's perception of North Korea's identity? Were there any other factors to consider, such as the matter of national interests, as realists would advocate? Or, does this pipeline shutdown, especially the second time, support the hypothesis of identity-driven foreign policy? This chapter delves into North Korea's provocations in 2006 by focusing on the Taepodong-2 missile test and the North Korea's first nuclear test in an attempt to answer the above questions.

Background

Origin of the SPT

On April 23–25, 2003, Beijing, Pyongyang, and Washington agreed to hold Three-Party Talks in Beijing to address the second North Korean nuclear

North Korea's TD-2 and nuclear test 111

crisis (also see Chapter 2).[2] The talks were mediated by China, which was a middle-ground strategy between the North Korean goal of a direct bilateral dialogue with the United States and the U.S. firm insistence on a multilateral approach to resolve the issue, with preference for exerting collective pressure (Moon and Bae 2003, 15–16). Moreover, China's proactive behavior during this time was in stark contrast to its stance during the first North Korean nuclear crisis.[3] On the eve of the Three-Party Talks, the Chinese Ministry of Foreign Affairs released a statement saying:

> China has always advocated the peaceful settlement of the Korean nuclear issue through dialogue. This is also the consensus of related parties and the international community. Based on such a consensus, China has invited the DPRK and the United States to send delegations to hold talks in China.
>
> (…, as cited in Fu 2017, 8)

Nevertheless, the talks could not produce any result. North Korea suggested a "new and bold" comprehensive approach by which the United States would offer diplomatic recognition and provide security assurances and economic assistance in return for North Korea's pledge to dismantle its nuclear weapons program, whereas the United States reiterated its position to start the negotiations, regarding demands by North Korea, only if the DPRK abandoned its nuclear program through a "verifiable and irreversible dismantlement" method, which was the precursor of later demands for "Complete, Verifiable, and Irreversible Dismantlement (CVID)" (Chinoy 2008, 171–172). Hence, a stalemate was reached.

Right after the failure of this round of talks, China began to prepare for another round of Three-Party Talks (Pritchard 2007, 101). But both North Korea and the United States were reluctant to have a second round. The United States preferred five-party talks with China, North Korea, South Korea, and Japan (Chinoy 2008, 166). North Korea still wanted to have a bilateral dialogue with the United States, and insisted on the participation of Russia as the next best option. However, it strongly opposed the participation of Japan. China preferred to only invite South Korea to the next talks (Shin 2005, 39–40). Thus was born the SPT – a multilateral dialogue framework involving China, North Korea, South Korea, Japan, Russia, and the United States that was especially designated to tackle North Korean issues. It was hoped that the SPT would meet all parties' satisfaction, and the first round of the SPT was held in Beijing on August 27–29, 2003. Due to a sharp gap in positions between the United States and North Korea, however, the participants could not reach agreement on a joint statement. Instead, the SPT chairman, Wang Yi, delivered an oral summary of the common understanding of the participants (Funabashi 2007, 345).[4]

Three points are noteworthy from the first round of the SPT in terms of the purpose of this case study. First is that China was satisfied with the issuance of the chairman's statement, despite the failure to draw up a joint statement. It seems that China was proud of hosting the SPT because it showed

112 *North Korea's TD-2 and nuclear test*

its diplomatic capabilities and its peace-loving image to the world (Lee 2005, 94–95). Second, China became the permanent host country after the parties could not agree on the choice of location for the talks; besides, China was growing accustomed to its role as a host, and it became a source of prestige (Funabashi 2007, 340).[5] Third, China employed the carrot rather than the stick, which was used for the Three-Party Talks, to bring North Korea back to the multilateral talks. It is said that China promised to provide 10,000 tons of diesel oil to North Korea for free when Dai Bingguo, chief deputy minister for Foreign Affairs of China, paid a visit to Pyongyang on July 12, 2003 (Shin 2005, 41–42).

The second round of the SPT was held on February 25–28, 2004 – originally scheduled for December 25–27, 2003. Because North Korea repeatedly maintained that participation in the SPT was meaningless and, thus, it was no longer interested in taking part in the SPT, China tried to coax Pyongyang into coming back to the table by suggesting the construction of a glass factory in North Korea free of cost (Funabashi 2007, 347). During the talks, North Korea proposed a so-called "comprehensive approach" that would temporarily freeze its overall nuclear program, albeit without complete dismantlement, in return for the U.S. security assurance. However, the United States reiterated its CVID requirement (Funabashi 2007, 349).[6]

The second SPT made some progress compared to the first one in that it released a chairman's statement that was a little more formal than a host's oral summary, which followed the first round. Furthermore, participants agreed to establish a working group to support future SPT (Funabashi 2007, 352–353). However, China revealed its intention to develop the SPT into a regional security regime (Shin 2005, 46).

To encourage North Korea to participate in the next round of SPT, China again dangled the carrot. At the summit between North Korean leader Kim Jong-il and Chinese President Hu Jintao on April 19–20, 2004, China promised to provide heavy oil, amounting to CN¥0.3 billion, to North Korea free of charge (Shin 2005, 48). Thanks to this offer, the third round of the SPT was held on June 23–26, 2004. In contrast to the previous SPTs that were more focused on dialogue to figure out the difference in positions between participants, the third round of the SPT made some headway in negotiations (Kwak 2004, 42–47). In this situation, Chairman Wang Yi had to use the phrase "for the first time" several times because North Korea and the United States seemed to be ready to negotiate "for the first time" (Funabashi 2007, 360).

After the third round, there was a hiatus for about 13 months. On February 10, 2005, North Korea suspended its further participation in the SPT on the grounds that the United States had called it "an outpost of tyranny", and also officially declared that it had nuclear weapons (Snyder 2007, 163). A North Korean official said that the only way North Korea would return to the SPT was if the United States formally retracted the naming of North

Korea as an outpost of tyranny (Funabashi 2007, 376). Although there was no official U.S. retraction, North Korea decided to return to the SPT without providing a justification (Hill 2014, 210–211). South Korea gave an ostensible reason to North Korea to return by providing the country with 500,000 metric tons of food, while China put constant pressure on North Korea as well (Pritchard 2007, 108–109).

The first session of the fourth round of the SPT was held on July 26–August 7, 2005, and the second session on September 13–19, 2005. The issue this time round was the North Korean demand for a light water reactor: the DPRK argued for the right to peaceful use of nuclear power, whereas the United States had concerns about nuclear proliferation (Kwak 2007, 16–17; Pritchard 2007, 120–123). The compromise was to insert the phrase "at an appropriate time" in the joint statement. However, the definition of appropriate time was ambiguous. For example, as the Chinese Foreign Ministry spokesperson said, "It requires further consultation among the six parties to define when will be the appropriate time" (Pritchard 2007, 125). For the United States, however, the appropriate time was to be determined by "North Korean action in fulfilling its denuclearization obligations" (Hill 2014, 240).

Further, at the end of the fourth round, a joint statement was issued for the first time since the SPT began in 2003. As one of the goals of the joint statement, the first session of the fifth round of the SPT was held on November 9–11, 2005. However, the talks ended in a stalemate due to two issues raised by North Korea. One was the demand to provide a light water reactor and the other was the request for the United States to lift financial sanctions, which were imposed in response to money laundering activities involving the Macau-based Banco Delta Asia Bank (Funabashi 2007, 401–415; Kwak 2007, 21–22; Pritchard 2007, 127–129).

Developments

Launch of Taepodong-2

Amid a tug-of-war between the United States and North Korea over the financial sanctions, when Kim Gye-gwan, deputy foreign minister of North Korea and SPT representative, visited Tokyo to attend the meeting of Northeast Asia Cooperation Dialogue on April 13, 2006, he said,

> We don't care about the delay of the SPT. We can have more deterrence [while delaying the talks]. As soon as the money [in the Banco Delta Asia Bank] comes into my hands, I will go to the meeting. No concession for this matter. If the U.S. wants to pressure us, we will take a stronger measure.
>
> (Jung 2006)

114 *North Korea's TD-2 and nuclear test*

A week later, Chinese President Hu Jintao during a visit to the United States met U.S. President George W. Bush to discuss the SPT. President Bush asked President Hu to tell Kim Jong-il that the United States was ready to work on a peace treaty if North Korea was willing (Funabashi 2007, 422). So, on April 27–28, 2006, State Councilor Tang Jiaxuan and Vice Foreign Minister Wu Dawei secretly visited North Korea. But there was no positive response from Kim Jong-il.[7]

From March to June, the Japanese news agency Kyodo News continually reported that a launch of the Taepodong-2 missile seemed to be pending. In response to these moves from North Korea, the U.S. Secretary of State Condoleezza Rice warned on June 19, 2006, that North Korea's missile launch would be regarded as a provocative act and a violation of moratorium responsibility under the joint statement of the fourth round of the SPT (Cooper and Onishi 2006). In response, the next day, Ri Pyong Dok, a researcher from North Korea's Foreign Ministry, asserted that Pyongyang did not have to keep any promises regarding missile tests, nor was it bound by any statement, because this issue concerned their autonomy (Cooper and Gordon 2006). On June 22, 2006, Han Song Ryol, deputy chief of North Korea's mission to the United Nations, aligned himself with Ri by saying, "North Korea as a sovereign state has the right to develop, deploy, test fire and export a missile." However, he also noted, "We are aware of the U.S. concerns about our missile test-launch. So, our position is that we should resolve the issue through negotiations" (Herman 2006).

On the same day, former Defense Secretary William J. Perry and Assistant Secretary of Defense Ashton B. Carter wrote an op-ed in the *Washington Post* urging President Bush to launch a pre-emptive strike against North Korea's long-range ballistic missile (Carter and Perry 2006). At the same time, the international community, including the other SPT members, exhorted North Korea not to launch any missiles. The UN Secretary-General Kofi Anan urged Pyongyang to halt test preparations: "I hope that the leaders of North Korea will listen to and hear what the world is saying. We are all worried" (…, as cited in Pritchard 2007, 147).

China's attitude was noteworthy. On June 27, 2006, Chinese Foreign Minister Li Zhaoxing had a meeting with South Korean Foreign Minister Ban Ki-moon. After the meeting, Chinese Foreign Ministry Spokesperson Jiang Yu said,

> Both sides believe that under the current situation relevant parties should stick to the direction of solving this issue through dialogue and peaceful means, avoid intensifying antagonism and tension, and to press ahead with the resumption of the six-party talks at an early date so as to maintain peace and stability in the Korean peninsula.
>
> (Voice of America 2006)

North Korea's TD-2 and nuclear test 115

On June 28, 2006, China offered a more resolute statement. Chinese Premier Wen Jiabao issued an unprecedented public warning.

> We are paying close attention to the information showing there might be a possible missile-testing launch by North Korea. We hope that the various parties will proceed for the greater interest of maintaining stability on the Korean Peninsula and *refrain from* taking measures that will worsen the situation [emphasis added].
>
> (..., as cited in Chinoy 2008, 280)

Despite the international community's unanimous demand that North Korea should stop its provocative missile test, North Korea eventually launched Taepodong-2 on July 5 (July 4, as per U.S. time), along with five Scud and Nodong missiles (Pritchard 2007, 145). North Korea said that the launching of missiles was a part of "routine military exercises to increase the nation's military capacity for self-defense" (Kwak 2007, 27). Although the Taepodong-2 launching seemed to fail technically because it fell into the East Sea right after firing, it still was seen as a serious threat due to its long range, which was presumed to be more than 10,000 km and could reach the U.S. West Coast (Ministry of National Defense of the Republic of Korea 2017, 33).

On July 7, Deputy Chief to the United Nations Han Song Ryol said that North Korea was willing to return to the SPT if the United States lifted sanctions against the Macau-based bank (Kwak 2007, 28). However, on July 15, the UNSC unanimously passed Resolution 1695, which meant that China voted for the resolution, though China had abstained from the previous resolution in 1993 that urged Pyongyang to reconsider its announcement of withdrawal from the NPT. Resolution 1695 condemned North Korea's launch of ballistic missiles and imposed sanctions by demanding that North Korea should stop producing and testing missiles, halt future launches, and unconditionally return to the six-party negotiations (UNSC 2006a; Hill 2014, 247).

In the process of making a draft for the resolution, China opposed invoking the provisions of Article 42 under Chapter VII of the UN Charter, which allowed UN member states to employ military measures (Pritchard 2007, 147). In September 2006, however, Beijing autonomously punished Pyongyang by reducing its oil exports to North Korea, which were previously restored after North Korea's promise to return to the SPT (Twomey 2008, 417; Chanlett-Avery and Rinehart 2013, 10).

The first nuclear test

The international community's condemnation of North Korea missile provocation continued. For example, the multilateral framework of the

116 *North Korea's TD-2 and nuclear test*

Association of Southeast Asian Nations (ASEAN) – the ASEAN Regional Forum (ARF) – which is the only regional regime to promote constructive dialogue and consultation on political and security issues in the region, issued a chairman's statement on August 1, 2006, saying,

> Most Ministers expressed concern over the test-firing of missiles by the DPRK on 5 July 2006 and believed that such tests could have adverse repercussions on peace, stability and security in the region….The Ministers urged the DPRK in this regard to re-establish its moratorium on missile testing.
>
> (ASEAN 2006)

Amid the constant criticism and concerns by the international community, the U.S. broadcasting company ABC News reported on August 17 that there was evidence of North Korea preparing for an underground test of a nuclear bomb (Karl 2006). On October 3, 2006, North Korea announced its plan for a nuclear test in a Foreign Ministry statement, "[T]he field of scientific research of the DPRK will in the future conduct a nuclear test under the condition where safety is firmly guaranteed" (Yonhap News Agency 2006). Three days later, the UNSC issued president's statement underlining that "such a test would bring universal condemnation by the international community and would not help the DPRK to address the stated concerns particularly with regard to strengthening its security" (UNSC 2006b).

Following the release of its plan, Pyongyang finally conducted an underground nuclear test on October 9, 2006. The Korean Central News Agency (KCNA), which is the largest news media run by the North Korean state, released a statement:

> The field of scientific research in the DPRK [North Korea] successfully conducted an underground nuclear test under secure conditions on October 9, Juche 95 (2006), at a stirring time when all the people of the country are making a great leap forward in the building of a great, prosperous, powerful socialist nation. It has been confirmed that there was no such danger as radioactive emission in the course of the nuclear test as it was carried out under scientific consideration and careful calculation.
>
> (…, as cited in Zhang 2007, 1)

The international community immediately responded. The UNSC had an emergency meeting the next morning and discussed whether it should impose sanctions against North Korea. Moreover, U.S. President Bush said that the North Korean nuclear test was "a threat to international peace and security" and denounced it as a "provocative act" (Hoge and Stolberg 2006). China reacted furiously by saying that North Korea had ignored the widespread opposition of the international community and conducted a nuclear test *brazenly*, and that "the Chinese government is firmly opposed to this" (Ministry of Foreign Affairs of PRC 2006b). President Hu Jintao ordered Foreign Minister Li Zhaoxing to covertly meet North Korean First Vice Foreign Minister Kang Sok-ju. On October 12, Foreign Minister Li expressed China's strong displeasure to his counterpart (Shin 2006a; Chinoy 2008, 295). Apart from that, the UNSC passed Resolution 1718 unanimously that required UN members to prevent any provision of nuclear technology, large-scale weapons, or luxury goods to North Korea and permitted inspection of cargo to ensure compliance (UNSC 2006c).

On October 19, Tang Jiaxuan visited Pyongyang and met with North Korean leader Kim Jong-il. Kim expressed regret to Tang for North Korea's nuclear test and also said that North Korea would return to the SPT if it could have some bilateral meetings with the United States (Kim 2006; Pritchard 2007, 156). However, China denied that Kim made an apology to the Chinese delegation. About a report by a Korean newspaper on Kim's apology, Chinese Foreign Ministry Spokesperson Liu Jianchao said, "These reports are certainly not accurate. We have not heard any information that Kim Jong Il apologized for the test" (Jeffries 2010, 168). On October 31, 2006, North Korea agreed to return to the SPT and the second session of the fifth round of the SPT was held on December 18–22, 2006 (Pritchard 2007, 155; Hill 2014, 252).

Analysis

North Korea's identity to China

Explaining China's reduction in oil supply and its vote for the UN sanctions requires close examination of how China identifies North Korea. Had their equation changed for China under the new circumstances? It is surely not impossible for identity to change dramatically, especially for a proclaimed identity that is announced by oneself. However, a rapid change in identity is practically implausible considering that identity is socially constructed. In particular, it is less feasible for perceived identity to change quickly, since the confirmation of such an identity needs sufficient social contacts that are only built over a period of time. For this reason, China's fury toward North Korea in this case should be considered as an exception rather than as evidence of China suddenly perceiving North Korea as a non-friend.

In this context, gleaning from Chinese statements and behaviors, one can say that for China the perceived identity of North Korea had not changed at all. For example, when the United States suggested on April 26, 2005, that China should shut down its oil pipeline to North Korea, China was reluctant to do so (Pritchard 2007, 111). Furthermore, China opposed invoking Chapter VII of the UN Charter that stipulates "action with respect to threats to the peace, breaches of the peace, and acts of aggression," despite its vote for UNSC resolutions condemning North Korea (Pritchard

118 North Korea's TD-2 and nuclear test

2007, 92). Also, China and North Korea had constant exchanges between high-ranking officials, including national leaders, regardless of Pyongyang's provocations in 2006.

As can be seen in Table 6.1, there have been constant exchanges of high-level officials between China and North Korea, though the lowest number of exchanges (six) was in 2007, a year after the nuclear test. However, the number is not too significant, given that only nine visits occurred in 2002 and 2003, and eight in 2000, long before the nuclear test. Yet, the lower number of visits in 2007 may be interpreted as friction between the two countries. Nevertheless, if we concluded that China saw North Korea as a non-friend based on this number, it would be inadequate proof. In fact, China's support for continued high-level visits between the two countries (including 10 visits in 2008, 19 in 2009, and 17 in 2010) substantiates that China's perceived identity of North Korea as a friend did not change.

In addition to these behaviors, China's statements show that it still regarded North Korea as a friend. As seen in Table 6.2, the Ministry of Foreign Affairs of PRC always described the relationship between China and North Korea as a relationship between good friends and neighbors. Even after the launch of the Taepodong-2 missile and the nuclear test, this description was used in official statements by spokespersons. Surprisingly, there were only 12 articles in the *People's Daily* from October 9 to November 8, 2006, regarding the nuclear test, which mainly covered responses from the international community (*People's Daily* Database). This again points to no change in perceived identity.

Table 6.1 High-Level Visits Between China and North Korea (2000–2010)

Year/bound for		Leader		Premier/ Vice-Premier Level		Ministerial Level		Total		
		China	NK	China	NK	China	NK	China	NK	Sum
2000		1	–	–	1	4	2	5	3	8
2001		2	1	–	2	7	2	9	5	14
2002		–	–	1	3	4	1	5	4	9
2003		1	–	3	2	1	2	5	4	9
2004		1	–	3	3	4	2	8	5	13
2005		–	1	2	4	2	2	4	7	11
2006	Before nuclear test	1	–	–	1	2	2	3	3	6
	After nuclear test	–	–	–	1	–	–	0	1	1
2007		–	–	–	–	2	4	2	4	6
2008		–	–	1	3	4	2	5	5	10
2009		–	–	3	4	6	6	9	10	19
2010		2	–	5	2	6	2	13	4	17

Sources: Lee (2017, 179); Hiraiwa (2013, 449–469); Ye (2017), Appendix F.

Table 6.2 China's Official Statements on North Korea as a Friend (2006)

Date (2006)	Statements by Chinese Foreign Ministry Spokespersons
January 19	– Although Sino-North Korean relations are in transformation in the 21st century, traditional friendship of parties and peoples between two countries has never changed – As good friends and neighbors, China and North Korea have the responsibility for common development – China and North Korea further strengthened the profound traditional friendship and cooperation between two parties and two peoples
February 14	China and North Korea are good friends and neighbors. Economic and personnel exchanges between the two countries are normal
April 4	China and North Korea have normal and friendly relations of states
April 18	China and North Korea have the traditional relationship of friends and cooperation. Two countries hold good cooperation and exchange in all areas
July 6	China and North Korea are good friends and neighbors. China has always pursued a good-neighbor policy
October 10	– North Korea's nuclear test has a negative impact on China-DPRK relationship. China and North Korea are good friends and neighbors. This policy is unwavering and has never changed – I do not agree with what you just said that China is in alliance with North Korea. China pursues the non-alignment policy and is not aligned with any other country. The relationship between China and the DPRK is a normal state-to-state relations based on the norms of IR – Regarding the second question [revision of the Sino-North Korean Mutual Aid and Cooperation Friendship Treaty], I did not hear any consideration of the revision
October 12	China is committed to developing friendly and cooperative relations between China and the DPRK. The friendship between the Chinese and Korean people is profound

Source: CFMSA.

In short, there are three important reasons that bolster my statement that Chinese perception of North Korea's identity as a friend did not alter despite North Korea's missile launch and nuclear test in 2006. First, the social bond of the Sino-North Korean Mutual Aid and Cooperation Friendship Treaty was not revised. Also, their diplomatic ties established in 1949 did not change. Second, social exchanges between the two states were not suspended. Third, the wordings of official statements still reflected social expressions of intimacy.

China's lost face

China's unexpected behavior of cutting off the oil supply and voting for the sanctions needs closer examination, especially since there was no change

120 *North Korea's TD-2 and nuclear test*

in North Korea's perceived identity of a friend. Can it be explained as loss of face? My answer is in the affirmative. Having been forced to deal with two North Korean provocations, there was sufficient cause for China to feel that it had lost face because of North Korea. There are two ways to confirm whether China lost its face. One is to determine whether this was a negative situation where China was unlikely to save its face. The other is to investigate whether mechanisms of restoring lost face can be observed, which in turn has two remedies: seeking another face or retaliating with fury (as discussed in Chapter 3).

Failure to save face

As discussed in Chapter 3, China's foreign policy is heavily influenced by its culture. This observation also applies to the Sino-North Korean relationship. Besides, "China's expectations of deference (*zunzhong*, 尊重) remain integral to Chinese policy toward North Korea because North Korea 'owes' China special respect" (Easley and Park 2016, 659). Deference in this case refers to saving another's face. However, China experienced a loss of face post the nuclear tests in 2006 as a result of the DPRK not respecting China's ambitions (seeking face as a responsible great power).[8]

In fact, China was ambivalent about hosting both the Three-Party Talks and the SPT in the beginning. Not only that China had to shoulder substantial financial and logistical burden to host the talks (Funabashi 2007, 340), but it was burdensome to convene representatives and mediate their positions through these negotiations. For instance, after the failure of the Three-Party Talks, one Chinese diplomat confessed as follows:

> We wish no more trilateral meetings. China will be bashed from both sides no matter what. We have an old saying in China, we are always expected to give them [North Korea] things with *haokan haochi* [with both good looks and good taste]. North Korea would be unhappy if both the appearance and the substance were not satisfactory. We have had enough. One cause of the failure might be that we had forcefully pulled a reluctant North Korea to the meeting.
>
> (Funabashi 2007, 336)

Nonetheless, China enjoyed projecting the image of being a responsible great power. When the first joint statement was issued following the second round of the SPT, it was "a diplomatic victory for China as host and mediator" (Kwak 2007, 18).

China's ambivalence about hosting the SPT might have been a derivative of its face culture. It is widely known that a Chinese person generally declines a gift two or three times before they receive it. Similarly, China may have wanted to be the host from the outset, but was vacillating in order to

North Korea's TD-2 and nuclear test 121

save face. The following comment by a Japanese government official highlights the same:

> Once during Japan-China bilateral consultations, the Chinese declared that they would stop hosting the six-party talks after two more rounds [that is, after the first round]. But they said nothing this time [the second round]. In its heart of hearts, China probably wants to remain the host. But it wants to be asked by other members to remain the host.
>
> (Funabashi 2007, 326)

Accordingly, China considered the inclusion of the following excerpt in the chairman's statements (second and third rounds of the SPT) as a great honor: "[T]he delegations of the DPRK, Japan, the ROK, Russia and the USA have expressed *their appreciation to the Chinese side* for the efforts aimed at the successful staging of the two [three] rounds of the Six-Party Talks" [emphasis added] (Ministry of Foreign Affairs of ROK 2004). One of the reasons for China's insistence on the resumption of the talks could be its desire to be appreciated by the international community.

However, China's sense of achievement did not last long because North Korea failed to save China's face. The launch of Taepodong-2 on July 5, 2006, made China lose face. First, this launch poured cold water on China's plan to hold another round of the SPT. In fact, before the launch, China had proposed an unofficial meeting of member states of the SPT to discuss the next round on June 28. Chinese Vice Foreign Minister Wu Dawei called the ambassadors of the six member nations and suggested an unofficial round of talks in mid-July (Hankyoreh 2006). A week after China's proposal, however, North Korea launched several missiles, including the Taepodong-2.

Second, North Korea did not pay China deference, and rubbed salt into the wound by ignoring its call for restraint. Premier Wen Jiabao had announced that "China expects North Korea to refrain from taking measures that would worsen the situation" (Funabashi 2007, 465). Instead of complying, North Korean Deputy Foreign Minister Kim Gye-gwan said, "What I hear is, Big Brother is telling Little Brother, 'Don't do that.' But we are not boys. We are a nuclear power" (Chinoy 2008, 280).

Third, North Korea not only ignored China's admonition but also did not notify China of the impending missile test. Though North Korea notified Wu Dawei, China's vice foreign minister, who had explained China's position to the North Korean ambassador to China three times, this notification occurred only one hour before the official announcement (Funabashi 2007, 465). When he met with Dennis Wilder, senior director for Asia at the National Security Council, after the missile launch, one Chinese general did not conceal his fury: "After all we've done for them, they couldn't give us any warning they were going to do this. How dare they?" (Chinoy 2008, 284).[9] What was worse was, on the same day as the missile launch (July 4),

122 *North Korea's TD-2 and nuclear test*

Chinese Foreign Ministry Spokesperson Jiang Yu had announced a Chinese delegation's visit to North Korea from July 10 to 15 to celebrate the 45th anniversary of the Sino-North Korean Mutual Aid and Cooperation Friendship Treaty that was signed in 1961 (CFMSA).[10]

The situation was more serious following the first nuclear test conducted by North Korea on October 9, 2006. Although the pattern of China losing face was similar to the case of the missile test, the level of Chinese humiliation and wrath was not comparable. There are four reasons to suggest that the impact of the loss of face following the missile launch was less severe: first, the missile test of Taepodong-2 dropped into the sea, no less than one minute after launch. Second, by firing other missiles along with Taepodong-2, North Korea argued that the test was just a part of normal military drills. Third, the date of the launch was July 4 as per the U.S. local time, which is U.S. Independence Day, one of its most significant national holidays. The missile launch was therefore obviously aimed at the United States. Fourth, this launch did not devastate the foundations of the SPT. Thus, China could save face to some extent.

However, the nuclear test completely violated international norms, and provoked a totally different response from China. First, the nuclear test frustrated China's efforts to reignite the SPT. Due to North Korea's provocative nuclear test, participant states in the SPT had to discuss severe punishment rather than friendly dialogue. The SPT was out of the limelight, and the UNSC drew more attention, which meant a loss of face for China, the host of the SPT. Second, North Korea notified China only 20 minutes before the test (Huntley 2010). China might have saved some face by apprising the United States of the same, through the U.S. embassy in Beijing, as soon as it was informed (Funabashi 2007, 463). But China did not think a 20-minute warning was sufficient to save its face at all. China felt North Korea had crossed a red line and violated a fundamental understanding of their relationship, which was that North Korea was expected to avoid a nuclear test without prior consultation with China (Chinoy 2008, 295). Third, North Korea intentionally defied China. In late February 2006, Chinese President Hu Jintao sent Wan Jiarui, head of the International Liaison Bureau of the CCP, to Kim Jong-il with a personal message that said, "It was in both China's and North Korea's vital interests to resolve the issue reasonably through negotiation." Kim responded by saying that North Korea was still interested in the SPT (Kim 2011, 149). In turn, North Korean Premier Park Bong-Ju visited Beijing on March 23, 2006, to have a meeting with President Hu (Kim 2011, 149). Furthermore, the date of the nuclear test humiliated China because it was the second day of the Sixth Plenary Session of the 16th Central Committee of the CCP, which was scheduled from October 8 to 11 in 2006 (Paltiel 2008, 96). The plenary session assumed greater importance at the time because President Hu was planning to consolidate his power through this event by announcing action plans for his goal of building a "harmonious society." North Korea's nuclear test overshadowed this critical event.

Restoring lost face

According to the dynamics of Chinese face culture, there are two kinds of remedies to recover a loss of face: (1) seeking another face and (2) retaliating against those who caused the damage. China employed both these two methods to restore its lost face in response to North Korean missile and nuclear tests. As per the first remedy, China made considerable efforts to be recognized as a responsible great power. In so doing, Beijing endeavored to resume the SPT. Right after the missile and nuclear tests, China dispatched high-level officials to persuade North Korea to refrain from further provocation and to return to the SPT. For example, Vice Foreign Minister Wu Dawei visited North Korea after the missile launch in July. He conveyed China's grave concerns to Kim Gye Gwan and urged Pyongyang to return to the SPT (Funabashi 2007, 467). State Councilor Tang Jiaxuan also went to Pyongyang after the nuclear test. He had a meeting with Kim Jong-il and discussed North Korea's return to the SPT in October (Pritchard 2007, 156). These efforts came to fruition in the second session of the fifth round of the SPT held on December 18–22, 2006.

In addition, China voted for UNSC Resolutions 1695 and 1718, which were adopted in response to North Korea's missile launch and nuclear test, respectively. China adhered to the notion that the role of a responsible great power in the international community should be played out in the United Nations (Funabashi 2007, 317). Against the backdrop of unanimous condemnation of North Korea's provocations, China was committed to acting as a responsible great power. Thus, China agreed to the adoption of resolutions of condemnation, in contrast to its previous abstentions against resolutions that were unfavorable to North Korea. For example, China had abstained from the vote on the IAEA resolution that was designated to report North Korea's nuclear program to the UNSC in 1994. It had also abstained from the UNSC resolution that asked North Korea to reconsider its announcement of withdrawal from the NPT in 1993.

In accordance with the second method to restore its lost face, China employed coercive measures (through both words and actions) against North Korea. First, China expressed its rage publicly – contrary to the terms of the Chinese face culture, which dictates that conflict be resolved behind the scenes, because revealing conflict causes a loss of face for all parties. One typical example is the conversation between Wu Dawei and Kim Gye Gwan during Wu's secret visit to Pyongyang after the missile launch:

Wu: This kind of conduct goes against the long friendship between North Korea and China.
Kim: We base every action on the principle of our being a sovereign state. As a sovereign state, we are allowed to develop and test missiles. Friendship has nothing to do with that principle.

124 *North Korea's TD-2 and nuclear test*

Wu: Friendship is a very basic principle. It is an important principle agreed upon by Chairman Mao Zedong and Chairman Kim Il Sung. You have no right to change this principle unilaterally.

Kim: China should go its own way. We will go our own way. Still, we will survive.

(Funabashi 2007, 467)

President Hu Jintao made a public statement that "North Korea should face severe criticism from international society" (Easley and Park 2016, 661). This response was an exception to the rule in that (1) it is uncommon for Chinese leaders to express their opinion publicly and (2) he did not conceal his feelings of outrage, which contradicts Chinese face culture.

After the nuclear test by North Korea, China responded with even greater fury. A significant marker of Chinese anger was the use of the word *hanran* (悍然) in official Chinese statements:[11]

> On 9 October, the Democratic People's Republic of Korea *flagrantly* conducted a nuclear test in disregard of the common opposition of the international community. The Chinese Government is firmly opposed to this act [emphasis added]. To bring about denuclearization of the Korean Peninsula and oppose nuclear proliferation is the firm and consistent stand of the Chinese Government. China strongly urges the DPRK to honor its commitment to denuclearization, stop all moves that may further worsen the situation and return to the Six-Party Talks. To safeguard peace and stability in Northeast Asia serves the interests of all parties involved. The Chinese Government calls on all parties concerned to be cool-headed in response and persist in seeking a peaceful solution through consultation and dialogue. China will continue to make every effort towards this goal.
>
> (CFMSA)

The Chinese word *hanran*, which is usually translated into "brazenly" or "flagrantly" in English, is a rare word to find in official documents and remarks.[12] It is mostly reserved for describing putative adversaries or non-socialist states (Swaine 2009, 4; Moore 2014, 88). As seen in Table 6.3, it is hard to find *hanran* in Chinese Foreign Ministry statements before it was used to describe North Korean actions in 2006. Other than describing the North Korean nuclear test in 2006, the word *hanran* appeared four times in the CFMSA for describing Japan, the Philippines, and India. All of them are used in cases that are perceived as challenges to China's territorial sovereignty.

In addition to expressing its fury with words, China took actions to exact revenge for its loss of face. As mentioned earlier, China voted for two UNSC resolutions against North Korea. Although China did not approve much

Table 6.3 Mentions of *Hanran* (悍然) in Official Press Conferences (2001–2018)

Date	Expressions
September 30, 2012	The Japanese government has *brazenly* made the wrong decision to "purchase" the Diaoyu Islands. This is gravely infringing on China's territorial sovereignty. It sparks the strong indignation of the entire Chinese people and also seriously damages Sino-Japanese relations
June 29, 2015	It is the expansion policy employed by the Philippines that *brazenly* infringes on China's sovereignty and rights and interests, causing disputes over the South China Sea
July 6, 2017	The purpose of the Indian side to provoke the incident is clear. On the pretext of so-called "security concerns" and the so-called "protection of Bhutan, it *brazenly* crossed the boundary of Sikkim delineated by the Convention Between Great Britain and China Relating to Sikkim and Tibet, which was recognized by both China and India
August 3, 2017	On June 18, more than 270 Indian border guards carrying weapons and two bulldozers *brazenly* crossed the boundary of the Sikkim section more than 100 meters in the Doka La pass and entered Chinese territory to obstruct the Chinese activities for constructing roads

Source: CFMSA.

stricter sanctions, including inspection of cargo to and from North Korea, it was meaningful that China voted for the sanctions against North Korea, which included an embargo on arms sales and luxury goods, as well as a freeze on North Korean assets. Although these votes can be seen as an expression of China's desire to play the role of a responsible great power, they could also be seen as an action to punish North Korea at the same time. According to the Chinese Permanent Representative to the United Nations Wang Guangya,

> On 9 October, the Democratic People's Republic of Korea had flagrantly conducted a nuclear test in disregard of the common opposition of the international community. China's Foreign Ministry had issued a statement on the same day, expressing firm opposition to that act. Proceeding from the overall interests of bringing about denuclearization of the Korean peninsula and maintaining peace and stability there and in North-East Asia, China supported the Council in making a firm and appropriate response.
>
> (UNSC 2006d)

126 *North Korea's TD-2 and nuclear test*

Apart from that, China also avenged itself by controlling the oil supply to North Korea. Despite the arguments regarding the level of North Korea's oil dependence on China due to inaccurate data, it is indisputable that China's suspension of oil supply to North Korea was detrimental to its economy and further survival.[13] As discussed in Chapter 4, China had earlier pressured North Korea into participating in the Three-Party Talks by threatening to close down the oil pipeline. Once again, China pulled out this card. In September 2006, China sharply reduced the oil supply to the degree where any further reduction could lead to a structural problem that the oil feed pipe would become unusable (Twomey 2008, 417). Instead, all of China's oil exports in September were sent to the United States (Moore 2014, 88).[14]

Further, China also stopped all financial transactions between its four largest banks – Bank of China, Shanghai Pudong Development Bank, China Construction Bank, and CITIC Bank – and North Korea after the nuclear test (Fairclough and King Jr. 2006; Moore 2014, 88–89).

Chinese core national interests

China's assertive attitude toward its friend North Korea also stemmed from North Korea's infringement on China's core interests (as also discussed in Chapter 2). In fact, China has frequently defended its core interests through acts of retaliation. As briefly mentioned in Chapter 1, Japan, Norway, France, Taiwan, and the Philippines all suffered from economic retaliation by China, because the country perceived that these nations were undermining its core interests.

China has repeatedly declared its willingness to use armed force when its core interests are infringed. Despite controversy over the exact definition of Chinese core interests, they are generally understood as what Dai Bingguo suggested in 2009, which are "1) preserving China's basic state system and national security; 2) national sovereignty and territorial integrity; and 3) the continued development of China's economy and society" (Swaine 2011, 4). Applying these initial core interests to explaining China's retaliation against Japan, Taiwan, and the Philippines shows that each of these retaliatory acts was related to "national sovereignty and territorial integrity" issues, because retaliation by China was caused by territorial disputes with these countries. Similarly, Norway and France were seen as challenging China's commitment to "preserving China's basic system" because they supported Chinese dissidents.

Does this same analysis apply to the North Korean case? At a glance, North Korea's missile launch and nuclear test are not directly related to the Chinese core interests. Nonetheless, a brief look into the term "core interests" in official Chinese documents, however, yields interesting findings. The first official entry of the term is found in the report of a meeting between Chinese Foreign Minister Tang Jiaxuan and the U.S. Secretary of State Colin Powell on January 19, 2003 (Swaine 2011, 3). In this meeting,

Tang said that "the Taiwan question is one of China's core interests and that handling the issue in a careful and appropriate way is critical to the stable development of Sino-US relations" (*China Daily* 2003). According to the records of the *People's Daily* from January 1, 2000, to October 27, 2016, Chinese core national interests have been expanding over time – from one core interest in 2004 (the Taiwan question) to 19 in 2016 (Lee 2017a).

There have been no Chinese core national interests directly, or even indirectly, related to North Korea's provocations in 2006, because the Korean Peninsula was included as a Chinese core interest only in 2016. As seen in Table 6.4, only Taiwan, sovereignty, territorial integrity, and history are mentioned as Chinese core national interests in the *People's Daily* around 2006 (Lee 2017a, 49–52). This result is in accordance with the outcome of content analysis using CFMSA, as seen in Table 6.5. The term "core interests" first appeared on CFMSA only in 2004. Before 2004, the term "fundamental interests" was generally used. All reference to *core interests* are made regarding Taiwan. "Sovereignty" and "territorial integrity" are mostly used along with references to Taiwan, rather than used separately, such as in the following sentence, typically: "The matter of Taiwan is related to sovereignty, territorial integrity, and core interests."

In short, there is no ground for claiming that China's retaliation against North Korea was caused by North Korea's infringement on China's core national interests. The missile launch and nuclear test in 2006 by North Korea

Table 6.4 Chinese Core National Interests That Appeared in the *People's Daily* (2004–2007)[15]

Year	Chinese Core National Interests	
	Existing	Newly Added
2004	Taiwan	–
2005	Taiwan	Sovereignty, territorial integrity
2006	Taiwan, sovereignty, territorial integrity	History
2007	Taiwan, sovereignty, territorial integrity	–

Source: Lee (2017b, 51).

Table 6.5 Chinese Core National Interests in CFMSA (2004–2007)

Year	Frequency	Chinese Core National Interests
2004	6	Taiwan
2005	4	Taiwan (sovereignty, territorial integrity)
2006	2	Taiwan (sovereignty, territorial integrity)
2007	4	Taiwan (sovereignty, territorial integrity)

Source: CFMSA.

128 *North Korea's TD-2 and nuclear test*

are not related to any Chinese core national interests such as Taiwan, sovereignty, territorial integrity, and history, which are the only terms in the *People's Daily* around the period of 2006 when North Korea's provocations were made.

Conclusion

Findings from the case study on North Korea's first nuclear test support Hypothesis 1a (*China's proclaimed identity of great power or responsible great power influences its policy toward North Korea*), Hypothesis 1c (*China behaves according to its perceived identity of North Korea in Sino-North Korean relations*), and Hypothesis 3a (*Chinese face culture leads to assertive Chinese foreign policy when China loses its face*). However, the findings reject Hypothesis 2a (*Chinese inconsistent behaviors on North Korea are influenced by Chinese core national interests*).

Thus, a summary of the dynamics of Chinese face culture that were in operation after the North Korean missile and nuclear tests is as follows: China felt it lost face because of North Korean provocations while it was seeking the face of a responsible great power. It then made an effort to restore its face by forcing North Korea to return to the SPT on the one hand; while, on the other hand, it tried to recover from the humiliation (loss of face) by expressing its rage through both words and actions. In other words, China's North Korean policy (inconsistent behavior toward North Korea) stemmed from its own proclaimed identity as a responsible great power and the perceived identity of North Korea as a friend.

Notes

1 From the North Korean perspective, however, China's identity is sometimes that of "not a good friend." This can be a good example to understand the discrepancy between state identity and national identity. Anti-Chinese sentiment among North Koreans is very strong and deep-rooted. North Korean leader Kim Jong-un allegedly argued that "Japan has been the deadly enemy for hundreds of years, but China has been the old enemy for thousands of years" (Denyer 2017). Similarly, there is an episode where the U.S. representative to the Six-Party Talks (SPT), Christopher R. Hill, said to Chinese Chairman Wu Dawei, "I know why they hate us. I know why they hate the Japanese. What I cannot understand is why they hate you" (Hill 2014, 231).

2 The Three-Party Talks were practically held for only two days, wrapping up one day earlier than the original schedule. However, China succeeded in making it a three-day talk, albeit formally, by holding the delegations on the same spot for additional minutes to have a farewell courtesy (Funabashi 2007, 334; Pritchard 2007, 65).

3 In general, three worst-case scenarios are known to be the causes of China's different approaches: "1) North Korean nuclear blackmail directed at China; 2) Japan's ambition to be a nuclear power; and 3) a U.S.-DPRK War" (Kim 2003b, 15).

North Korea's TD-2 and nuclear test   129

4 Pritchard (2007, 104) regarded the summary as the chairman's statement, but it was different from a typical chairman's statement because it was not a written document.
5 At first, some countries thought the host could be rotated and China itself complained about organizing the talks because of the financial burden and uncooperative attitudes of participants (Funabashi 2007, 340).
6 South Korea proposed a compromise with a three-stage process: the first stage is a nuclear dismantlement proclamation of North Korea and oral commitment of security assurance by the United States; the second stage is a freeze of nuclear programs by North Korea and corresponding measures by the other five participants; and the third stage would be the complete dismantlement of nuclear programs by North Korea and implementation of the corresponding measures (Lee 2008). For the details of the South Korean position at the SPT in the beginning, see Lee (2008) and Moon (2008).
7 There are several different stories regarding Tang's visit to Pyongyang. One is that Kim Jong-il was outraged due to China's coercive tactics (Pritchard 2007, 160). Another is that Tang was told that the return to the SPT was only possible when the United States unfroze $24 million at Macao bank (Lee 2006), and yet another is that Kim seemed not to believe China's real intention (Funabashi 2007, 423).
8 In fact, the role of China was intentionally administered by the United States because the latter wanted to put more pressure on China to play an active role in tackling the North Korean issue. For example, Deputy Secretary of State Robert Zoellick believed that China, as a responsible stakeholder, should prove that it was pursuing a peaceful rise not only in words but also in action (Funabashi 2007, 316).
9 North Korea often challenges China in this way. When North Korea declared that it had nuclear weapons, it did not give prior notice of its announcement to China, which, as a result, lost face in the world (Funabashi 2007, 323)
10 The delegation went to Pyongyang as scheduled despite the nuclear test. But the head of the delegation, Vice Premier Hui Liangyu, was not received by Kim Jong-il, which was regarded by China as losing face (Cheow 2006, 34–35).
11 The English translation that follows is by the Ministry of Foreign Affairs of PRC, http://www.china-embassy.org/eng/fyrth/t275508.htm
12 The Chinese Foreign Ministry translated it into "flagrantly," while *China Daily* and Xinhua News Agency translated it into "brazenly" and "brazen," respectively.
13 The expected dependence varies from 50 to 100 percent depending on the energy expert consulted.
14 For this reason, Cheow (2006, 36) used the word "delayed" instead of "cutting off."
15 However, sovereignty and national integration also appeared in the *People's Daily* in 2004, according to its own database. This difference stems from the databases used, because Lee (2017) used the Chinese National Knowledge Infrastructure (CNKI) database.

7 Conclusion

When Chinese President Xi Jinping delivered a speech at the Seoul National University, ROK, in 2014, he mentioned eight historical persons: four were Chinese and four were Korean, dating from 219 B.C. to the 1900s. They all left significant marks on the history of Sino-Korean relations. Although China and South Korea had gone to war with each other, President Xi's speech was a reminder that China and Korea have had a long and close relationship, dating from ancient times.[1] This historically close relationship has continued to shape relations between China and both North Korea and South Korea even today.

The PRC and the DPRK have been friends forged in blood since the establishment of their governing parties and modern states. When these states were founded, they immediately recognized and established diplomatic ties with each other. Also, China signed a treaty of alliance with North Korea in 1961. In contrast, the PRC and the ROK have officially been friends since their normalization of diplomatic relations in 1992. Based on these traditional relations, in his Seoul address, President Xi addressed North Korean Leader Kim Jong-un as "comrade" and South Korean President Park Geun-hye as "an old friend." Furthermore, he described the Sino-South Korean relationship as follows:

> Historically, whenever the two nations have been in a perilous situation, they helped each other out and overcame the difficulties. Now the two nations clearly have a strategic cooperative partnership and the relationship is *better than ever before* [emphasis added].
>
> (Xi 2014b; Han and Lim 2014)

Regarding Sino-North Korean relations, he said:

> [North Korean Leader Kim Jong-un's visit to China] fully showed his fixed will to attach great importance to the strengthened strategic communication between the two parties of China and the DPRK and to develop the traditional friendship of the two countries and demonstrated

Conclusion 131

to the whole world the *invincibility of the relations* between the two parties and two countries [emphasis added].

(North Korea Leadership Watch 2018)

However, despite PRC's proclamations of friendship with both North and South Korea, Sino-North Korean as well as Sino-South Korean relations have experienced grave conflicts beyond simple frictions and quarrels (as already discussed in earlier chapters). China's excessive attacks on its friends are difficult to understand. In order to better comprehend the puzzling behavior, let us consider a contrasting example: South Korea (which has pursued differing policies toward North Korea according to the government in power) has often treated North Korea as a friendly partner worthy of dialogue and cooperation, despite provocations by the latter. For example, the Kim Dae-jung government pursued the so-called Sunshine Policy of engagement even in the face of two naval skirmishes. So, why does South Korea behave according to the perceived identity of friendship between nations, despite challenges, but China does not? Is China's foreign policy not influenced by identity? Or is there another factor influencing China's foreign policy, in addition to the significant role of identity?

As mentioned earlier, China's unexpected behavior toward its friends becomes more puzzling when considering its not-so aggressive behavior toward Japan in response to the THAAD deployment. Why did China not take any stringent measures against Japan? Is it because China thinks of Japan as a friend more than as an enemy? Or is it something else altogether? The book has attempted to explore the above questions, among others.

This concluding chapter presents my arguments based on the findings from the case studies discussed in previous chapters.

Key findings

From the theories and observations presented in previous chapters, three major hypotheses and ten sub-hypotheses can be drawn, as seen in Table 7.1. The alternative hypotheses are used to test, and eventually support, my arguments on identity and Chinese face culture. The null hypotheses serve as the counterargument to my claims about the influence of culture and identity on China's foreign policy.

To test hypotheses using the mixed systems research design, three cases were selected: North Korea's Taepodong-2 missile launch and first nuclear test in 2006 and resultant Sino-North Korean relations, South Korea's deployment of the THAAD system and resultant Sino-South Korean relations, and Japan's deployment of the X-band radars from 2005 to 2014 and resultant Sino-Japanese relations. Three measurements are used for identifying friendship between states in these case studies: social bonds, social contacts, and expressions of intimacy. Regardless of the degree of intimacy,

132　*Conclusion*

Table 7.1 Hypotheses of the Book

Category	Major Hypotheses	Sub-Hypotheses
Alternative hypotheses	H1: China's foreign policy is influenced by its proclaimed identity and the perceived identities of others	H1a: China's proclaimed identity of great power or responsible great power influences its policy toward North Korea
		H1b: China's proclaimed identity of great power or responsible great power influences its policy toward South Korea
		H1c: China's proclaimed identity of great power or responsible great power influences its policy toward Japan
		H1d: China behaves according to its perceived identity of North Korea in Sino-North Korean relations
		H1e: China behaves according to its perceived identity of South Korea in Sino-South Korean relations
		H1f: China behaves according to its perceived identity of Japan in Sino-Japanese relations
	H3: China's foreign policy is moderated by Chinese face culture	H3a: Chinese face culture leads to assertive Chinese foreign policy when China loses its face
Null hypotheses	H2: Chinese foreign policy is influenced by Chinese core national interests	H2a: Chinese inconsistent behaviors regarding North Korea are influenced by Chinese core national interests
		H2b: Chinese inconsistent behaviors regarding South Korea are influenced by Chinese core national interests
		H2c: Chinese inconsistent behaviors regarding Japan are influenced by Chinese core national interests

the relationship is treated as friendly when these three measurements are fulfilled to some extent. Additionally, public statements and behaviors are used as evidence to support or reject the hypotheses throughout the case studies.

The effect of identity on Chinese foreign policy

Using observations and theory, the study has tested whether China's foreign policymaking is influenced by identity – proclaimed or perceived, or both. A brief summary for each of the aforementioned three cases is as follows.

The North Korean Case. When the first North Korean nuclear crisis occurred in 1993, China acted as a bystander. In 1994, tensions between North Korea and South Korea increased to such a degree that Pyongyang

Conclusion 133

threatened to turn Seoul into a "sea of fire," resulting in scared Seoulites rushing to buy and store instant noodles, water, and other necessities (Williams 2013). The United States and South Korea asked China to exert influence on North Korea so as to ease tensions in the Korean Peninsula. Nevertheless, China adhered to the position of a third party and did not ratchet up pressure on North Korea (Snyder 2009, 117–118).

In contrast, China was, however, willing to take on a mediator's role in the second nuclear crisis, and accepted the U.S. request to play a proactive role. China was encouraged to take on this new role by its own proclaimed identity of a responsible great power. Yet, notwithstanding the mediator's role, China still considered North Korea its friend. It even tried to defend and speak on behalf of North Korea at international gatherings. Thus, there was no change in North Korea's perceived identity as friend to China during the second nuclear crisis. This conclusion is substantiated by China's official words and actions during this time. The social bond of friendship between China and North Korea is symbolized by the enduring Sino-North Korean Mutual Aid and Cooperation Friendship Treaty. The treaty has never been revised or abrogated, even after North Korea's arguably treacherous behavior. Furthermore, social exchanges, as represented by mutual inter-state visits of leaders and high-ranking officials, were never halted. Despite the decrease in their overall number, mutual visits between political elites of China and North Korea continued. Moreover, official Chinese statements never described Sino-North Korean relations in unfriendly terms. Therefore, China's punitive economic retaliation was targeted at a friend, not at a non-friend.

Thus, the North Korean case strongly supports H1a (*China's proclaimed identity of great power or responsible great power influences its policy toward North Korea*) and H1d (*China behaves according to its perceived identity of North Korea in Sino-North Korean relations*), as seen in Table 7.1.

The South Korean Case. As stated earlier, China perceives South Korea as a friend. In accordance with that the Sino-South Korean relationship has been continuously upgraded since the normalization of diplomatic relations in 1992. The two nations have even concluded a Korea-China Free Trade Agreement and established a military hotline. And although the THAAD deployment caused a souring of relationship, it did not escalate to a point that China changed its perception of South Korea as a friend. This unchanged identity is confirmed by China's behavior, through words and actions, post the deployment. The social contacts through exchanges of high-level officials continued; official Chinese statements on Sino-South Korean relations did not show any deep hostility; and most importantly, joint communiques establishing and continuing diplomatic relations – an important symbol of social bonds between two states – were never revised or abrogated. Thus, the South Korean case supports Hypothesis H1e (*China behaves according to its perceived identity of South Korea in Sino-South Korean relations*).

134 *Conclusion*

However, this study failed to find any evidence supporting Hypothesis H1b (*China's proclaimed identity of great power or responsible great power influences its policy toward South Korea*). There were no prominent statements or behaviors relating to China's proclaimed identity as a responsible great power before or after the South Korean THAAD issue. At the same time, the South Korean case also does not provide evidence to reject H1b, because the lack of claims of responsible great power status does not necessarily mean that China's behavior stems from an absence of such claims.

The Japanese Case. It strongly supports H1f (*China behaves according to its perceived identity of Japan in Sino-Japanese relations*). China has developed two ambivalent perceived identities of Japan in recent years: a partner identity in economic relations and a rival identity, in effect a potential adversary, in political relations. The partner identity is often overwhelmed by the rival identity.

However, regarding H1c (*China's proclaimed identity of great power or responsible great power influences its policy toward Japan*) direct evidence is not found. Although the identity of Japan as a rival might be likely to have formed partly due to Chinese proclaimed identity of great power status for itself, no specific evidence of this Chinese proclaimed great power identity can be found in the context of the Japanese radar case.

The effect of Chinese face culture on Chinese foreign policy

Remarks by national leaders and political elites provide substantial evidence of the influence of Chinese culture on foreign policy. As a corollary, Chinese face culture also influences foreign policy. The North Korean case well demonstrates not only the importance of seeking face (China's dedication to the proclaimed identity of responsible great power), but also the direct and important effects of the dynamics of losing face (a result of DPRK's missile and nuclear tests). Therefore, Hypothesis H3a (*Chinese face culture leads to assertive Chinese foreign policy when China loses its face*) is strongly supported by the North Korean case.

The South Korean case also strongly supports H3a: when China lost face in the events after the deployment of THAAD, it launched economic and political retaliation against South Korea.

However, the effect of Chinese face culture on foreign policy is limited, compared to the effect of identity. As seen in Figures 7.1 and 7.2, below, Chinese face culture only influences certain moments in the history of Sino-North Korean and Sino-South Korean relations. It does not create or sustain a long-term foreign policy trend. In this context, the role of face culture in foreign policymaking is to affect the foreign policy that is more fundamentally shaped by identity. Therefore, the two cases also strongly support H3 (*China's foreign policy is moderated by Chinese face culture*).

However, no dynamics of Chinese face culture were found to influence China's response to the Japanese deployment of X-band radars. However,

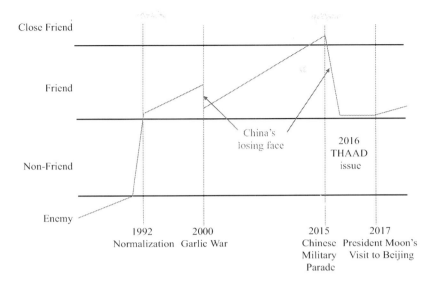

Figure 7.1 Fluctuations in Sino-South Korean Relations.

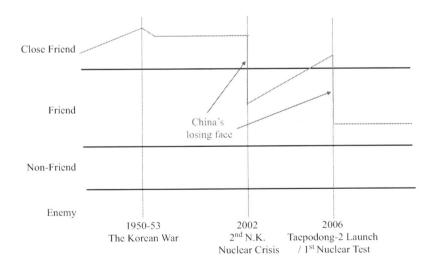

Figure 7.2 Fluctuations in Sino-North Korean Relations.

this does not mean that the Japanese case undermines claims about the importance of Chinese face culture. In fact, in the Japanese case, the dynamics of face culture were not at all at play: China did not expect any deference from Japan (a non-friend), and thus did not risk a loss of face due to the radar deployment (disrespectful action).

136 *Conclusion*

Effect of core national interests on Chinese foreign policy

About the mainstream realist counterargument that Chinese core national interests account for foreign policy decisions, the three cases produce mixed results.

The North Korean case rejects H2a (*Chinese inconsistent behaviors regarding North Korea are influenced by Chinese core interests*). In terms of Chinese reactions during the second North Korean nuclear crisis, it was arguably too early in its period of national development for China to apply the logic of core national interests to its retaliation against North Korea's misbehaviors. Moreover, North Korean defense and its development of a nuclear program had never been discussed by Chinese officials in terms of their relationship to Chinese core national interests. Although had North Korea's nuclear missiles been targeted at Beijing, or if North Korea's nuclear program would have led to more active and deep U.S. engagement on the Korean Peninsula, it could have posed a potential threat to China's security. Nonetheless, national security as a core national interest was not much discussed by Chinese spokespersons until after 2006. Thus, the argument that China's coercive measures were employed because of national interests is not supported by the North Korean case.

The South Korean case, however, shows a different result. It "slightly supports" H2b (*Chinese inconsistent behaviors regarding South Korea are influenced by Chinese core interests*). China has argued that the THAAD deployment undermines Chinese strategic security interests (core national interests), and had suggested that the protection of national security was a core national interest even before the THAAD controversy began in earnest. However, the argument is insufficient to fully support H2b. Rather, China seemed to use the argument of protecting core national interests as an excuse to justify retaliation. But China's excessive retaliation against South Korea can be explained by the dynamics of Chinese face culture. After all, findings from the case study do not weaken the hypothesis regarding the effect of Chinese face culture and do not strongly support H2b. As a result, the South Korean case only "slightly" supports H2b.

However, the Japanese case strongly rejects H2c (*Chinese inconsistent behaviors regarding Japan are influenced by Chinese core interests*), although for different reasons than the North Korean case. It is true that the X-band radars in Japan (non-friend) could be seen as challenging Chinese national interests in terms of undermining national security and stability. So, naturally, China should have taken extremely harsh actions against Japan. However, China did not launch any meaningful retaliation at all, suggesting that a defense of Chinese core interests cannot explain Chinese reactions to Japan's THAAD deployment.

Conclusion 137

Table 7.2 Test Results of the Hypotheses

Category	Hypotheses	North Korean Case	South Korean Case	Japanese Case
Alternative hypotheses	H1: China's foreign policy is influenced by its proclaimed identity and the perceived identities of others	Strongly support	Support	Support
	H1a/b/c: China's proclaimed identity of great power or responsible great power influences its policy toward North Korea/South Korea/ Japan	Strongly support	Unknown	Unknown
	H1d/e/f: China behaves according to its perceived identities of North Korea in Sino-North Korean relations/ South Korea in Sino-South Korean relations/Japan in Sino-Japanese relations	Strongly support	Strongly support	Strongly support
	H3: China's foreign policy is moderated by Chinese face culture	Strongly support	Strongly support	Unknown (possibly support)
	H3a: Chinese face culture leads to assertive Chinese foreign policy when China loses its face	Strongly support	Strongly support	Unknown (possibly support)
Null hypotheses	H2: Chinese foreign policy is influenced by Chinese core national interests	Strongly reject	Slightly support	Strongly reject
	H2a/b/c: Chinese inconsistent behaviors on North Korea/ South Korea/Japan are influenced by Chinese core national interests	Strongly reject	Slightly support	Strongly reject

Summary of findings

Table 7.2 lists the hypotheses results discussed in the above sections.

According to the comparable case study method, the North Korean and the South Korean cases are considered as "most different" cases. North and South Korea have many differences in regime types, economic systems, alliance with either China or the United States, and their perceived impact on Chinese core national interests. However, both countries are friends with

138 *Conclusion*

China and both experienced vigorous retaliation by China in response to its loss of face due to their actions (perceived as provocations).

In contrast, the South Korean and the Japanese cases are considered as "most similar" cases. Although South Korea (friend) and Japan (rival) are perceived differently by China, they share many things in common such as democratic political systems, liberal market economies, close trade relations with China, and identity as friends of the United States.[2] Therefore, these three cases are good candidates for mixed systems research, based on methods of analyzing reasons for convergent and divergent results between *most different* and *most similar* cases. The comparison of the three cases is summarized in Table 7.3.

Table 7.3 Features of the Three Cases

	North Korean Case (2006)	South Korean Case (2016)	Japanese Case (2005, 2014)
Perceived identity to China	Friend	Friend	Rival
Retaliation by China	Yes	Yes	No
Regime type	Autocracy	Democracy	Democracy
Economy system	Socialist closed economy	Capitalist open market economy	Capitalist open market economy
Alliance with China	Yes	No	No
Relationship with the United States	Enemy	Friend	Friend
Economic relations with China	Dependency	Interdependent	Interdependent
Geographic proximity	Bordering country	Neighboring country	Neighboring country
China's core national interests	No	Yes	Yes
China's face	Lost	Lost	No
Pattern of losing face	Increased tension → premier's visit to China → meeting with Chinese President →no prior consultation/ notification → return to Pyongyang → action against China's wish	Increased tension → prime minister's visit to China → meeting with Chinese President → no prior consultation/ notification → return to Seoul → action against China's wish	-

This book's contribution to existing literature

Discussions and findings from this book intend to contribute to existing theories of IR and FPA, as well as to area studies on China and relations between China and the two Koreas. The following are some of the recommendations.

First, this book suggests the worthiness of culture- and identity-based approaches to Chinese foreign policy. In particular, it provides new insight to understanding the Sino-North Korean and the Sino-South Korean relationships, by exploring how Chinese culture and identity shape Chinese policy toward these two countries and by contrasting them to the Sino-Japanese relationship. Traditionally, much attention has been paid to Sino-North Korean relations on the Korean Peninsula. However, Sino-South Korean relations have long been neglected in the studies of Northeast Asian security. By examining Sino-North Korean relations and Sino-South Korean relations in a balanced manner, my research foregrounds the impact of Chinese motivations and interests across the entire peninsula.

Second, it provides a multidimensional approach to the study of the effect of identity on foreign policy. In studies of identity and foreign policy, many works have emphasized a state's own proclaimed identity. This book offers the possibility to understand identity from various angles by suggesting two types of state identities: proclaimed and perceived. How a state perceives itself and how it projects itself are important in shaping the state's active behavior, but it is also true that how a state perceives the identity of others is significant in shaping that state's proactive and reactive behavior. To understand a state's foreign policy, both proclaimed and perceived identities are important. Additionally, the book suggests three criteria to measure the perceived identity of friendship between nations: social bonds, social contacts, and expressions of intimacy.

Third, the book proposes three vital dynamics of Chinese face culture at the state level. In previous studies of Chinese face culture, there has been no clear distinction between the dynamics of saving face and losing face. By more clearly distinguishing these two dynamics and adding the dynamic of seeking face, I offer a more robust understanding of Chinese face culture and suggest tools for exploring the operation of Chinese face culture through these three mechanisms. Moreover, the analysis reveals how feeling or cognition is realized as behavior. These dynamics can be seen in operation through mechanisms of reputation or naming and shaming in IR.

Fourth, although this book focuses on Chinese behaviors vis-à-vis North Korea, South Korea, and Japan, findings from this study can be generalized to other cases. For example, in a conflict between China and another state, it would be wholesome to take into account the dynamics of Chinese face culture, too, rather than simply concentrating on infringement of China's core national interests in order to understand the causes of Chinese retaliation.

Lastly, other than theoretical and empirical contributions, the book provides useful insights for policymakers. One tip is that they should not make a minor issue into a major one by humiliating China unconsciously

140 *Conclusion*

due to their ignorance of Chinese face culture. Many issues with China can be solved just by paying proper attention to Chinese face culture. What if the South Korean Prime Minister sincerely had sought the perspective of Chinese leaders before the decision to install THAAD? Moreover, it is necessary not to misunderstand China's real intention in attempting to establish the actual cause of discontent. Practically speaking, China's behavior and responses might not be understood from a traditionally "realist" perspective. But a cultural understanding might explain the motivations behind immediate behaviors. The following example that is commonly found in the business guidebooks on China is quite illustrative: in Chinese culture, it is customary to refuse a gift at least three times before accepting. If the gift-givers misunderstand the first refusal as real, and immediately infer that the receiver does not like to receive a gift, they cannot survive in the Chinese business community. This same insight leads to the conclusion that understanding the culture of a country is significant for foreign policymakers seeking productive international relationships.

The other tip is that it is wise to tackle an issue before it becomes a matter of Chinese face culture. It should also be understood that China's face is directly linked to its leader's face. Hence, understanding the verbal and non-verbal cues offered by the leader becomes important.

Nonetheless, trying to avoid a negative situation does not mean that a state should be obsequious in its relations with China. Rather, policymakers should simply be aware of practically useful methods to work with China – it may sometimes just be wise for a state to withhold its assertive stance.

Future of Chinese foreign policy with identity and culture

The influence of identity and culture on Chinese foreign policy will assume greater importance in the future as China consolidates its position as a global superpower. It means that the world will continue to witness rational and emotional China, all at the same time.

Let us go back to the episode mentioned at the beginning of this book: China's expulsion of the *Wall Street Journal* news reporters. The objectionable phrase in the column, "sick man of Asia," hit China where it hurt the most – its image. During the novel coronavirus pandemic, despite initial failings and amidst growing mistrust toward China in the international community, China has been making efforts to project an image of a winner, a successful controller, and a benevolent global leader providing support to other countries in a difficult situation – shifting the focus from its image as the initial epicenter of the outbreak. So, China regarded the opinion piece as a loss of face. Rather than pursuing or building a new face as a means of restoring its face, it chose to retaliate by expelling the journalists, as a result of the humiliation.

Conclusion 141

Notes

1 China and Korea also fought many times against a common enemy in the Second World War, which has frequently been Japan, as irony would have it.
2 China, Japan, and South Korea have highly close economic relations, especially in trade. For example, China was the top trading partner, and Japan was a top three trading partner with South Korea as of 2016. Japan and South Korea, respectively, are the top two and three trading partners with China as of 2016 (Korea International Trade Association 2016). However, they have political/ security conflicts at the same time. China and Japan have a territorial dispute over the Senkaku Islands/*Diaoyudao*. Japan claims the Dokdo Island and China claims the Ieodo rock, while South Korea also claims sovereignty over both islands. Furthermore, there are conflicts over history textbook issues between China and South Korea, and between China, South Korea, and Japan over the colonial past, such as conflicts over how to accurately present the history of sex slaves during Japanese occupation.

Bibliography

Abrams, Elliot. 2016. "Naming Names–and Naming Streets." *Council on Foreign Relations*. Retrieved from https://www.cfr.org/blog/naming-names-and-naming-streets

Akimoto, Daisuke. 2013. "A Theoretical Analysis of Japan's Changing Security Identity: Through the Application of Analytical Eclecticism." *Electronic Journal of Contemporary Japanese Studies* 13 (1). Retrieved from http://www.japanesestudies.org.uk/ejcjs/vol13/iss1/akimoto.html

Almond, Gabriel A., and Sidney Verba. 1965. *The Civic Culture*. Boston, MA: Little, Brown and Company.

Amako, Satoshi. 2014. "China's Diplomatic Philosophy and View of the International Order in the 21st Century." *Journal of Contemporary East Asia Studies* 3 (2): 3–33.

Anderson, Benedict. 1991. *Imagined Communities*. London: Verso.

Aoyama, Rumi. 2007a. "Chinese Diplomacy in the Multimedia Age." In Kazuko Mori and Kenichiro Hirano (eds.) *A New East Asia: Toward a Regional Community* (pp. 156–182). Singapore: NUS Press.

———. 2007b. "China's Public Diplomacy." *Working Paper* 41. Center of Excellence-Contemporary Asian Studies. Waseda University. Retrieved from http://jairo.nii.ac.jp/0069/00018869/en

Arms Control Association. 2019. "Chronology of U.S.-North Korean Nuclear and Missile Diplomacy." Retrieved from https://www.armscontrol.org/factsheets/dprkchron

Association of Southeast Asian Nations (ASEAN). 2006. "Chairman's Statement of the Thirteenth ASEAN Regional Forum Kuala Lumpur." Retrieved from https://asean.org/chairman-s-statement-of-the-thirteenth-asean-regional-forum-kuala-lumpur/

Ausderan, Jacob. 2013. "How Naming and Shaming Affects Human Rights Perceptions in the Shamed Country." *Journal of Peace Research* 51 (1): 81–95.

Azuma, Yasushi. 2013. "Hagel Vows Defense Commitments to Japan, Including Nuclear Umbrella." *Kyodo News*. Retrieved from https://www.japantimes.co.jp/news/2013/04/30/national/politics-diplomacy/hagel-vows-defense-commitments-to-japan-including-nuclear-umbrella/

Bae, Jong-Yun, and Chung-In Moon. 2014. "South Korea's Engagement Policy: Revisiting a Human Rights Policy." *Critical Asian Studies* 45 (1): 15–38.

Baek, Jongho. 2018. "Korea-China-Japan Garlic Three-Way Battle: Garlic Girls & Curling Game." *Young Nong Shinmun* (The Agriculture Management News).

144 *Bibliography*

Retrieved from http://www.youngnong.co.kr/news/articleView.html?idxno=7278 (In Korean).

Baker, Peter, and Choe Sang-Hun. 2017. "Trump Threatens 'Fire and Fury' against North Korea if It Endangers U.S." *The New York Times.* Retrieved from https://www.nytimes.com/2017/08/08/world/asia/north-korea-un-sanctions-nuclear-missile-united-nations.html

Barnes, Julian E. 2012. "Panetta Announces U.S. Expansion of Missile Defense." *The Wall Street Journal.* (September 17). Retrieved from https://www.wsj.com/articles/SB10000872396390443816804578001750835566198

Baum, Matthew A. 2002. "The Constituent Foundations of the Rally-Round-the-Flag Phenomenon." *International Studies Quarterly* 46 (2): 263–298.

BBC. 2015. "Is Japan Abandoning Its Pacifism?" Retrieved from https://www.bbc.com/news/world-asia-34278846

Berger, Thomas U. 1996. "Norms, Identity and National Security in Germany and Japan." In P. J. Katzenstein (ed.) *The Culture of National Security: Norms and Identity in World Politics* (pp. 317–356). New York: Columbia University Press.

Brady, Anne-Marie. 2015. "China's Foreign Propaganda Machine." *Journal of Democracy* 26 (4): 51–59.

———. 2017. *China as a Polar Great Power.* Cambridge: Cambridge University Press.

Breuning, Marijke. 2007. *Foreign Policy Analysis: A Comparative Introduction.* New York: Palgrave Macmillan.

Brewster, Rachel. 2009. "Unpacking the State's Reputation." *Harvard International Law Journal* 50 (2): 231–269.

Broomfield, Emma V. 2003. "Perceptions of Danger: The China Threat Theory." *Journal of Contemporary China* 12 (35): 265–284.

Brown, Penelope, and Stephen C. Levinson. 1987. *Politeness: Some Universals in Language Usage.* New York: Cambridge University Press.

Brunnstrom, David, and Lesley Wroughton. 2016. "China Calls Obama, Xi Talks 'Constructive.'" *Reuters.* Retrieved from https://www.reuters.com/article/us-nuclear-summit-obama-xi-idUSKCN0WX2RV

Burns, Katherine G. 2000. "China and Japan: Economic Partnership to Political Ends." In Michael Krepon and Chris Gagne (eds.) *Economic Confidence-Building and Regional Security* (pp. 27–58). Washington, DC: Henry L. Stimson Center.

Byman, Daniel L., and Kenneth M. Pollack. 2001. "Let Us Now Praise Great Men: Bringing the Statesman Back in." *International Security* 25: 107–146.

Byun, See-Won. 2017. "The Impact of Chinese National Identity on Sino-South Korean Relations." *Joint U.S. Korea Academic Studies 2017.* Retrieved from http://www.keia.org/publication/impact-chinese-national-identity-sino-south-korean-relations

Cabestan, Jean-Pierre. 2010. "Introduction: China's New Diplomacy: Old Wine in a New Bottle?" In Shaun Breslin (ed.) *Handbook of China's International Relations* (pp. 1–10). London & New York: Routledge.

Callahan, William A. 2010. *China: The Pessoptimist Nation.* New York: Oxford University Press.

Campbell, David. 1992. *Writing Security: United States Foreign Policy and the Politics of Identity.* Minneapolis: University of Minnesota Press.

Cao, Kun, and Cheng Yang. 2016. "*Huanbaobuzaizhangbaishanchenglichaoheyingjizhihuibuquebaofushehuanjinganquan* (环保部在长白山成立朝核应急指挥部确保辐射环境安全)." *The People's Daily.* Retrieved from http://politics.people.com.cn/n1/2016/0111/c1001-28038422.html (In Chinese).

Bibliography 145

Carson, Austin. 2016. "Facing off and Saving Face: Covert Intervention and Escalation Management in the Korean War." *International Organization* 70 (1): 103–131.

Carter, Ashton B., and William J. Perry. 2006. "If Necessary, Strike and Destroy." *The Washington Post*. (June 22). Retrieved from http://www.washingtonpost.com/wp-dyn/content/article/2006/06/21/AR2006062101518.html

Chan, Alvin. 2006. "The Chinese Concepts of Guanxi, Mianzi, Renqing and Bao: Their Interrelationships and Implications for International Business." *ANZMAC 2006 Proceedings: Advancing Theory, Maintaining Relevance*. Brisbane: ANZMAC. Retrieved from http://handle.uws.edu.au:8081/1959.7/44970

Chan, Gerald. 2001. "Power and Responsibility in China's International Relations." In Yongjin Zhang and Greg Austin (eds.) *Power and Responsibility in Chinese Foreign Policy*. Canberra: Australian University Press, 48–68.

Chanlett-Avery, Emma, and Ian E. Rinehart. 2014. "North Korea: US Relations, Nuclear Diplomacy, and Internal Situation." *CRS Report*.

Chang, Hong, Kang Denghui, and Chen Bingjie. 2016. "*zongshu: xijinpingde 'xinxingdaguoguanxi' waijiaozhanlueshizheyanglianchengde* (综述：习近平的"新型大国关系"外交战略是这样炼成的)." *The People's Daily*. Retrieved from http://world.people.com.cn/n1/2016/0213/c1002-28120530.html (In Chinese).

Chen, Dingding, and Jianwei Wang. 2011. "Lying Low No More?: China's New Thinking on the Tao Guang Yang Hui Strategy." *China: An International Journal* 9 (2): 195–216.

Chen, Gina Masullo. 2015. "Losing Face on Social Media: Threats to Positive Face Lead to an Indirect Effect on Retaliatory Aggression through Negative Affect." *Communication Research* 42 (6): 819–838.

Chen, Jian. 2003. "Limits of the 'Lips and Teeth' Alliance: An Historical Review of Chinese-North Korean Relations." *Asia Program Special Report* (Woodrow Wilson International Center for Scholars) 115: 4–10.

Cheng, Joseph Y. S. 1984/85. "China's Japan Policy in the 1980s." *International Affairs* 61 (1): 91–107.

Cheng, Joseph Y. S., and King-Lun Ngok. 2004. "The 2001 'Spy' Plane Incident Revisited: The Chinese Perspective." *Journal of Chinese Political Science* 9 (1): 63–83.

Cheng, Xiaohe. 2015. "The Evolution of the Lips and Teeth Relationship: China-North Korea Relations in the 1960s." In Carla P. Freeman (ed.) *China and North Korea: Strategic and Policy Perspectives from a Changing China* (pp. 119–138). New York: Palgrave Macmillan.

Cheow, Eric T. C. 2006. "The North Korean Missile and Nuclear Crises: China's Historic and Strategic Stakes on the Korean Peninsula." *The Korean Journal of Defense Analysis* 18 (4): 31–50.

Cheung, Han. 2015. "The Day China Joined the UN." *Taipei Times*. Retrieved from http://www.taipeitimes.com/News/feat/archives/2015/10/18/2003630319

Chilcote, Ronald H. 1981. *Theories of Comparative Politics: The Search for a Paradigm*. Boulder, CO: Westview Press.

China Daily. 2003. "Tang, Powell Pledge to Enhance Cooperation." Retrieved from china.org.cn/english/international/54052.htm

China FTA Network. 2015. "Chinese President Xi Jinping and Korean President Park Geun-hye Exchange Congratulatory Letters on the Official Signing of the China-Korea FTA." Retrieved from http://fta.mofcom.gov.cn/enarticle/enkorea/enkoreanews/201506/21937_1.html

Chinese Foreign Ministry Spokespersons Archive (CFMSA) 2001–2018 (each year)

146 *Bibliography*

Chinoy, Mike. 2008. *Meltdown: The Inside Story of the North Korean Nuclear Crisis.* New York: St. Martin's Griffin.

Cho, Seungho. 2015. "[Best Scene in Korean Diplomacy History] Two Breakthroughs after the Korean War." *Donga Ilbo.* Retrieved from http://news.donga.com/List/Series_70000000000588/3/70000000000588/20150824/73207269/1

Cho, Yong-sung. 2016. "THAAD on the Korean Peninsula Will Be Primary Target of PLA." *Aju Business Daily.* Retrieved from http://www.ajunews.com/view/20160217141248473 (In Korean).

Cho, Young Chul. 2012. "State Identity Formation in Constructivist Security Studies: A Suggestive Essay." *Japanese Journal of Political Science* 13 (3): 299–316.

Cho, Young Nam, and Jung Ho Jeong. 2008. "China's Soft Power: Discussions, Resources, and Prospects." *Asian Survey* 48 (3): 453–472.

Cho, Yun Young. 2018. "Kim Jong Un Ordered Internal Guidance to Propagate the Status of Nuclear Power." *Newsis.* Retrieved from http://www.newsis.com/view/?id=NISX20180424_0000289820

Choe, Sang-Hun. 2016. "South Korea and U.S. Agree to Deploy Missile Defense System." *The New York Times.* Retrieved from https://www.nytimes.com/2016/07/08/world/asia/south-korea-and-us-agree-to-deploy-missile-defense-system.html

Choi, Byong-ok, Wontae Kim, Sungchul Shin, Changsu Kim, Jisuk Kang, and Dajeong Kim. 2019. "Trends and Prospects in Supply and Demand of Vegetables for Seasoning." In KREI (ed.) *2019 Agriculture Prospects* (pp. 673–747). Naju: Korea Rural Economic Institute.

Choi, Seunghwan. 2000. "Law and Policy of the Settlement of Korea-China Garlic Dispute." *Trade Law* 34: 83–104 (In Korean).

Choi, Seung-pyo. 2017. "Chinese Tourists Reduced by 64% after THAAD Retaliation." *Joongang Daily.* Retrieved from https://news.joins.com/article/21467437

Choon, Chang May. 2017. "North Korea's Fabled Mount Baekdu Bloodline." *The Straits Times.* Retrieved from https://www.straitstimes.com/asia/east-asia/north-koreas-fabled-mount-baekdu-bloodline

Christensen, Thomas J. 1996. *Useful Adversaries: Grand Strategy, Domestic Mobilization, and Sino-American Conflict, 1947–1958.* Princeton, NJ: Princeton University Press.

Chun, Hye-won. 2017. "President Park Ignored the Possibility of China's Retaliation." *Sisain.* Retrieved from https://www.sisain.co.kr/?mod=news&act=articleView&idxno=28286 (In Korean).

Chung, Chien-Peng. 2012. "China-Japan Relations in the Post-Koizumi Era: A Brightening Half-Decade?" *Asia-Pacific Review* 19 (1): 88–107.

Chung, Jae Ho. 2003/4. "From a Special Relationship to a Normal Partnership? Interpreting the 'Garlic Battle' inSino-South Korean Relations." *Pacific Affairs* 76 (4): 549–568.

———. 2007. *Between Ally and Partner: Korea-China Relations and the United States.* New York: Columbia University Press.

Chung, Jaeho, and Myunghae Choi. 2013. "Uncertain Allies or Uncomfortable Neighbors? Making Sense of China-North Korea Relations, 1949–2010." *The Pacific Review* 26 (3): 243–264.

Chung, Wa Dae. 2017. "Address by President Moon Jae-in at the Körber Foundation, Germany." Retrieved from http://www.korea.net/Government/Briefing-Room/Presidential-Speeches/view?articleId=156591&pageIndex=10

Confucius. 2015. *The Analects*. Translated by Robert Eno. Retrieved from http://www.indiana.edu/~p374/Analects_of_Confucius_(Eno-2015).pdf

Cooper, Helene, and Michael R. Gordon. 2006. "North Korea Disavows Its Moratorium on Testing of Long-Range Missiles." *The New York Times*. Retrieved from https://www.nytimes.com/2006/06/21/world/asia/21korea.html

Cooper, Helene, and Norimitsu Onishi. 2006. "Rice Says North Korean Missile Test Would Be 'Provocative Act.'" *The New York Times*. Retrieved from https://www.nytimes.com/2006/06/20/world/asia/20korea.html

Copeland, Dale C. 1997. "Do Reputations Matter?" *Security Studies* 7: 33–71.

Cotton, James. 1993. *Korea under Roh Tae-Woo: Democratization, Northern Policy, and Inter-Korean Relations*. St. Leonards: Allen & Unwin.

———. 2003. "The Second North Korean Nuclear Crisis." *Austrian Journal of International Affairs* 57 (2): 261–279.

Crescenzi, Mark J. C. 2018. *Of Friends and Foes: Reputation and Learning in International Politics*. New York: Oxford University Press.

Cronin, Richard P. 2002. "Japan-U.S. Cooperation on Ballistic Missile Defense: Issues and Prospects." *CRS Report for Congress* No. 9186. Retrieved from https://archive.org/stream/9186Japan-USCooperationonBallisticMissileDefenseIssuesandProspects-crs/9186%20Japan-U.S.%20Cooperation%20on%20Ballistic%20Missile%20Defense_%20Issues%20and%20Prospects_djvu.txt

Deborah, Welch A. 2003. "Culture and Emotion as Obstacles to Good Judgment." In Stanley A. Renshon and Deborah Welch Larson (eds.) *Good Judgment in Foreign Policy: Theory and Application* (pp. 3–24). Lanham, MD: Rowman & Littlefield Publishers.

Deng, Xiaoping. 1990. "Seize the Opportunity to Develop the Economy." Retrieved from https://dengxiaopingworks.wordpress.com/2013/03/18/seize-the-opportunity-to-develop-the-economy/

———. 1994. "With Stable Policies of Reform and Opening to the Outside World, China Can Have Great Hopes for the Future." *Selected Works of Deng Xiaoping, Vol. III (1982–1992)*. Beijing: Foreign Languages Press. Retrieved from https://dengxiaopingworks.wordpress.com/2013/03/18/with-stable-policies-of-reform-and-opening-to-the-outside-world-china-can-have-great-hopes-for-the-future/

Deng, Yong. 2015. "China: The Post Responsible Power." *The Washington Quarterly* 37 (4): 117–132.

Deng, Yuwen. 2013. "China Should Abandon North Korea." *Financial Times*, February 27. Retrieved from https://www.ft.com/content/9e2f68b2-7c5c-11e2-99f0-00144feabdc0

Denyer, Simon. 2017. "In China, a Sense of Betrayal after the Assassination of Kim Jong Nam." *The Washington Post*. Retrieved from https://www.washingtonpost.com/world/in-china-a-sense-of-betrayal-after-the-assassination-of-kim-jong-nam/2017/02/17/434d7626-f4f0-11e6-8873-a962f11835fb_story.html?utm_term=.cbb6a56c42cf

d'Hooghe, Ingrid. 2005. "Public Diplomacy in the People's Republic of China." In J. Melissen (eds) *The New Public Diplomacy. Studies in Diplomacy and International Relations*. London: Palgrave Macmillan.

Dittmer, Lowell, and Samuel S. Kim. 1993. *China's Quest for National Identity*. Ithaca, NY: Cornell University Press.

Dobson, Hugo. 2016. "Is Japan Really Back? The 'Abe Doctrine' and Global Governance." *Journal of Contemporary Asia* 47 (2): 199–224.

148 Bibliography

Doshi, Rush. 2017. "Xi Jinping Just Made It Clear Where China's Foreign Policy Is Headed." *The Washington Post.* Retrieved from https://www.washingtonpost.com/news/monkey-cage/wp/2017/10/25/xi-jinping-just-made-it-clear-where-chinas-foreign-policy-is-headed/?utm_term=.bd7b55970b0b

———. 2019. "Hu's to Blame for China's Foreign Assertiveness?" *Brookings Institute.* Retrieved from https://www.brookings.edu/articles/hus-to-blame-for-chinas-foreign-assertiveness/

Downs, E. S., and P. C. Saunders. 1998/1999. "Legitimacy and the Limits of Nationalism: China and the Diaoyu Islands." *International Security* 23 (3): 114–146.

Draudt, Darcie. 2015. "The Park-Xi Friendship and South Korea's New Focus on China." *China Brief* 15 (18). Retrieved from https://jamestown.org/program/the-park-xi-friendship-and-south-koreas-new-focus-on-china/

Dreyer, June Teufel. 2016. *Middle Kingdom and Empire of the Rising Sun: Sino-Japanese Relations, Past and Present.* Oxford: Oxford University Press.

Du, Jing. 2005. "Hu Addresses ROK's National Assembly." Retrieved from http://www.gov.cn/misc/2005-11/17/content_101300.htm

Duan, Xiaolin. 2017. "Unanswered Questions: Why We May Be Wrong about Chinese Nationalism and Its Foreign Policy Implications." *Journal of Contemporary China* 26 (108): 886–900.

Dueck, Colin. 2006. *Reluctant Crusaders: Power, Culture, and Change in American Grand Strategy.* Princeton, NJ: Princeton University Press.

Easley, Leif-Eric, and In Young Park. 2016. "China's Norms in Its Near Abroad: Understanding Beijing's North Korea Policy." *Journal of Contemporary China* 25 (101): 651–668.

Ebel, R. H., R. Taras, and J. D. Cochrane. 1991. *Political Culture and Foreign Policy in Latin America: Case Studies from the Circum-Caribbean.* Albany: State University of New York Press.

Edelmann, Robert J. 1985. "Individual Differences in Embarrassment: Self-Consciousness, Self-Monitoring and Embarrassability." *Personality and Individual Differences* 6: 223–230.

Editorial Board. 2018. "Editorial: Xi Jinping Dreams of World Power for Himself and China." *The New York Times.* Retrieved from https://www.nytimes.com/2018/02/27/opinion/xi-jinping-power-china.html

Editors. 2019. "Boxer Rebellion." *Encyclopedia Britannica.* Retrieved from https://www.britannica.com/event/Boxer-Rebellion

Entous, Adam, and Julian E. Barnes. 2012. "U.S. Plans New Asia Missile Defenses." *The Wall Street Journal.* Retrieved from https://www.wsj.com/articles/SB10000872396390444812704577605591629039400

Fairbank, John K. 1942. "Tributary Trade and China's Relations with the West." *The Far Eastern Quarterly* 1(2): 129–149.

Fairclough, Gordon, and Neil King Jr. 2006. "China Banks to Halt Dealings with North Korea." *Wall Street Journal.* Retrieved from https://www.wsj.com/articles/SB116124405366997523

Fearon, James D. 1999. "What Is Identity (As We Now Use the Word)?" Retrieved from http://www.stanford.edu/~jfearon/papers/idn1v2.pdf

Feng, Huiyun. 2007. *Chinese Strategic Culture and Foreign Policy Decision-Making.* New York: Routledge.

Fenghuangwang (凤凰网). 2010. "1983*nianzhuochangrenjiejian: xijuxingkaipizhonghanjiaotongdao* (1983年卓长仁劫机案: 戏剧性开辟中韩外交通道)." Retrieved from http://news.ifeng.com/history/zhongguoxiandaishi/201002/0201_7179_1532268_1.shtml

Festinger, Leon. 1957. *A Theory of Cognitive Dissonance*. Stanford, CA: Stanford University Press.

Fletcher, Joseph F. 1968. "China and Central Asia, 1368–1884." In John K. Fairbank (ed.) *The Chinese World Order: Traditional China's Foreign Relations* (pp. 206–224). Cambridge, MA: Harvard University Press.

Foster, Paul B. 2006. *Ah Q Archaeology: Lu Xun, Ah Q, A Q Progeny and National Character Discourse in Twentieth Century China*. Lanham, MD: Lexington Books.

Francovic, Kathy. 2018. "The President and the American people see North Korea differently." Yougov. Retrieved from https://today.yougov.com/topics/politics/articles-reports/2018/09/27/president-and-american-people-see-north-korea-diff

Frendreis, John P. 1983. "Explanation of Variation and Detection of Covariation: The Purpose and Logic of Comparative Analysis." *Comparative Political Studies* 16 (2): 255–272.

Friedberg, Aaron L. 2012. *A Contest for Supremacy: China, America, and the Struggle for Mastery in Asia*. New York: W.W. Norton & Company.

Friman, Richard H. 2015. "Introduction: Unpacking the Mobilization of Shame." In Richard H. Friman (ed.) *The Politics of Leverage in International Relations: Name, Shame, and Sanction* (pp. 1–29). London: Palgrave Macmillan.

Fu, Ying. 2017. "The North Korean Nuclear Issue: Past, Present, and Future: A Chinese Perspective." *Strategy Paper* 3: 1–27. Retrieved from https://www.brookings.edu/wp-content/uploads/2017/04/north-korean-nuclear-issue-fu-ying.pdf

Fu, Yiqin. 2018. "Data Analysis: Who Votes with China, and Who Votes with the US and Europe at the UN?" Retrieved from https://yiqinfu.github.io/posts/united-nations-general-assembly/

Funabashi, Yoichi. 2007. *The Peninsula Question: A Chronicle of the Second Korean Nuclear Crisis*. Washington, DC: Brookings Institution Press.

Galbraith, Andrew. 2019. "China Will Never Yield on Core National Interests: People's Daily." *Reuters*. Retrieved from https://www.reuters.com/article/us-usa-trade-china/china-will-never-yield-on-core-national-interests-peoples-daily-idUSKCN1OW026

Gao, Charlotte. 2017. "China and South Korea Hail 'New Start' Amid Scuffle." *The Diplomat*. Retrieved from https://thediplomat.com/2017/12/china-and-south-korea-hail-new-start-amid-scuffle/

Gartzke, Erik, and Alex Weisiger. 2012. "Fading Friendships: Alliances, Affinities and the Activation of International Identities." *British Journal of Political Science* 43: 25–52.

Geddes, Barbara. 2003. *Paradigms and Sand Castles: Theory Building and Research Design in Comparative Politics*. Ann Arbor: University of Michigan Press.

Gellner, Ernest. 1983. *Nations and Nationalism*. Ithaca, NY: Cornell University Press.

Geva, Nehemia, and D. Christopher Hanson. 1999. "Cultural Similarity, Foreign Policy Actions, and Regime Perception: An Experimental Study of International Cues and Democratic Peace." *Political Psychology* 20 (4): 803–827.

Glaser, Bonnie S., and Brittany Billingsley. 2012. "Reordering Chinese Priorities on the Korean Peninsula." A Report of the CSIS Freeman Chair in China Studies. Retrieved from https://www.csis.org/analysis/reordering-chinese-priorities-korean-peninsula

150 *Bibliography*

Glaser, Bonnie S., and Lisa Collins. 2017. "China's Rapprochement with South Korea: Who Won the THAAD Dispute?" *Foreign Affairs*. Retrieved from https://www. foreignaffairs.com/articles/china/2017-11-07/chinas-rapprochement-south-korea

Global Times. 2016. "Sanctions Should Target North Korea's Nuclear Ambition, Not Public Livelihoods." Retrieved from http://www.globaltimes.cn/content/965818. shtml

Goffman, Erving. 1955. "On Face-Work: An Analysis of Ritual Elements in Social Interaction." *Psychiatry* 18 (3): 213–231.

Goldstein, Judith, and Robert O. Keohane. 1993. "Ideas and Foreign Policy: An Analytical Framework." In Judith Goldstein and Robert O. Keohane (eds.) *Ideas and Foreign Policy: Beliefs, Institutions, and Political Change* (pp. 3–30). Ithaca, NY: Cornell University Press.

Green, Michael, Kathleen Hicks, Zack Cooper, John Schaus, and Jake Douglas. 2017. *Countering Coercion in Maritime Asia*. CSIS. Retrieved from https://amti. csis.org/countering-coercion-hub/

Greenfeld, L., and J. Eastwood. 2007. "National Identity." In C. Boix and S. Stokes (eds.) *The Oxford Handbook of Comparative Politics* (pp. 256–273). New York: Oxford University Press.

Grieco, Joseph M. 1993. "Anarchy and the Limits of Cooperation: A Realist Critique of the Newest Liberal Institutionalism." In David A. Baldwin (ed.) *Neorealism and Neoliberalism: The Contemporary Debate* (pp. 116–169). New York: Columbia University Press.

Gries, Peter Hays. 2004. *China's New Nationalism: Pride, Politics, and Diplomacy.* Berkeley & London University of California Press.

Gries, Peter Hays. 2010. "Experimental Methods and Psychological Measures in the Study of Chinese Foreign Policy." In Allen Carlson, Mary Gallagher, Kenneth Lieberthal, Melanie Manion (eds.) *Contemporary Chinese Politics: New Sources, Methods, and Field Strategies* (pp. 69–87). Cambridge, MA: Cambridge University Press.

Gries, Peter Hays, Kaiping Peng, and Michael H. Crowson. 2012. "Determinants of Security and Insecurity in International Relations: A Cross-National Experimental Analysis of Symbolic and Material Gains and Losses." In Vaughn P. Shannon and Paul A. Kowert (eds.) *Psychology and Constructivism in International Relations: An Ideational Alliance* (pp. 170–193). Ann Arbor: University of Michigan Press.

Gries, Peter Hays, Qingmin Zhang, H. Michael Crowson, and Huajian Cai. 2011. "Patriotism, Nationalism and China's US Policy: Structures and Consequences of Chinese National Identity." *The China Quarterly* 205: 1–17.

Grove, Andrea. 2010. "Culture and Foreign Policy Analysis." In R. Denmark (ed.) *International Studies Encyclopedia* (pp. 764–781). Oxford: Oxford University Press.

Guangxu. 1901. "Imperial Decree on Events Leading to the Signing of Boxer Protocol (光緒二十六年十二月二十六日諭)." Wikisource. Retrieved from https:// en.wikisource.org/wiki/Translation:Imperial_Decree_on_events_leading_to_ the_signing_of_Boxer_Protocol

Gustafsson, Karl. 2015. "Identity and Recognition: Remembering and Forgetting the Post-War in Sino-Japanese Relations." *The Pacific Review* 28 (1): 117–138.

Haberman, Clyde. 1983. "Chinese Jet Is Hijacked to South Korea." *The New York Times*. Retrieved from https://www.nytimes.com/1983/05/06/world/chinese-jet-is-hijacked-to-south-korea.html

Hage, Jerald, and Barbara F. Meeker. 1988. *Social Causality*. New York: Routledge.

Hagström, Linus. 2015. "The 'Abnormal' State: Identity, Norm/Exception and Japan." *European Journal of International Relations* 21(1): 122–145.

Ham, Gyowon. 2018. "Korea's Nappa Cabbage Production Is Top 4 in the World." *Nongmin Shinmun* (The Farmers Newspaper). Retrieved from https://www.nongmin.com/news/NEWS/POL/GOV/292828/view (In Korean).

Hamashita, Takeshi. 2008. *China, East Asia and the Global Economy: Regional and Historical Perspectives*. New York: Routledge.

Han, Jeon, and Jae-Un Lim. 2014. "President Xi, 'Korea-China Relations Better than Ever.'" Retrieved from http://www.korea.net/NewsFocus/Society/view?articleId=120421

Han, Kuei-Hsiang. 2016. "The Feeling of 'Face' in Confucian Society: From a Perspective of Psychosocial Equilibrium." *Frontiers in Psychology* 7 (1055): 1–9.

Han, Sukhee. 2009. "China's Position on North Korean Nuclear Issues." *EAI Issue Briefing* 2009-03 (In Korean).

Hankyoreh. 2006. "China Proposes Informal Six-Party Talks on N.K. Nuclear Issue." Retrieved from http://english.hani.co.kr/arti/english_edition/e_international/137955.html

Harding, Harry. 2013. "American Visions of the Future of U.S.-China Relations: Competition, Cooperation, and Conflict." In David Shambaugh (ed.) *Tangled Titans: The United States and China* (pp. 389–409). New York: Rowman & Littlefield.

Hafner-Burton, Emilie M. 2008. "Sticks and Stones: Naming and Shaming the Human Rights Enforcement Problem." *International Organization* 62 (4): 689–716.

Harrison, Selig S. 2005. "Did North Korea Cheat?" *Foreign Affairs*. Retrieved from https://www.foreignaffairs.com/articles/asia/2005-01-01/did-north-korea-cheat

Hartig, Falk. 2016. *Chinese Public Diplomacy: The Rise of the Confucius Institute*. London & New York: Routledge.

He, Yinan. 2013. "War, Myths, and National Identity Formation: Chinese Attitudes toward Japan." In Gérard Bouchard (ed.) *National Myths: Constructed Pasts, Contested Presents* (pp. 223–242). New York: Routledge.

Herman, Burt. 2006. "White House Rejects N. Korea Plea for Talks about a Missile Test." *Deseret News*. Retrieved from https://www.deseretnews.com/article/640188969/White-House-rejects-N-Korea-plea-for-talks-about-a-missile-test.html

Hill, Christopher. 2007. "Bringing War Home: Foreign Policy-Making in Multicultural Societies." *International Relations* 21 (3): 259–283.

Hill, Christopher R. 2014. *Outpost: Life on the Frontlines of American Diplomacy*. New York: Simon & Schuster.

Hinze, Carl G. 2012. "Chinese Politeness Is not about 'Face': Evidence from the Business World." *Journal of Politeness Research* 8 (1): 11–27.

Hiraiwa, Shunji. 2013. *The Democratic People's Republic of Korea and the People's Republic of China*. Translated by Jongkuk Lee. Seoul: Sunin (In Korean).

Ho, Benjamin Tze Ern. 2016. "About Face – The Relational Dimension in Chinese IR Discourse." *Journal of Contemporary China* 25 (98): 307–320.

Ho, David Yau-fai. 1976. "On the Concept of Face." *American Journal of Sociology* 81 (4): 867–884.

Hoef, Yuri V., and Andrea Oelsner. 2018. "Friendship and Positive Peace: Conceptualising Friendship in Politics and International Relations." *Politics and Governance* 6 (4): 115–124.

152 Bibliography

Hoge, Warren, and Sheryl G. Stolberg. 2006. "Bush Rebukes North Korea: U.S. Seek New U.N. Sanctions." *The New York Times* Retrieved from https://search-proquest-com.du.idm.oclc.org/docview/93071935?accountid=14608

Hoo, Tiang Boon. 2018. *China's Global Identity: Considering the Responsibilities of Great Power.* Washington, DC: Georgetown University Press.

Hornung, Jeffrey W., and Kenneth M. McElwain. 2017. "Abe's Victory and Constitutional Revision." *Foreign Affairs.* Retrieved from https://www.foreignaffairs.com/articles/japan/2017-10-31/abes-victory-and-constitutional-revision

Hu, Hsien-Chin. 1944. "The Chinese Concepts of 'face.'" *American Anthropologist* 46 (1): 45–64.

Hu, Weixing. 2019. "Xi Jinping's 'Major Country Diplomacy': The Role of Leadership in Foreign Policy Transformation." *Journal of Contemporary China* 28 (115): 1–14.

Hu, Xiao, and Wenwei Song. 2005. "Japanese Textbook Distorts History, Stirs Fury." *China Daily.* Retrieved from http://www.chinadaily.com.cn/english/doc/2005-04/06/content_431575.htm

Huang, Yi-Hui, and Olwen Bedford. 2009. "The Role of Cross-Cultural Factors in Integrative Conflict Resolution and Crisis Communication: The Hainan Incident." *American Behavioral Scientist* 53 (4): 565–578.

Hudson, Valerie M. 1997. *Culture and Foreign Policy.* Boulder, CO: Rienner.

Hudson, Valerie M. 2014. *Foreign Policy Analysis: Classic and Contemporary Theory.* Lanham, MD: Rowman & Littlefield.

Hughes, Christopher W. 2016. "Japan's 'Resentful Realism' and Balancing China's Rise." *The Chinese Journal of International Politics* 9 (2): 109–150.

Hui, Victoria K.-Y., and Michael. H. Bond. 2009. "Target's Face Loss, Motivations, and Forgiveness Following Relational Transgression: Comparing Chinese and US Cultures." *Journal of Social and Personal Relationships* 26 (2–3): 123–140.

Huntley, Wade L. 2010. "Bucks for the Bang: North Korea's Nuclear Program and Northeast Asian Military Spending." *Institute for Policy Studies.* Retrieved from https://ips-dc.org/north_koreas_nuclear_program/

Huntington, Samuel P. 1993. "The Clash of Civilizations?" *Foreign Affairs*, 72 (3), 1993: 22–49.

Hwang, Kyung-sang. 2014. "North Korea's Rodong Missile Launching Targeted at South Korea." *Kyunghyang Shinmun.* Retrieved from https://www.kinds.or.kr/news/detailSearch.do (In Korean).

Igarashi, Aya. 2006. "U.S. to Deploy Radar System Here within 6 Months." *Yomiuri Shimbun.* Retrieved from https://infoweb-newsbank-com.du.idm.oclc.org/apps/news/document-view?p=WORLDNEWS&t=continent%3AAsia%21Asia/country%3AJapan%21Japan/year%3A2006%212006&sort=YMD_date%3AA&maxresults=20&f=advanced&val-base-0=%22X%20band%22&fld-base-0=alltext&docref=news/10FA7081E7F74ED8

Inglehart, Ronald. 1988. "The Renaissance of Political Culture." *American Political Science Review* 82: 1203–1230.

Inoguchi, Takashi. 2005. "Japan's Ambition for Normal Statehood." In Jorge I. Domínguez and Byung-kook Kim (eds.) *Between Compliance and Conflict: East Asia, Latin America, and the New "Pax" Americana* (pp. 135–164). New York & London: Routledge.

Inoue, Masaya. 2009. "Yoshida Shigeru's 'Counter Infiltration' Plan Against China: The Plan for Japanese Intelligence Activities in Mainland China 1952–1954." *World Political Science* 5 (1): 1–24.

Bibliography 153

International Crisis Group. 2009. "Shades of Red: China's Debate over North Korea." *Asia Report N°179*. Retrieved from https://d2071andvip0wj.cloudfront. net/179-shades-of-red-china-s-debate-over-north-korea.pdf

Inuzuka, Ako. 2013. "Remembering Japanese Militarism through the Fusosha Textbook: The Collective Memory of the Asian-Pacific War in Japan." *Communication Quarterly* 61 (2): 131–150.

Jangseogak Royal Archives. "Ikilwugyunhongseobonggeumtanguk (翌ㅣㅣ又遣 洪瑞鳳金盡國)." Retrieved from http://yoksa.aks.ac.kr/jsp/aa/VolView.jsp?- mode=&page=&fcs=&fcsd=&cf=&cd=&gb=&aa10up=&aa10no=kh2_je_a_ vsu_20037_020&aa15no=020&aa20no=20037_020_0016&gnd1=&gnd2= &keywords=%E6%9D%8E%E6%83%87 (In Classical Chinese).

Japan Times. 2013. "U.S. Radar to Counter North's Missiles." Retrieved from https://www.japantimes.co.jp/news/2013/02/24/national/politics-diplomacy/u- s-x-band-radar-to-be-installed-at-asdf-base-to-counter-n-korea-missiles/#. XMJrGOhKi00

Jarvie, Ian C., and Joseph Agassi. (eds.). 1969. *Hong Kong: A Society in Transition*. New York: Frederick A. Praeger.

Jeffries, Ian. 2010. *Contemporary North Korea: A Guide to Economic and Political Developments*. London & New York: Routledge.

Jeon, Sumi. 2018. "Preemptive Strike on North Korea: Explaining the Sino-North Korean Mutual Aid and Cooperation Friendship Treaty." *The Korean Journal of Defense Analysis* 30 (2): 247–263.

Jepperson, Ronald, Alexander Wendt, and Peter J. Katzenstein. 1996. "Norms, Identity, and Culture in National Security." In Peter. J. Katzenstein (ed.) *The Culture of National Security: Norms and Identity in World Politics* (pp. 33–78). New York: Columbia University Press.

Jervis, Robert. 1968. "Hypotheses on Misperception." *World Politics* 20 (3): 454–479.

Jiang, Wenran. 2007. "New Dynamics of Sino-Japanese Relations." *Asian Perspective* 31 (1): 15–41.

Jiang, Yan. 2009. "Exploratory Study on Chinese only Child Generation's Motives of Conspicuous Consumption." *Journal of Dalian Maritime University* 8: 54–58.

Jimbo, Ken. 2002. "A Japanese Perspective on Missile Defense and Strategic Co- ordination." *The Nonproliferation Review*: 56–62. Retrieved from https://www. nonproliferation.org/wp-content/uploads/npr/92jimbo.pdf

Jin, Jingyi. 2015. "China's Anti-Japanese War and the Independence Movement on the Korean Peninsula." In Carla P. Freeman (ed.). *China and North Korea: Strategic and Policy Perspectives from a Changing China* (pp. 109–118). New York: Palgrave Macmillan.

Jin, Jingyi, and Jun Jaewoo. 2012. "Twenty-Years of China-Korea Amity: Retro- spect and Prospects." *The Quarterly Journal of Defense Policy Studies* 95: 45–66 (In Korean).

Jo, Jun-hyung. 2016. "Why President Xi Mentioned Traditional Idiom?" Yonhap News Agency. Retrieved from https://www.yna.co.kr/view/AKR20160905125100014

Jo, Min hee. 2018. "South Korea's Tough Choice on THAAD." *The National Interest*. Retrieved from https://nationalinterest.org/feature/south-koreas-tough- choice-thaad-26132

Joffe, Ellis G. H. 1987. *The Chinese Army after Mao*. Cambridge, MA: Harvard University Press.

Johnston, Alastair Iain. 1995. *Cultural Realism: Strategic Culture and Grand Strategy in Chinese History*. Princeton, NJ: Princeton University Press.

154 *Bibliography*

Johnston, Alastair Iain. 2013. "How New and Assertive Is China's New Assertiveness?" *International Security* 37 (4): 7–48.

Ju, Minuk. 2016. "A Practical Study of the Chinese Face Types." *The Journal of Chinese Studies* 75: 275–297 (In Korean).

Jung, Chol-Ho. 2015. "Strategic Approach to ROK-China Military Cooperation: Limits and Utility." *Sejong Institute.* Retrieved from http://www.sejong.org/boad/1/egoread.php?bd=17&itm=&txt=&pg=1&seq=798 (In Korean).

Jung, Kwonhyun. 2006. "If I Have Macao Funds Frozen by the U.S. in My Hand, I Will Go to the Meeting." *Chosun Ilbo.* Retrieved from http://news.chosun.com/site/data/html_dir/2006/04/14/2006041470026.html?related_all (In Korean).

Kaarbo, Juliet. 2003. "Foreign Policy Analysis in the Twenty-First Century: Back to Comparison, Forward to Identity and Ideas." *International Studies Review* 5 (2): 156–202.

Kaneda, Hideaki, Kazumasa Kobayashi, Hiroshi Tajima, and Hirofumi Tosaki. 2007. "Japan's Missile Defense: Diplomatic and Security Policies in a Changing Strategic Environment." *The Japan Institute of International Affairs.* Retrieved from http://www2.jiia.or.jp/en/pdf/polcy_report/pr200703-jmd.pdf

Kang, Won-Taek (ed). 2012. *Reconsidering the Roh Tae Woo Era: South Korea at the Crossroads.* Paju: Nanam (In Korean).

Karl, Jonathan. 2006. "N. Korea Appears to Be Preparing for Nuclear Test." ABC News. Retrieved from https://abcnews.go.com/International/story?id=2326083&page=1

Katahara, Eiichi. 2007. "Japan's Leap toward a "Normal State" and Its Impact on East Asia." *The Journal of Strategic Studies* 14 (3): 109–136.

Katzenstein, L. C. 1997. "Change, Myth, and the Reunification of China." In Valerie M. Hudson (ed.) *Culture and Foreign Policy* (pp. 45–72). Boulder, CO: Rienner.

Katzenstein, Peter J. (ed.) 1996. *The Culture of National Security. Norms and Identity in World Politics.* New York: Columbia University Press.

Keren, Yarhi-Milo. 2018. *Who Fights for Reputation: The Psychology of Leaders in International Conflict.* Princeton, NJ: Princeton University Press.

Khan, Joseph. 2003. "China Offers Its help in U.S.–North Korea Nuclear Talks." *The New York Times.* Retrieved from https://www.nytimes.com/2003/04/24/world/china-offers-its-help-in-us-north-korea-nuclear-talks.html

———. 2006. "China Cut Off Exports of Oil to North Korea." *The New York Times.* Retrieved from https://www.nytimes.com/2006/10/30/world/asia/30iht-oil.3334398.html?mtrref=www.google.com&gwh=68E7D189AD23167250F0551F882E51B5&gwt=pay

Kim, Ae-kyung. 2004. "The Change in China's Perception of Foreign Identity." *National Strategy* 10 (4): 33–60 (In Korean).

Kim, Chun-Sig. 2014a. "The Effects of Nationalism and Statism in Korean Unification Policies." *Journal of Peace and Unification Studies* 6 (2): 3–38 (In Korean).

Kim, Doo Seung. 2016a. "The Abe administration's China Policy and South Korea." *Journal of Korean-Japanese Military and Culture* 21 (0): 31–60 (In Korean).

Kim, Eun-sik. 2016b. *Chung Yul-Song: The Soldier from Korean Independence Army Who Later Became a Star in China.* Seoul: Isang Media (In Korean).

Kim, Heungkyu. 2009. "China's 'Partnership' Diplomacy: Concept, Process, and Implication." *Korean Political Science Review* 43 (2): 287–305.

Kim, Heungkyu. 2010. "From a Buffer Zone to a Strategic Burden: Evolving Sino-North Korea Relations during the Hu Jintao era." *The Korean Journal of Defense Analysis* 22 (1): 57–74.

Kim, Heungkyu. 2012. "Enemy, Homager or Equal Partner? Evolving Korea-China Relations." *Journal of International and Area Studies* 19 (2): 47–62.
———. 2017a. "China and the U.S.-ROK Alliance: Promoting a Trilateral Dialogue." Discussion Paper at the Council on Foreign Relations. Retrieved from https://www.cfr.org/sites/default/files/report_pdf/Discussion_Paper_Kim_US-China-ROK_OR.pdf
Kim, Hong Youl. 2001. "Comparing the Response by Korea and Japan for China's Safeguard Retaliation." *World Economy* (KIEP) (August): 82–90 (In Korean).
Kim, Hyun Jung. 2019. "South Korea's Use of Force against Chinese Illegal Fishing in the Course of Law Enforcement in the Yellow Sea." *Marine Policy* 99: 148–156.
Kim, Hyung-Suk. 2017b. "The Possibility of Policy Integration on North Korea between Conservative Government and Progressive Government." *The Korean Journal of Unification Affairs* 29 (2): 241–269 (In Korean).
Kim, Inhan. 2018. "No More Sunshine: The Limits of Engagement with North Korea." *The Washington Quarterly* 40 (4): 165–181.
Kim, James D. 2017c. "Empirical Study on South Korean Presidents' Understanding on North Korea: Comparing Operational Code Beliefs of Kim, Roh, Lee and Park (1998–2016)." *Journal of Political Science* 1 (1): 1–15.
Kim, Ji-eun. 2017d. "US Flatly Refuses to Recognize North Korea as a Nuclear State." *Hankyoreh*. Retrieved from http://english.hani.co.kr/arti/english_edition/e_northkorea/822138.html
Kim, Joo Yup, and Sang Hoon Nam. 1998. "The Concept and Dynamics of Face: Implications for Organizational Behavior in Asia." *Organization Science* 9 (4): 522–534.
Kim, Ki Jung. 2008. "Six Illusion of Preoccupation for the U.S.-ROK Alliance." *Pressian*. Retrieved from http://www.pressian.com/news/article.html?no=56605#09T0
Kim, Myungho. 2014b. "60 Years of the Relations between North Korea and China." *Hankyoreh Newspaper Special Series* (In Korean).
Kim, Oui-hyun. 2013. "Park Geun-hye Will Send First Special Envoys to China." *Hankyoreh*. Retrieved from http://english.hani.co.kr/arti/english_edition/e_international/570129.html
———. 2017e. "Special Envoy Holds Meeting in China, Takes First Steps to Healing THAAD Rift." *Hankyoreh*. Retrieved from http://english.hani.co.kr/arti/english_edition/e_international/795723.html
Kim, Samuel S. 2003a. "China's Path to Great Power Status in the Globalization Era." *Asian Perspective* 27 (1): 35–75.
———. 2003b. "China and North Korea in a Changing World." *Asia Program Special Report* 115: 11–17.
———. 2006. *The Two Koreas and the Great Powers*. Cambridge: Cambridge University Press.
Kim, Sung-mi. 2016c. "South Korea's Middle-Power Diplomacy: Changes and Challenges." *Chathamhouse*. Retrieved from https://www.chathamhouse.org/publication/south-koreas-middle-power-diplomacy-changes-and-challenges
Kim, Yanghee. 2006. "Kim Jong Il Apology for Nuclear Test." *Joonang Ilbo*. Retrieved from https://news.joins.com/article/2622082
Kim, Yongho. 2011. *North Korean Foreign Policy: Security Dilemma and Succession*. Plymouth: Lexington Books.
Kim, Young Jae. 2014c. "An Analysis of the Park Geun-hye Government's North Korea Policy." *The Journal of Political Science & Communication* 17 (2): 31–55 (In Korean).

156   *Bibliography*

Kim, Young-kown. 2017g. "China Ordered to Stop Selling Tour Packages for South Korea." VOA Korea. Retrieved from https://www.voakorea.com/a/3748830.html

Kim, Young-nam. 2017f. "US DOD, China Should Express Its Fury to Pyongyang." VOA Korea. Retrieved from https://www.voakorea.com/a/4141258.html

King Ambrose Y. C., and John T. Myers. 1977. "Shame as an Incomplete Conception of Chinese Culture: A Study of Face." Working Paper presented at Social Research Centre. Hong Kong: The Chinese University of Hong Kong.

Kirchner, Alexander, Michael Boiger, Yukiko Uchida, Vinai Norasakkunkit, Philippe Verduyn, and Batja Mesquita. 2017. "Humiliated Fury Is Not Universal: The Co-Occurrence of Anger and Shame in the United States and Japan." *Cognition and Emotion* 32 (6): 1317–1328.

Kirk, Don. 2000. "Just a Little Garlic Overpowers Asian Trade Ties." *The New York Times*. Retrieved from https://www.nytimes.com/2000/07/08/news/just-a-little-garlic-overpowers-asian-trade-ties.html

Kissinger, Henry. 2011. *On China*. New York: The Penguin Press.

Kitchen, Nicolas. 2010. "Systemic Pressures and Domestic Ideas: A Neoclassical Realist Model of Grand Strategy Formation." *Review of International Studies* 36 (1): 117–143.

Klingner, Bruce. 2015. "The Importance of THAAD Missile Defense." *Journal of East Asian Affairs* 29 (2): 21–41.

Koliev, Faradj, and James H. Lebovic. 2018. "Selecting for Shame: The Monitoring of Workers' Rights by the International Labour Organization, 1989 to 2011." *International Studies Quarterly* 62 (2): 437–452.

Konish, Weston S., and Mark E. Manyin. 2009. "South Korea: Its Domestic Politics and Foreign Policy Outlook." CRS Report No. 40851. Retrieved from https://www.hsdl.org/?abstract&did=32756

Korea International Trade Association. 2016. "Trade Statistics." Retrieved from http://stat.kita.net/main.screen#

Korea Tourism Organization. 2018. "Statistics of Korea Tourism," Retrieved from https://kto.visitkorea.or.kr/kor/notice/data.kto

Kwak, Tae-Hwan. 2004. "The Six-Party Nuclear Talks: An Evaluation and Policy Recommendations." *Pacific Focus* 19 (2): 7–55.

———. 2007. "North Korea's Second Nuclear Crisis and the Six-Party Talks." In Seung-Ho Joo and Tae-Hwan Kwak (eds.) *North Korea's Second Nuclear Crisis and Northeast Asian Security* (pp. 15–44). Burlington, VT: Ashgate.

Kwak, Tae-Hwan, and Seung-Ho Joo. 2007. "Introduction." In Seung-Ho Joo and Tae-Hwan Kwak (eds.) *North Korea's Second Nuclear Crisis and Northeast Asian Security* (pp. 1–14). Burlington, VT: Ashgate.

Kwon, K. J. 2012. "North Korea Proclaims Itself a Nuclear State in New Constitution." CNN. Retrieved from https://www.cnn.com/2012/05/31/world/asia/north-korea-nuclear-constitution/index.html

Kyodo News. 2013. "U.S. X-Band Radar to Be Installed at ASDF Base."

Kyunghyang Shinmun. 1965. "South Korea Competes with PRC at the 28th World Table Tennis Championship." Naver News Library. Retrieved from https://newslibrary.naver.com (In Korean).

———. 1968. "PRC Officially Invited to UN Non-Nuclear Conference." Naver News Library. Retrieved from https://newslibrary.naver.com (In Korean).

———. 1969. "South Korea Belongs to the Same Group with PRC and North Korea." Naver News Library. Retrieved from https://newslibrary.naver.com (In Korean).

———. 1971. "Foreign Minister Kim Says Trade with PRC Is Possible." Naver News Library. Retrieved from https://newslibrary.naver.com (In Korean).

———. 1981. "Beijing and Seoul Expand Their Trade." Naver News Library. Retrieved from https://newslibrary.naver.com (In Korean).

Lai, Him M. 2010. *Chinese American Transnational Politics*. Urbana: University of Illinois Press.

Lai, Mark W. 2012. "Chinese Foreign Policy Making 2010–2011: Using the Cultural Approach to Explain Complexity." *Journal of Chinese Political Science* 17: 187–205.

Laitin, David D. 2007. *Nations, States, and Violence*. Oxford & New York: Oxford University Press.

Lao-Tzu. 2010. *Daodejing*. Translated by Robert Eno. Retrieved from http://www.fang.ece.ufl.edu/daodejing.pdf

Larson, Deborah W. 2011. "How Identities Form and Change: Supplementing Constructivism with Social Psychology." In Vaughn P. Shannon and Paul A. Kower (eds.) *Psychology and Constructivism in International Relations: An Ideational Alliance* (pp. 57–75). Ann Arbor: University of Michigan Press.

———. 2015. "Will China Be a New Type of Great Power?" *The Chinese Journal of International Politics* 8 (4): 323–348.

Larson, Deborah W., and Alexei Shevchenko. 2014. "Russia Says No: Power, Status, and Emotions in Foreign Policy." *Communist and Post-Communist Studies* 47 (3/4): 269–279.

Lee, Chae-Jin. 1984. *China and Japan: New Economic Diplomacy*. Stanford, CA: Hoover Institution Press.

Lee, Changhyung. 2012. "Development Direction of ROK-China Military Relations in the Era of Strategic Cooperative Partner." *KIDA Defense Weekly* 1420: 1–8 (In Korean).

Lee, Dong-hui. 2015a. "Chinese Deputy Chief of Staff for the PLA concerned about THAAD." *Chosun Ilbo*. Retrieved from http://news.chosun.com/site/data/html_dir/2015/05/31/2015053101362.html

Lee, Geun. 2018a. "Identity, Threat Perception, and Trust-Building in Northeast Asia," In Kevin P. Clements (ed.) *Identity, Trust, and Reconciliation in East Asia: Dealing with Painful History to Create a Peaceful Present* (pp. 29–46). London: Palgrave Macmillan.

Lee, Gil-sung. 2018b. "China Explained Diplomatic Mishap as a New Practice." *Chosun Ilbo*. Retrieved from http://news.chosun.com/site/data/html_dir/2018/03/27/2018032700193.html

Lee, Heeok. 2010. "China's Policy toward (South) Korea: Objectives of and Obstacles to the Strategic Partnership." *The Korean Journal of Defense Analysis* 22 (3): 283–301.

Lee, Hochul. 2013. "China in the North Korean Nuclear Crises: 'Interest' and 'Identity' in Foreign Behavior." *Journal of Contemporary China* 22 (80): 312–331.

Lee, Hyejoo. 2015c. *The Influence of Face and Luxury Consumption Values on Luxury Consumption among Korean, Chinese, and Japanese Consumers*. Doctoral Book. Retrieved from http://hdl.handle.net/10371/120283 (In Korean).

Lee, Hyo-won. 2011. "Analysis on the Judicial Precedents about the Relationship between South and North Korea." *Seoul Law Journal* 52 (3): 1–36 (In Korean).

Lee, Jiyoung. 2018c. "Service Account Surplus in Korean Culture Increased Due to BTS and Lifting the Ban on Korean Culture." *Joongang Daily*. Retrieved from https://news.joins.com/article/23043944

158   Bibliography

Lee, Kangkyu, and Myeongchul Lee. 2012. "Security on Korean Peninsula and Korean-China Relations: Chinese Perspective." *Northeast Asia Strategic Analysis*. Retrieved from http://www.kida.re.kr/frt/board/frtNormalBoard.do?sidx=2184&depth=2 (In Korean).

Lee, Kee-Jong. 1997. "The Determining Factors and Prospect of North Korean Policy toward South Korea." *The Korean Journal of International Studies* 37 (2): 181–207 (In Korean).

Lee, Kihyun, and Jangho Kim. 2017. "Cooperation and Limitations of China's Sanctions on North Korea: Perception, Interest and Institutional Environment." *North Korean Review* 13 (1): 28–44.

Lee, Kwang-ho. 2017a. "GDP 1% Decreased by THAAD Retaliation." *The Asia Economy Daily*. Retrieved from http://www.asiae.co.kr/news/view.htm?idxno=2017092912580503224

Lee, Mingyu. 2017b. "Periodic Characteristics and Issues of China's Core Interests' Expansion." *Sino-Soviet Affairs* 41 (1): 41–75 (In Korean).

———. 2017e. "Scrutiny on China's Change in Korea Policy Given THADD Deployment: Analysis Based on China's 'Core Interests.'" *The Quarterly Journal of Defense Policy Studies* 33 (2): 10–34 (In Korean).

Lee, Sangsuk. 2016. "A Study on North Korea's Economic and Social Cooperation with Chinese Communist Party during the Chinese Civil War." *North Korean Studies Review* 20 (1): 209–231 (In Korean).

Lee, Seongbong. 2017c. "A Study on Relations between China and North Korea Viewed through the Interchange of High-Level Personnel (2000–2016)." *Korean National Studies* 70: 168–189 (In Korean).

Lee, Seong-hyon. 2017d. "PacNet #43 – Envoy, THAAD and Korea-China Relations Under Moon Jae-in." *PacNet Commentary*. Retrieved from https://pacforum.org/publication/pacnet-43-envoy-thaad-and-korea-china-relations-under-moon-jae-in

Lee, Seungchul. 2006. "The Secret of Tang Jiaxuan's Visit to North Korea." *Kyunghyang Shinmun*. Retrieved from http://news.khan.co.kr/kh_news/khan_art_view.html?art_id=200606051802321 (In Korean).

Lee, Seung-Ook. 2015b. "A Geo-Economic Object or an Object of Geo-Political Absorption? Competing Visions of North Korea in South Korean Politics." *Journal of Contemporary Asia* 45 (4): 693–714.

Lee, Soo-Hyuk. 2008. *Transforming Events: An In-Depth Analysis of North Korean Nuclear Problem*. Seoul: Joongang Books (In Korean),

———. 2011. *North Korea is Reality*. Paju: Book21 [E-Book] (In Korean).

Lee, Taehwan. 2010. "Sino-Korean Strategic Cooperative Partnership: Evaluation and Prospects." *Sejong Policy Studies* 6 (2): 123–157 (In Korean).

Lee, Won Bong. 2005. "Six Party Talks and China." *The Journal of Political Science & Communication* 8 (2): 85–109.

Legro, Jeffrey W., and Andrew Moravcsik. 1999. "Is Anybody Still a Realist?" *International Security* 24 (2): 5–55.

Lester, Simon, and Huan Zhu. 2018. "What Trump Gets Right about China and Trade." Cato Institute. Retrieved from https://www.cato.org/publications/commentary/what-trump-gets-right-about-china-trade

Li, Cheng-Ri. 2009. "Study on the Impact of the Case of 1983 China Airplane in Terms of the Korea-China Relationship: From Chinese Point of View." *Journal of Northeast Asian Cultures* 20: 394–412 (In Korean).

Bibliography 159

Li, Dunqiu. 2017. "*2016nian, Pujinhuichedigaoluanlehanguo* (2016年，朴槿惠彻底搞乱了韩国)" *Huanqiu Shibao*. Retrieved from http://opinion.huanqiu.com/opinion_world/2017-01/9892107.html?agt=1 (In Chinese).

Li, Hongxiu. 2018. "Public Diplomacy in the Belt and Road Initiative within the New Media: Theories and Practices." *Athens Journal of Mass Media and Communications* 4 (3): 219–236.

Li, Julie Juan, and Chenting Su. 2007. "How Face Influences Consumption: A Comparative Study of American and Chinese Consumers." *International Journal of Market Research* 49 (2): 237–256.

Li, Kwok-sing. 1995. *A Glossary of Political Terms of the People's Republic of China*. Hong Kong: Chinese University Press.

Lim, Anday, and Victor Cha. 2017. "Dataset: China-DPRK High Level Visits since 1953." Retrieved from https://beyondparallel.csis.org/china-dprk-high-level-visits-since-1953/

Lim, Chun-young. 2012. "Chinese Face Practice with Cases from Biographies of Records of History." *The Journal of Chinese Studies* 59: 295–318 (In Korean).

Lin, Yutang. 1936. *My Country and My People*. London & Toronto: William Heinemann.

Lind, Jeniffer. 2016. "Japan's Security Evolution." *Policy Analysis* (Caito Institute) 788: 1–10. Retrieved from https://object.cato.org/sites/cato.org/files/pubs/pdf/pa-788.pdf

Liu, Ge, and Lulu Zhang. 2013. "*Rihanteshifanhuazhuanjia: Sanguoyouhaoliyudiqujushi* (日韩特使访华 专家：三国友好利于地区局势)." *HuanQiuWang*. Retrieved from http://world.huanqiu.com/regions/2013-01/3569013.html?agt=61 (In Chinese).

Liu, To-hai. 1991. "Sino-South Korean Relations since 1983: Toward Normalization." *The Journal of East Asian Affairs* V: 49–78.

Loewenberg, Peter. 2011. "Matteo Ricci, Psychoanalysis, and 'Face' in Chinese Culture and Diplomacy." *American Imago* 68 (4): 689–706.

Ma, Sang-yoon. 2011. "Achievements, Celebration and Homework: South Korean President Lee Myung-bak's State Visit to the United States." Brookings Institute. Retrieved from https://www.brookings.edu/opinions/achievements-celebration-and-homework-south-korean-president-lee-myung-baks-state-visit-to-the-united-states/

Mansfield, Edward, and Jack Snyder. 1995. "Democratization and the Danger of War." *International Security* 20 (1): 5–38.

Mao, Zedong. 1938. *On Protracted War*. Retrieved from https://www.marxists.org/reference/archive/mao/selected-works/volume-2/mswv2_09.htm

———. 1949. "The Chinese People Have Stood Up!" Retrieved from https://www.marxists.org/reference/archive/mao/selected-works/volume-5/mswv5_01.htm

McCauley, Clark. 2017. "Toward a Psychology of Humiliation in Asymmetric Conflict." *American Psychologist* 72 (3): 255–265.

McCormick, Barrett L. 2000. "Introduction." In Edward Friedman and Barrett L. McCormick (eds.) *What If China Doesn't Democratize? Implications for War and Peace* (pp. 3–18). Armonk, NY: M. E. Sharpe.

McKee, Ian, and Norman T. Feather. 2008. "Revenge, Retribution, and Values: Social Attitudes and Punitive Sentencing." *Social Justice Research* 21 (2): 138–163.

McKeon, James, and Meyer Thalheimer. 2017. "North Korea Is a Nuclear State – US Foreign Policy Must Recognize That." *The Hill*. Retrieved from https://thehill.

160 *Bibliography*

com/opinion/national-security/356399-north-korea-is-a-nuclear-state-american-foreign-policy-needs-to

Mead, Walter Russell. 2020. "China Is the Real Sick Man of Asia." *The Wall Street Journal.* http://wsj.com/articles/china-is-the-real-sick-man-of-asia-11580773677

Mearsheimer, John J. 2001. *The Tragedy of Great Power Politics.* New York: W.W. Norton.

Meick, Ethan, and Nargiza Salidjanova. 2017. "China's Response to U.S.-South Korean Missile Defense System Deployment and Its Implications." *Staff Research Report* (U.S.-China Economic and Security Review Commission). Retrieved from https://www.uscc.gov/sites/default/files/Research/Report_China%27s%20Response%20to%20THAAD%20Deployment%20and%20its%20Implications.pdf

Mencius. 2016. *Mengzi.* Translated by Robert Eno. Retrieved from https://scholarworks.iu.edu/dspace/handle/2022/23421

Mercer, Jonathan. 1996. *Reputation and International Politics.* Ithaca, NY: Cornell University Press.

Mierzejewski, Dominik. 2012. "The Quandary of China's Soft-Power Rhetoric: The 'Peaceful-Rise' Concept and Internal Debate." In Hongyi Lai and Yiyi Lu (eds.) *China's Soft Power and International Relations* (pp. 64–82). London & New York: Routledge.

Ministry of Defense of Japan. 2017. *Defense of Japan 2017* (Annual White Paper). Retrieved from http://www.mod.go.jp/e/publ/w_paper/2017.html

———. 2018. *Defense of Japan 2018* (Annual White Paper). Retrieved from http://www.mod.go.jp/e/publ/w_paper/2018.html

Ministry of Foreign Affairs of Japan. 2005. "Security Consultative Committee Document U.S.-Japan Alliance: Transformation and Realignment for the Future." Retrieved from https://www.mofa.go.jp/region/n-america/us/security/scc/doc0510.html

———. 2006a. "Japan-China Joint Press Statement, October 8, 2006." Retrieved from http://www.mofa.go.jp/region/asia-paci/china/joint0610.html

———. 2006b. "United States-Japan Roadmap for Realignment Implementation." Retrieved from https://www.mofa.go.jp/region/n-america/us/security/scc/doc0605.html

Ministry of Foreign Affairs of PRC. 2004. "Struggle to Restore China's Lawful Seat in the United Nations." Retrieved from http://ee.china-embassy.org/eng/zggk/xzgwjjs/t110281.htm

———. 2005a. "Hu Jintao Holds Talks with ROK President Lee Myung-bak." Retrieved from https://www.fmprc.gov.cn/mfa_eng/wjb_663304/zzjg_663340/yzs_663350/gjlb_663354/2767_663538/2769_663542/t460009.shtml

———. 2005b. "Topics: President Hu Jintao Pays a State Visit to Russia and Kazakhstan and Attends the Shanghai Cooperation Organization (SCO) Summit in Astana and the Dialogue of Leaders of G8." Retrieved from https://www.fmprc.gov.cn/mfa_eng/topics_665678/hzxcfels_665834

———. 2006a. "Foreign Ministry Spokesman Liu Jianchao's Regular Press Conference on 26 October 2006." Retrieved from http://www.china-botschaft.de/det/fyrth/t278406.htm

———. 2006b. "*Waijiaobu Shengming: Zhongguozhengbuduichaoxianshishiheshiyanjianjuefandui* (外交部声明: 中国政府对朝鲜实施核试验坚决反对)." Retrieved from http://www.gov.cn/gzdt/2006-10/09/content_407836.htm (In Chinese).

Bibliography   161

———. 2014. "Foreign Ministry Spokesperson Hua Chunying's Regular Press Conference on February 25, 2014." Retrieved from http://www.china-embassy.org/eng/fyrth/t1132459.htm

———. 2016. "Xi Jinping Meets with Prime Minister Hwang Kyo-ahn of ROK." Retrieved from http://www.china-embassy.org/eng/zgyw/t1377229.htm

———. 2018. "*Zhongguotonghanguodeguanxi(*中国同韩国的关系*)*" Retrieved from https://www.fmprc.gov.cn/web/gjhdq_676201/gj_676203/yz_676205/1206_676524/sbgx_676528

Ministry of Foreign Affairs of Republic of Korea. 2000. "Sign the Agreement on the Trade of Garlic between Korea and China (Press Release)." Retrieved from http://www.mofa.go.kr/www/brd/m_4080/view.do?seq=290182&srchFr=&srchTo=&-srchWord=&srchTp=&multi_itm_seq=0&itm_seq_1=0&itm_seq_2=0&company_cd=&company_nm=&page=1485 (In Korean).

———. 2004. "Main Documents." Retrieved from http://www.mofa.go.kr/www/brd/m_3973/list.do

———. 2014. *2014 Diplomatic White Paper*. Retrieved from http://www.mofa.go.kr/www/brd/m_4105/list.do

Ministry of National Defense of PRC. 2015. "Defense Ministry's Regular Press Conference on Dec.31." Retrieved from http://eng.mod.gov.cn/Press/2015-12/31/content_4634720.htm

———. 2016. "Defense Ministry's Regular Press Conference on July 28." Retrieved from http://eng.mod.gov.cn/Press/2016-07/28/content_4703117.htm

Ministry of National Defense of Republic of Korea. 1995. *1995 White Paper*. Seoul: Ministry of National Defense (In Korean).

———. 2006. *2004 White Paper*. Seoul: Ministry of National Defense.

———. 2017. *2016 White Paper*. Seoul: Ministry of National Defense.

———. 2018. *2018 White Paper*. Seoul: Ministry of National Defense (In Korean).

Ministry of Oceans and Fisheries of ROK. 2018. "Korea-China Fisheries Negotiations Reached an Agreement." Retrieved from http://www.mof.go.kr/article/view.do?articleKey=23857&searchSelect=title&searchValue=%EC%96%B4%EC%97%85%ED%98%91%EC%83%81&boardKey=10&menuKey=376&currentPageNo=1 (In Korean).

Mitzen, Jeniffer. 2006, "Ontological Security in World Politics: State Identity and the Security Dilemma." *European Journal of International Relations* 12 (3): 341–370.

Modigliani, Andre. 1971. "Embarrassment, Facework, and Eye Contact: Testing a Theory of Embarrassment." *Journal of Personality and Social Psychology* 17: 15–24.

Moon, Chung-in. 2008. "Diplomacy of Defiance and Facilitation: The Six Party Talks and the Roh Moo Hyun Government." *Asian Perspective* 32 (4): 71–105.

Moon, Chung-in, and Jong-Yun Bae. 2003. "The Bush Doctrine and the North Korean Nuclear Crisis." *Asian Perspective* 27 (4): 9–45.

Moon, Chung-in, and Seung-won Suh. 2018. "Historical Analogy and Democratization of Others: Memories of 1930s Japanese Militarism and Its Contemporary Implications." In Kevin P. Clements (ed.) *Identity, Trust, and Reconciliation in East Asia: Dealing with Painful History to Create a Peaceful Present*. London: Palgrave Macmillan, 75–104.

Moore, Gregory J. 2014. "Beijing's Problem with an Operationally Nuclear North Korea." In Gregory J. Moore (ed.) *North Korean Nuclear Operationality: Regional*

162 *Bibliography*

Security & Nonproliferation (pp. 77–103). Baltimore, MD: Johns Hopkins University Press.

Mueller, Gotelind. 2013. *Documentary, World History, and National Power in the PRC: Global Rise in Chinese Eyes.* London: Routledge.

Mulgan, Aurelia George. 2005. "Japan's Defence Dilemma." *Security Challenges* 1 (1): 59–72.

Munck, Gerardo L. 2007. "The Past and Present of Comparative Politics." In Gerardo L. Munck and Richard Snyder. *Passion, Craft, and Method in Comparative Politics* (pp. 32–59). Baltimore, MD: Johns Hopkins University Press.

Nagy, Stephen R. 2014. "Nationalism, Domestic Politics, and the Japan Economic Rejuvenation." *East Asia* 31 (1): 5–21.

Nam, Chang-hee & Jongsung Lee. 2010. "Japan's Response to North Korea's Nuclear and Missile Threats: Patterns and Prospects." *National Strategy* 16 (2): 63–94.

Narang, Vipin, and Ankit Panda. 2018. "North Korea Is a Nuclear Power. Get Used to It." *The New York Times.* https://www.nytimes.com/2018/06/12/opinion/trump-kim-summit-denuclearization-north-korea.html

Narizny, Kevin. 2017. "On Systemic Paradigms and Domestic Politics: A Critique of the Newest Realism." *International Security* 42 (2): 155–190.

Nathan, Andrew J., and Andrew Scobell. 2012. *China's Search for Security.* New York: Columbia University Press.

National Archives of Korea. 2006. "Korea-China Garlic Trade Dispute." Retrieved from http://www.archives.go.kr/next/search/listSubjectDescription.do?id=003099&pageFlag=&sitePage=1-2-1 (In Korean).

———. 2017. "North Korean Nuclear Issues." Retrieved from http://www.archives.go.kr/next/search/listSubjectDescription.do?id=003350&pageFlag=A&sitePage=1-2-1 (In Korean).

Newman, Alex. 2017. "Lawmakers: Name Chinese Embassy Plaza after Dissident Liu Xiaobo." *NewAmerican.* Retrieved from https://www.thenewamerican.com/usnews/congress/item/26706-lawmakers-name-chinese-embassy-plaza-after-dissident-liu-xiaobo

Nikitin, Mary B. D., Emma Chanlett-Avery, and Mark E. Manyin. 2017. "Nuclear Negotiations with North Korea: In Brief." CRS Report No.R45033. Retrieved from https://fas.org/sgp/crs/nuke/R45033.pdf.

Noh, Jiwon. 2018. "Chinese Aircraft Enters Korean Air Space without Advance Notice." *Hankyoreh.* Retrieved from http://english.hani.co.kr/arti/english_edition/e_international/872190.html

North Korea Leadership Watch. 2018. "KJU Does Beijing (A Good Year for the Roses)." Retrieved from http://www.nkleadershipwatch.org/2018/06/24/kju-does-beijing-a-good-year-for-the-roses/

O'Dowd, Edward C. 2007. *Chinese Military Strategy in the Third Indochina War: The Last Maoist War.* New York: Routledge.

Oetzel, J. G., and Ting-Toomey, S. 2003. "Face Concerns in Interpersonal Conflict: A Cross-Cultural Empirical Test of the Face Negotiation Theory." *Communication Research* 30: 599–624.

Oh, Soo-hyun, and Park Manwon. 2017. "China Mistreated a State Guest from South Korea." *Maeil Business Newspaper.* (In Korean). Retrieved from https://www.mk.co.kr/news/politics/view/2017/12/826200/

Paik, Hak-soon. 2012. *Comparison of North Korean Policy between the Kim Young-sam Government and the Ro Tae-Woo Government.* Seongnam: Sejong Institute (In Korean).

Paltiel, Jeremy. 2008. "China and the North Korean Crisis: The Diplomacy of Great Power Transition." In Seung-Ho Joo and Tae-Hwan Kwak (eds.) *North Korea's Second Nuclear Crisis and Northeast Asian Security* (pp. 95–109). Burlington, VT: Ashgate.

Panda, Ankit. 2017. "Chinese Defense Ministry: Opposition to THAAD 'Will Definitely Not Stay on Words Only.'" *The Diplomat*. Retrieved from https://thediplomat.com/2017/03/chinese-defense-ministry-opposition-to-thaad-will-definitely-not-stay-on-words-only/

Park, Byungkwang. 2014a. "The Trust-Building Process on the Korean Peninsula and Korea-China Cooperation." *The State and Politics* 20: 69–97 (In Korean).

Park, Byung-soo. 2014b. "USFK Commander Says Deployment of THAAD Is in Initial Review." *Hankyoreh*. Retrieved from http://www.hani.co.kr/arti/english_edition/e_international/640706.html

———. 2016. "Park Says Government Will Review Possibility of Deploying THAAD in South Korea." *Hankyuoreh*. http://english.hani.co.kr/arti/english_edition/e_national/726204.html

Park, Byung-soo, and Hye-jeong Choi. 2016. "[Analysis] South Korea, US Announce Beginning of Consultations on THAAD Deployment." *Hankyoreh*. Retrieved from http://english.hani.co.kr/arti/english_edition/e_international/729924.html

Park, Ji-Hyun. 2015. "Reason of China's Opposition to the THAAD." *Monthly Joongang*. Retrieved from https://jmagazine.joins.com/monthly/view/305867 (In Korean).

Park, Jong-Chul. 2008. "Lee Myung-Bak Administration's North Korea Policy: Challenges and Tasks." *The Journal of East Asian Affairs* 22 (2): 39–61.

Park, Ju-Jin, and Youngho Kim. 2014. "A Review of the China-North Korea Alliance." *Korea Focus*. Retrieved from http://www.koreafocus.or.kr/design2/layout/content_print.asp?group_id=105360

Park, Juneyong. 2017a. "THAAD Retaliation Just Started, Diplomatic Solution Needed." *Sisa Journal*. Retrieved from http://www.sisapress.com/news/articleView.html?idxno=163606 (In Korean).

Park, Kun Young. 1998. "A New North Korea Policy." *The Korean Journal of International Studies* 38 (2): 87–107 (In Korean).

Park, No-hwang. 2006. "U.S. Sees South Korea as Candidate for Another X-Band Radar." *Yonhap News Agency*. Retrieved from https://news.naver.com/main/read.nhn?mode=LSD&mid=sec&sid1=104&oid=001&aid=0001389465 (In Korean).

Park, Soo-jin. 2017b. "Bank of Korea Said the Shock by THAAD Retaliation Became More Serious." *SBS News*. https://news.sbs.co.kr/news/endPage.do?news_id=N1004443358 (In Korean).

Parker, Jeffrey G., and Steven R. Asher. 1993. "Friendship and Friendship Quality in Middle Childhood: Links with Peer Group Acceptance and Feelings of Loneliness and Social Dissatisfaction." *Developmental Psychology* 29 (4): 611–621.

Peking Review. 1961. "Sino-Korean Treaty of Friendship, Cooperation and Mutual Assistance." Retrieved from https://www.marxists.org/subject/china/peking-review/1961/PR1961-28.pdf

Pekkanen, Saadia M., and Paul Kallender-Umezu. 2010. *In Defense of Japan: From the Market to the Military in Space Policy*. Stanford, CA: Stanford University Press.

People's Daily. 1948. "*Meidizhichengnanxiankuileichengfu hanjianlichengwanrenweizongtong* (美帝制成南鲜傀儡政府　韩奸李承晚任伪总统)." Retrieved from http://data.people.com.cn/rmrb/pd.html (In Chinese).

164 *Bibliography*

———. 2012. "*Lengjingguancha, Chenzhuoyingfu, Taoguangyanghui, Shanyushou-zhuo, Juebudangtou, Yousuozuowei* (冷静观察、沉着应付、韬光养晦、决不当头、有所作为)." Retrieved from http://theory.people.com.cn/ (In Chinese).

Peyrefitte, Alain. 2013. *The Immortal Empire*. New York: Vintage Books.

Pharr, Susan J. 1990. *Losing Face: Status Politics in Japan*. Berkeley & Los Angeles: University of California Press.

Pizano, Pedro. 2014. "The Power of Naming and Shaming." *Foreign Policy*. https://foreignpolicy.com/2014/08/05/the-power-of-naming-and-shaming/

Posen, Barry R. 1993. "The Security Dilemma and Ethnic Conflict." *Survival* 35 (1): 27–47.

Pratt, Keith. 2006. *Everlasting Flower: A History of Korea*. London: Reaktion Books.

Prime Minister of Japan and His Cabinet. 2006. "Press Conference by Prime Minister Shinzo Abe Following His Visit to China." Retrieved from japan.kantei.go.jp/abespeech/2006/10/08chinapress_e.html

Pritchard, Charles L. 2007. *Failed Diplomacy: The Tragic Story of How North Korea Got the Bomb*. Washington, DC: Brookings Institute.

Prizel, Ilya. 1998. *National Identity and Foreign Policy: Nationalism and leadership in Poland, Russia and Ukraine*. Cambridge: Cambridge University Press.

Pu, Xiaoyu. 2017. "Controversial Identity of a Rising China." *The Chinese Journal of International Politics* 10 (2): 131–149.

Pye, Lucian W. 1965. "Introduction: Political Culture and Political Development." In Lucian W. Pye and Sidney Verba (eds.) *Political Culture and Political Development* (pp. 3–26). Princeton, NJ: Princeton University Press.

Pye, Lucian W. 1985. *Asian Power and Politics: The Cultural Dimensions of Authority*. Cambridge, MA: Harvard University Press.

Pye, Lucian W. 1988. *The Mandarin and the Cadre: China's Political Cultures*. Ann Arbor: University of Michigan (Center for Chinese Studies).

Qi, Xiaoying. 2017. "Reconstructing the Concept of Face in Cultural Sociology: In Goffman's Footsteps, Following the Chinese Case." *The Journal of Chinese Sociology* 4 (19): 1–17.

Qin, Amy, and Sang-Hun Choe. 2016. "South Korean Missile Defense Deal Appears to Sour China's Taste for K-Pop." *The New York Times*. Retrieved from https://www.nytimes.com/2016/08/08/world/asia/china-korea-thaad.html

Qin, Yaqing. 2011. "Chinese Culture and Its Implications for Foreign Policy-Making." *China International Studies* 5: 21–33. (Chinese)

Qiu, Guohong. 2014. "Ambassador: Let Our Dreams Brighten the Future of China-ROK Friendship." *People's Daily*. Retrieved from http://en.people.cn/n/2014/0703/c98649-8750330.html

Quah, Jon S. T. 2007. "Combating Corruption Singapore-Style: Lessons for Other Asian Countries." *Maryland Series in Contemporary Asian Studies* 2 (189): 1–56.

Quang, Nguyen Minh. 2017. "The Bitter Legacy of the 1979 China-Vietnam War." *The Diplomat*. Retrieved from https://thediplomat.com/2017/02/the-bitter-legacy-of-the-1979-china-vietnam-war/

Renshon, Jonathan, Allan Dafoe, and Paul Huth. 2018. "Leader Influence and Reputation Formation in World Politics." *American Journal of Political Science* 62 (2): 325–339.

Reyes, Sebastian. 2015. "Singapore's Stubborn Authoritarianism." *Harvard Political Review*. Retrieved from http://harvardpolitics.com/world/singapores-stubborn-authoritarianism/

Reynolds, Isabel, and Emi Nobuhiro. 2018. "Abe Set to Become Japan's Longest-Serving Premier after Victory." Bloomberg. Retrieved from https://www.bloomberg.com/news/articles/2018-09-20/abe-wins-japan-ruling-party-vote-extending-six-year-term

Rinna, Anthony V. 2018. "Russia's Strategic Partnerships with China and South Korea: The Impact of THAAD." *Asia Policy* 13 (3): 79–99.

Roberts, Brad. 2004. "China and Ballistic Missile Defense: 1955 to 2002 and Beyond." *IDA Paper P-3826*. Retrieved from https://fas.org/nuke/guide/china/doctrine/bmd.pdf

Robertson, Jeffrey. 2018. "Is South Korea Really a Middle Power?" East Asia Forum. Retrieved from http://www.eastasiaforum.org/2018/05/02/is-south-korea-really-a-middle-power/

Roblin, Sebastien. 2017. "A U.S. Bombing Run in North Korea Wiped Out Mao Zedong's Dynasty." *The National Interest*. Retrieved from https://nationalinterest.org/blog/the-buzz/us-bombing-run-north-korea-wiped-out-mao-zedongs-dynasty-20550

Rodrigo, Chris M. 2018. "Trump: Kim Jong Un and I 'Fell in Love.'" *The Hill*. Retrieved from https://thehill.com/blogs/ballot-box/409104-trump-kim-jong-un-and-i-fell-in-love

Roh, Hyodong, and Myojeong Jung. 2011. "Behind Diplomacy: Chinese Missile Expert on Hijacked Airplane." *Yonhap News Agency*. Retrieved from https://www.yna.co.kr/view/AKR20110701139600043

Romberg, Alan D., and Michael McDevitt. 2003. *China and Missile Defense: Managing US-PRC Strategic Relations*. Washington, DC: The Stimson Center.

Rose, Gideon. 1998. "Neoclassical Realism and Theories of Foreign Policy." *World Politics* 51 (1): 144–172.

Rose, Caroline, and Jan Sýkora. 2017. "The Trust Deficit in Sion-Japanese Relations." *Japan Forum* 29 (1): 100–124.

Ross, Marc H. 2009. "Culture and Comparative Political Analysis." In Mark Lichbach and Allan S. Zuckerman (eds.) *Comparative Politics: Rationality, Culture and Structure* (pp. 134–161). Cambridge: Cambridge University Press.

Ross, Robert. 1988. *The Indochina Tangle. China's Vietnam Policy 1975–1979*. New York: Columbia University Press.

Rozman, Gilbert. 1999. "China's Quest for Great Power Identity." *Orbis* 43 (3): 383–402.

Rozman, Gilbert (ed.). 2012. *East Asian National Identities: Common Roots and Chinese Exceptionalism*. Stanford, CA: Stanford University Press.

Sakaki, Alexandra. 2015. "Japan's Security Policy: A Shift in Direction under Abe?" SWP Research Paper. Retrieved from https://www.swp-berlin.org/fileadmin/contents/products/research_papers/2015_RP02_skk.pdf

Sanger, David E. 2002. "North Korea Says It Has a Program on Nuclear Arms." *The New York Times*. Retrieved from https://www.nytimes.com/2002/10/17/world/north-korea-says-it-has-a-program-on-nuclear-arms.html

Sankaran, Jaganath, and Bryan L. Fearey. 2017. "Missile Defense and Strategic Stability: Terminal High Altitude Area Defense (THAAD) in South Korea." *Contemporary Security Policy* 38 (3): 321–344.

Sartori, Anne. 2005. *Deterrence and Diplomacy*. Princeton, NJ: Princeton University Press.

Scheff, Thomas J. 1988. "Shame and Conformity: The Deference-Emotion System." *American Sociological Review* 53 (3): 395–406.

166   *Bibliography*

Schelling, Thomas. 1960. *The Strategy of Conflict.* Cambridge, MA: Harvard University Press.

Shelling, Thomas C. 1966. *Arms and Influence.* New Haven, CT: Yale University Press.

Schlenker, Barry R., and Mark R. Leary. 1982. "Social Anxiety and Self-Presentation: A Conceptualization and Model." *Psychological Bulletin* 92 (3): 641–669.

Seong, Yeon-Cheol. 2014. "Source: Xi Jinping Voiced Concerns about Missile Defense during Summit." *Hankyoreh.* Retrieved from http://www.hani.co.kr/arti/english_edition/e_international/652992.html

———. 2016. "US and China Jousting over North Korea's Actions." *Hankyoreh.* Retrieved from http://english.hani.co.kr/arti/english_edition/e_international/730402.html

Shaffer, Brenda (ed.). 2006. *The Limits of Culture: Islam and Foreign Policy.* Cambridge, MA: MIT Press.

Shambaugh, David. 2007. "China's Propaganda System: Institutions, Processes and Efficacy." *China Journal* 57: 25–58.

———. 2013. *China Goes Global: The Partial Power.* Oxford: Oxford University Press.

Sharabany, Ruth. 1994. "Intimate Friendship Scale: Conceptual Underpinnings, Psychometric Properties and Construct Validity." *Journal of Social Personal Relationships* 11 (3): 449–469.

Sharp, Paul. 2004. "The Idea of Diplomatic Cultures and Its Sources." In Hannh Slavik (ed.) *Intercultural Communication and Diplomacy* (pp. 93–106). Malta: Diplo Foundation.

Shen, Chuanliang. 2014. *Decision-Making China – The Historical Evolution of the Chinese Decision-Making System since Reform and Opening up.* Beijing: People's University Press. (Chinese)

Shen, Zhihua. 2013. *A Forced Choice: The Cold War and the Fate of the Sino-Soviet Alliance* (无奈的选择: 冷战与中苏同盟的命运). Beijing: Shehui Kexue Wenxian.

Shen, Zhihua, and Yafeng Xia. 2015. "Refuting Two Historical Myths: A New Interpretation of China-North Korean Relations." In Carla P. Freeman (ed.) *China and North Korea: Strategic and Policy Perspectives from a Changing China* (pp. 91–108). New York: Palgrave Macmillan.

———. 2018. *A Misunderstood Friendship: Mao Zedong, Kim Il-Sung, and Sino-North Korean Relations, 1949–1976.* New York: Columbia University Press.

Sheng, Michael. 2014. "Mao's Role in the Korean Conflict: A Revision." *Twentieth-Century China* 39 (3): 269–290.

Shi, Yinhong. 2009. "China and the North Korean Nuclear Issue: Competing Interests and Persistent Policy Dilemmas." *The Korean Journal of Defense Analysis* 21 (1): 33–47.

Shih, Chih-yu. 1993. *China's just World: The Morality of Chinese Foreign Policy.* Boulder, CO: Lynne Rienner.

Shim, Elizabeth. 2018a. "North Korea Hails History of 'Amicable' Relations with China." United Press International (UPI). Retrieved from https://www.upi.com/North-Korea-hails-history-of-amicable-relations-with-China/3881523297772/

———. 2018b. "Chinese Military Dismisses South Korea Concerns over Trespassing Spy Plane." UPI. Retrieved from https://www.upi.com/Chinese-military-dismisses-South-Korea-concerns-over-trespassing-spy-plane/7091543598674/

Shin, Jihong. 2006a. "Kang and Li Had a Secret Meeting after Three Day of Nuclear Test." *Hankyoreh*. Retrieved from http://www.hani.co.kr/arti/politics/defense/168996.html

———. 2006b. "U.S. Deploy Another X-Band Radar in Japan." *Yonhap News Agency*. Retrieved from https://news.naver.com/main/read.nhn?mode=LSD&mid=sec&sid1=104&oid=001&aid=0001505671

Shin, Sang-Jin. 2005. "China's Six-Party Talks Strategy." *National Strategy* 12 (2): 29–54 (In Korean).

Shirk, Susan L. 2007. *China: Fragile Superpower*. New York: Oxford University Press.

Sinha, Akash. 2018. "THAAD: The Fear of China, Anxiety of Russia." *The Economic Times*. Retrieved from economictimes.indiatimes.com/articleshow/57273866.cms?utm_source=contentofinterest&utm_medium=text&utm_campaign=cppst

Siu, Noel Yee-Man, Ho Yan Kwan, and Celeste Yunru Zeng. 2016. "The Role of Brand Equity and Face Saving in Chinese Luxury Consumption." *Journal of Consumer Marketing* 33 (4): 245–256.

Smits, Gregory. 1999. *Visions of Ryukyu: Identity and Ideology in Early-Modern Thought and Politics*. Honolulu: University of Hawaii Press.

Snyder, Glenn H. 1984. "The Security Dilemma in Alliance Politics." *World Politics* 36 (4): 461–495.

———. 1997. *Alliance Politics*. Ithaca, NY: Cornell University Press.

Snyder, Scott. 2007. "U.S.-North Korean Negotiating Behavior and the Six-Party Talks." In Seung-Ho Joo and Tae-Hwan Kwak (eds.) *North Korea's Second Nuclear Crisis and Northeast Asian Security* (pp. 151–166). Burlington, VT: Ashgate.

———. 2009. *China's Rise and the Two Koreas: Politics, Economics, Security*. Boulder, CO: Lynne Rienner.

Snyder, Scott, and See-Won Byun. 2010. "China-ROK Trade Disputes and Implications for Managing Security Relations." *KEI Academic Paper Series* 5 (8): 1–10.

Solomon, Richard H. 1971. *Mao's Revolution and the Chinese Political Culture*. Berkeley & Los Angeles: University of California Press.

Son, Il-sun, Dae-ki Kim, and Kang-rae Kim. 2016. "Chinese Retaliation Started?" *Maeil Business Newspaper*. Retrieved from http://news.mk.co.kr/newsRead.php?no=556842&year=2016 (In Korean).

Song, Hogyun. 2008. "ROK-China Upgrade Their Relations to Strategic Cooperative Partnership." *Pressian*. Retrieved from http://www.pressian.com/news/article.html?no=13524

Soon, Lau Teik. 1980. "The Soviet-Vietnamese Treaty: A Giant Step Forward." *Southeast Asian Affairs*: 54–65.

Spencer-Oatey, Helen. 2012. "What Is Culture? A Compilation of Quotations." *GlobalPAD Core Concepts*. Retrieved from http://www2.warwick.ac.uk/fac/soc/al/globalpad/interculturalskills/

Sterling, Dahlia Patricia. 2018. "A New Era in Cultural Diplomacy: Promoting the Image of China's 'Belt and Road' Initiative in Asia." *Open Journal of Social Science* 6: 102–116.

Stevenson, Alexandra. 2020. "China Expels 3 Wall Street Journal Reporters as Media Relations Sour." *The New York Times*. https://www.nytimes.com/2020/02/19/business/media/china-wall-street-journal.html

168 *Bibliography*

Su, Xiaohui. 2018. "Major-Country Diplomacy with Chinese Characteristics." *China Institute of International Studies.* Retrieved from http://www.ciis.org.cn/english/2018-03/14/content_40251823.htm

Suh, Jae Jean. 2009. *The Lee Myung-Bak Government's North Korea Policy: A Study on Its Historical and Theoretical Foundation.* Seoul: Korea Institute for National Unification.

Sullivan, Eileen. 2019. "Trump Calls Intelligence Officials 'Naive' after They Contradict Him." *The New York Times.* Retrieved from https://www.nytimes.com/2019/01/30/us/politics/trump-intelligence.html

Svan, Jennifer H. 2006. "High-Tech Missile-Tracking System Unveiled at Misawa." *Stars and Stripes.* Retrieved from https://www.stripes.com/news/army-showing-off-new-x-band-radar-in-japan-1.50062

Svolik, Milan W. 2012. *The Politics of Authoritarian Rule.* Cambridge: Cambridge University Press.

Swaine, Michael. 2009. "China's North Korea Dilemma." *China Leadership Monitor* 30: 1–27.

———. 2011. "China's Assertive Behavior: Part One: On 'Core Interests.'" *China Leadership Monitor* 34: 1–25.

———. 2017. "Chinese Views on South Korea's Deployment of THAAD." *China Leadership Monitor* 52: 1–15.

Swaine, Michael D., Rachel M. Swanger, and Takashi Kawakami. 2001. "Japan and Ballistic Missile Defense." RAND Corporation. Retrieved from https://www.rand.org/pubs/monograph_reports/MR1374.html#toc

Syring, James D. 2014. "Unclassified Statement of Vice Admiral James D. Syring, USN Director, Missile Defense Agency before the Senate Appropriations Committee Defense Subcommittee." Retrieved from https://www.mda.mil/global/documents/pdf/ps_syring_061114_sacd.pdf

Tadokoro, Masayuki. 2011. "Change and Continuity in Japan's 'Abnormalcy': An Emerging External Attitude of the Japanese Public." In Yoshihide Soeya, Masayuki Tadokoro, and David A. Welch (eds.) *Japan as a "Normal Country"? A Nation in Search of Its Place in the World* (pp. 38–71). Toronto: University of Toronto Press.

Takahashi, Sugio. 2012. "Ballistic Missile Defense in Japan: Deterrence and Military Transformation." *Proliferation Papers* 44: 7–27. Retrieved from https://www.ifri.org/sites/default/files/atoms/files/pp44av59takahashi.pdf

Tang, Janice. 2006. "China, N. Korea Concerns for Japan, U.S. Security Alliance." *Kyodo News.*

Tang, Jiaxuan. 2002. "*Zhongguokuashijiwaijiaodeguanghuilicheng* (中国跨世纪外交的光辉历程)" *The People's Daily.* Retrieved from http://www.people.com.cn/GB/guoji/24/20021010/838700.html (In Chinese).

Tao, Lin. 2017. "Face Perception in Chinese and Japanese." *Intercultural Communication Studies* 24 (1): 151–167.

Teng, Jianqun. 2015. "Why Is China Unhappy with the Deployment of THAAD in the ROK?" *China Institute for International Studies.* Retrieved from http://www.ciis.org.cn/english/2015-04/01/content_7793314.htm

Tianshanwang(天山网). 2014. "*wangshi: 1970nianjinrichengyonggourouyanzhaodaizhouenlai* (往事: 1970年金日成用狗肉宴招待周恩来)." Retrieved from http://books.sina.com/gb/funny/focus/20130401/184043795.html

Tiezzi, Shannon. 2015. "It's Official: China, South Korea Sign Free Trade Agreement." *The Diplomat*. Retrieved from https://thediplomat.com/2015/06/its-official-china-south-korea-sign-free-trade-agreement/

———. 2016. "China Warns THAAD Deployment Could Destroy South Korea Ties 'in an Instant.'" *The Diplomat*. Retrieved from https://thediplomat.com/2016/02/china-warns-thaad-deployment-could-destroy-south-korea-ties-in-an-instant/

Ting-Toomey, Stella, and John G. Oetzel 2001. *Managing Intercultural Conflict Effectively*. Thousand Oaks, CA: Sage Publications.

Toki, Masako. 2009. "Japan's Evolving Security Policies: Along Came North Korea's Threats." Nuclear Threat Initiative (NTI). Retrieved from https://www.nti.org/analysis/articles/japans-evolving-security-policies/

Tomz, Michael. 2007. *Reputation and International Cooperation*. Princeton, NJ: Princeton University Press.

Topping, Audrey R. 2013. *China Mission: A Personal History from the Last Imperial Dynasty to the People's Republic*. Baton Rouge: Louisiana State University Press.

TransparencyInternational.2018."CorruptionPerceptionIndex2017."Retrievedfrom https://www.transparency.org/news/feature/corruption_perceptions_index_2017

Tsang, Kwok Kuen. 2016. "A Theoretical Analysis of Chinese Ingratiation." *Journal of Social Sciences* 12 (1): 55–63.

Tselichtchev, Ivan. 2017. "Beyond THAAD: The Real Reason Why China Is Angry with South Korea." *South China Morning Post*. Retrieved from https://www.scmp.com/week-asia/politics/article/2114232/beyond-thaad-real-reason-why-china-angry-south-korea

Tsunekawa, Jun. 2006. "Toward a Stable Relationship between Japan and China: From a Bilateral to a Multilateral Approach." In Masafumi Iida (ed.) *China's Shift: Global Strategy of the Rising Power* (pp. 99–124). Tokyo: National Institute for Defense Studies.

———. 2009. "Introduction: Japan's Policy Toward China." In Jun Tsunekawa (ed.) *The Rise of China: Responses from Southeast Asia and Japan*. Tokyo: National Institute for Defense Studies: 9–20.

Twomey, Christopher. 2008. "Explaining Chinese Foreign Policy toward North Korea: Navigating between the Scylla and Charybdis of Proliferation and Instability." *Journal of Contemporary China* 17 (56): 401–423.

Tyler, Patrick E. 2004. "Annan Says Iraq War Was 'Illegal.'" *The New York Times*. Retrieved from https://www.nytimes.com/2004/09/16/international/annan-says-iraq-war-was-illegal.html

U.N. 1971. "The U.N. General Assembly Resolution 2578." October 25. Retrieved from https://documents-dds-ny.un.org/doc/RESOLUTION/GEN/NR0/327/74/IMG/NR032774.pdf?OpenElement

U.N. Bibliographic Information System (UNBIS). "Voting Record Search." Retrieved from https://digitallibrary.un.org/search?ln=en&cc=Voting+Data

U.N. Security Council (UNSC). 1993. "Resolution 825." Retrieved from http://www.securitycouncilreport.org/atf/cf/%7B65BFCF9B-6D27-4E9C-8CD3-CF6E4FF96FF9%7D/Disarm%20SRES825.pdf

———. 2006a. "Resolution 1695." July 15. Retrieved from http://www.securitycouncilreport.org/atf/cf/%7B65BFCF9B-6D27-4E9C-8CD3-CF6E4FF96FF9%7D/Disarm%20SRES1695.pdf

170 Bibliography

———. 2006b. "Statement by the President of the Security Council." October 6. Retrieved from http://www.securitycouncilreport.org/atf/cf/%7B65BFCF9B-6D27-4E9C-8CD3-CF6E4FF96FF9%7D/NKorea%20SPRST%202006%2041.pdf

———. 2006c. "Resolution 1718." October 14. Retrieved from http://www.securitycouncilreport.org/atf/cf/%7B65BFCF9B-6D27-4E9C-8CD3-CF6E4FF96FF9%7D/NKorea%20SRES%201718.pdf

———. 2006d. "Security Council Condemns Nuclear Test by Democratic People's Republic of Korea, Unanimously Adopting Resolution 1718 (2006)." October 14. Retrieved from https://www.un.org/press/en/2006/sc8853.doc.htm

UPI. 1992. "South Korea, China Communique on Diplomatic Ties." Retrieved from https://www.upi.com/Archives/1992/08/23/South-Korea-China-communique-on-diplomatic-ties/9864714542400/

———. 2012. "S. Korea: N. Korea Can't Be Nuclear Nation." Retrieved from https://www.upi.com/S-Korea-N-Korea-cant-be-nuclear-nation/54281338474789/

U.S. Army. 2017. "An Alliance Forged in Blood." Retrieved from https://www.army.mil/article/183561/an_alliance_forged_in_blood

U.S. Department of Defense. 2014. "Second Missile Defense Radar Deployed to Japan." Retrieved from https://dod.defense.gov/News/News-Releases/News-Release-View/Article/605330/second-missile-defense-radar-deployed-to-japan/

U.S. Joint Forces Command. 2008. "The Joint Operating Environment 2008: Challenges and Implications for the Future Joint Force." Retrieved from https://fas.org/man/eprint/joe2008.pdf

U.S. News & World Report. 2019. "Overall Best Countries Ranking." Retrieved from https://www.usnews.com/news/best-countries/overall-rankings

Varshney, Ashutosh. 2007. "Ethnicity and Ethnic Conflict." In C. Boix and S. Stokes (eds.) *The Oxford Handbook of Comparative Politics* (pp. 274–294), New York: Oxford University Press.

Viotti, Paul R. 2010. *American Foreign Policy.* Cambridge and Malden, MA: Polity Press.

Viotti, Paul R., and Mark V. Kauppi. 2012. *International Relations Theory.* New York: Pearson.

Vlahos, Michael. 1991. "Culture and Foreign Policy." *Foreign Policy* 82: 59–78.

Vogel, Ezra F. 2011. *Deng Xiaoping and the Transformation of China.* Cambridge, MA: Harvard University Press.

Voice of America (VOA). 2006. "The South Korean Foreign Minister Has Urged China to Use Its Influence." Retrieved from https://www.voakorea.com/a/a-35-2006-06-27-voa2-91224399/1300188.html

———. 2016. "South Korea, US to Discuss Deploying Missile Defense System." Retrieved from https://www.voanews.com/a/korea-us-to-discuss-deploying-missile-defense-system/3180470.html

Volodzko, David. 2017a. "China Wins Its War against South Korea's US THAAD Missile Shield – Without Firing a Shot." *South China Morning Post.* November 18. Retrieved from https://www.scmp.com/week-asia/geopolitics/article/2120452/china-wins-its-war-against-south-koreas-us-thaad-missile

———. 2017b. "Did Beijing Just Give South Korea's Moon the Cold Shoulder?" *South China Morning Post.* December 24. Retrieved from https://www.scmp.com/week-asia/politics/article/2125443/did-beijing-just-give-south-koreas-moon-cold-shoulder

Bibliography

Vucetic, Srdjan. 2017. "Identity and Foreign Policy." *Oxford Research Encyclopedia of Politics.*

Walker, Julian, and Victoria Knauer. 2011. "Humiliation, Self-Esteem and Violence." *The Journal of Forensic Psychiatry & Psychology* 22 (5): 724–741.

Waltz, Kenneth. 1954. *Man, the State, and War: A Theoretical Analysis.* New York: Columbia University Press.

———. 1979. *Theory of International Politics.* Long Grove, IL: Waveland Press.

———. 1993. "The Emerging Structure of International Politics." *International Security* 18 (2): 75–76.

———. 2000. "Structural Realism after the Cold War." *International Security* 25 (1): 5–41.

Wang, Hongying. 2003. "National Image-Building and Chinese Foreign Policy." *China: An International Journal* 1 (1): 46–72.

Wang, Jisi. 2011. "China's Search for a Grand Strategy: A Rising Great Power Finds Its Way." *Foreign Affairs* 90 (2): 68–79.

Wang, Junsheng. 2015. "Park Has Good Reason to Attend Sept 3 Parade." *China Daily.* Retrieved from http://m.chinadaily.com.cn/en/2015-08/18/content_2163 0065.htm

Wang, Tianyi. 2014a. "Small State, Big Influence: China's North Korea Policy Dilemma." *Georgetown Journal of Asian Affairs* 1 (1): 5–27.

Wang, Wei. 2016. "*Pujinhuishengrishoudaozhongguozhufufensituansongshang-tailiheka* (朴槿惠生日收到"中国祝福" 粉丝团送上台历贺卡)" *Huangqiu Shibao.* Retrieved from http://world.huanqiu.com/exclusive/2016-02/8487834.html (In Chinese).

Wang, Yi. 2013. "Exploring the Path of Major-Country Diplomacy with Chinese Characteristics." Ministry of Foreign Affairs of China. Retrieved from https://www.fmprc.gov.cn/mfa_eng/wjb_663304/wjbz_663308/2461_663310/t1053908.shtml

———. 2014b. "Full Text of Foreign Minister Wang Yi's Speech on China's Diplomacy in 2014." Ministry of Foreign Affairs of China. Retrieved from https://newyork.china-consulate.org/eng/xw/t1223262.htm

———. 2014c. "China and South Korea Should Promote Prosperity and Development Together." Retrieved from http://kr.china-embassy.org/kor/sgxx/t1162407.htm (In Korean).

———. 2018. "China's Diplomacy in the New Era: Opening Up New Horizons with a New Outlook (进入新时代的中国外交: 开启新航程 展现新气象)." *China International Studies* (国际问题研究) 68. Retrieved from http://www.ciis.org.cn/gyzz/2018-01/22/content_40197444.htm (In Chinese).

Wang, Yiwei. 2008. "Public Diplomacy and the Rise of Chinese Soft Power." *The Annals of the American Academy of Political and Social Science* 616: 257–273.

Wang, Yuan-Kang. 2011. *Harmony and War: Confucian Culture and Chinese Power Politics.* New York: Columbia University Press.

———. 2013. "Explaining the Tribute System: Power, Confucianism, and War in Medieval East Asia." *Journal of East Asian Studies* 13: 207–232.

Websdale, Neil. 2010. "Of Nuclear Missiles and Love Objects: The Humiliated Fury of Kevin Jones." *Journal of Contemporary Ethnography* 39 (4): 388–420.

Wedeman, Andrew. 2012. *Double Paradox: Rapid Growth and Rising Corruption in China.* Ithaca, NY: Cornell University Press.

172　*Bibliography*

Weiss, Jessica Chen. 2014. *Powerful Patriots: Nationalist Protest in China's Foreign Relations.* Oxford: Oxford University Press.

Weiss, Robert Stuart. 1994. *Learning from Strangers: The Art and Method of Qualitative Interview Studies.* New York: Free Press.

Weitz, Richard. 2012a. "A Way Forward on Ballistic Missile Defenses." China-US Focus. Retrieved from https://www.chinausfocus.com/peace-security/a-way-forward-on-ballistic-missile-defenses

———. 2012b. "China Steps up Rhetoric against U.S. Missile Defense." *China Brief* 12 (20): 11–14.

Wendt, Alexander. 1992. "Anarchy Is What States Make of It: The Social Construction of Power Politics." *International Organization* 46 (2): 391–425.

———. 1994. "Collective Identity Formation and the International State." *The American Political Science Review* 88 (2): 384–396.

———. 1995. "Constructing International Politics." *International Security* 20 (1): 71–81.

———. 1999. *Social Theory of International Politics.* Cambridge: Cambridge University Press.

Wertz, Danile, J. J. Oh, and Kim Insung. 2016. "DPRK Diplomatic Relations." *Issue Brief.* National Committee on North Korea. Retrieved from https://www.ncnk.org/resources/briefing-papers/all-briefing-papers/dprk-diplomatic-relations

Wiarda, Howard J. 2014. *Political Culture, Political Science, and Identity Politics.* Farnham: Ashgate.

Wilhelm, Richard. 1928. *The Soul of China.* Translated by John H. Reece and Arthur Waley. New York: Harcourt Brace and Co.

Williams, Rob. 2013. "Fiery Seas and Sacred Wars: A History of North Korea's Blustery Threats." *Independent.* Retrieved from https://www.independent.co.uk/news/world/asia/fiery-seas-and-sacred-wars-a-history-of-north-koreas-blustery-threats-8526243.html

Wilson, Ernest J. 2004. "Introduction: Framing the Discussion of Globalization, Diversity, and U.S. International Affairs." In Ernest J. Wilson (ed.) *Diversity and U.S. Foreign Policy: A Reader* (pp. 1–15). New York: Routledge.

Work, Robert O. 2014. "Deputy Secretary of Defense Work Delivers Remarks at the Council on Foreign Relations." U.S. Department of Defense. Retrieved from https://dod.defense.gov/News/Transcripts/Transcript-View/Article/606935/deputy-secretary-of-defense-work-delivers-remarks-at-the-council-on-foreign-rel/

Workman, Daniel. 2019. "China's Top Trading Partners." Retrieved from http://www.worldstopexports.com/chinas-top-import-partners/

Wu, Jackson. 2013. *Saving God's Face: A Chinese Contextualization of Salvation through Honor.* Pasadena, CA: William Carey International University Press.

Wu, Xinbo. 2004. "Four Contradictions Constraining China's Foreign Policy Behavior." In Zhao Suisheng (ed.) *Chinese Foreign Policy: Pragmatism and Strategic Behavior* (pp. 58–65). New York: M.E. Sharpe.

Xi, Jinping. 2014a. "Xi: China to Promote Cultural Soft Power." Retrieved from http://np.china-embassy.org/eng/News/t1113938.htm

———. 2014b. "Xijinpingzaihanguoguolishou'erdaxuedeyanjiang (习近平在韩国国立首尔大学的演讲)." Retrieved from http://www.xinhuanet.com/politics/2014-07/04/c_1111468087.htm

————. 2015. "Full Text of Chinese President's Speech at Boao Forum for Asia." Retrieved from https://www.fmprc.gov.cn/mfa_eng/topics_665678/xjpcxbayzlt2015nnh/t1250690.shtml

————. 2018a. "Jointly Write a New Chapter of China-Brunei Relations." *Borneo Bulletin*. Retrieved from https://borneobulletin.com.bn/jointly-write-a-new-chapter-of-china-brunei-relations/

————. 2018b. "*Xieshoupuxiezhongguotongwenlaiguanxixinhuazhang.*" *People's Daily*. Retrieved from http://politics.people.com.cn/n1/2018/1118/c1024-30406389.html (In Chinese).

————. 2018c. "Full Text of Chinese President Xi Jinping's Speech at the 18th SCO Qingdao Summit." *Global Times*. Retrieved from http://www.globaltimes.cn/content/1106320.shtml

Xiao, Huanrong. 2003. "Zhongguodedaguozerenyudiquzhuyizhanlue (中国的大国责任与地区主义战略)." 战略研究 1: 46–51 (In Chinese).

Yan. 2018. "Xi Urges Breaking New Ground in Major Country Diplomacy with Chinese Characteristics." Xinhua News Agency. Retrieved from http://xinhuanet.com/english/2018-06/24/c_137276269.htm

Ye, Min. 2017. *China–South Korea Relations in the New Era: Challenges and Opportunities*. Lanham, MD: Lexington Books.

Ye, Young-jun. 2016. "Putin and Xi Announce Joint Statements on Opposing THAAD Twice in Three Days." *Joongang Daily*. Retrieved from https://news.joins.com/article/20224025 (In Korean).

Yellen, Jeremy A. 2014. "Shinzo Abe's Constitutional Ambitions." *The Diplomat*. Retrieved from https://thediplomat.com/2014/06/shinzo-abes-constitutional-ambitions/

Yonhap News Agency. 2000. "Chronology of the Garlic Dispute between Korea and China." Retrieved from https://www.yna.co.kr/view/AKR20000715000400003 (In Korean).

————. 2006. "N. Korea Says It Will Conduct Nuclear Test." Retrieved from http://www.hani.co.kr/arti/english_edition/e_international/162011.html

————. 2015. "(LEAD) S. Korea Keeps Strategic Ambiguity over THAAD Missile Defense System." Retrieved from https://en.yna.co.kr/view/AEN20150311002551315

————. 2016. "THAAD Could Destroy Seoul-Beijing Relations: Chinese Envoy." Retrieved from https://en.yna.co.kr/view/AEN20160223010000315

Yoo, Hee-moon. 2017. "[China Insight] To Tackle THAAD Retaliation, You Have to Know Chuaimoshangyi Culture in China." *Joongang Daily*. Retrieved from https://news.joins.com/article/22042027

Yoo, Ji-hye. 2016. "China Suspends to Issue the Commercial Visa?" *Joongang Daily*. Retrieved from https://news.joins.com/article/20395918 (In Korean).

You, Sang-chul. 2017. "Why President Moon Mistreated?" *Joongang Daily*. Retrieved from https://news.joins.com/article/22215461

Yu, Bin. 1999. "China and Its Asian Neighbors: Implications for Sino-Korean Relations." In Yong Deng and Fei-Ling Wang (eds.) *In the Eyes of the Dragon: China Views the World* (pp. 183–210). Boulder, CO: Rowman & Littlefield Publishers.

Yu, Shin-mo. 2015. "Liu Jianchao in Korea, 'Take into Consideration China's Concerns on Placement of THAAD System.'" *Kyunghyang Shinmun*. http://english.khan.co.kr/khan_art_view.html?artid=201503171734037&code=710100#csidx4f47e20d12cc68487f8afb8266a09df

174 *Bibliography*

Yu, Tiejun, Ren Yuanzhe, and Wang Junsheng. 2016. *Chinese Perspectives towards the Korean Peninsula.* Washington, DC: Stimson Center.

Yuan, Jing-Dong. 2003. "Chinese Responses to U.S. Missile Defenses: Implications for Arms Control and Regional Security." *The Proliferation Review* (Spring): 75–96.

Zakaria, Fareed. 1998. *From Wealth to Power: The Unusual Origins of America's World Role.* Princeton, NJ: Princeton University Press.

Zeng, Jinghan, Yuefan Xiao, and Shaun Breslin. 2015. "Securing China's Core Interests: The State of the Debate in China." *International Affairs* 91 (2): 245–266.

Zeng, Jinghan. 2016. "Constructing a 'New Type of Great Power Relations': The State of Debate in China (1998–2014)." *The British Journal of Politics and International Relations* 18 (2): 422–442.

Zhang, Feng. 2015. "Confucian Foreign Policy Traditions in Chinese History." *The Chinese Journal of International Politics* 8 (2): 197–218.

Zhang, Hui. 2007. "North Korea's Oct. 9 Nuclear Test: Successful or Failed?" Retrieved from https://www.belfercenter.org/sites/default/files/legacy/files/NKtest_1NMM07_Hui.pdf

Zhang, Rui. 2017. *China Struggles for International Recognition – An Explanation from Chinese Face Culture.* Retrieved from https://biblio.ugent.be/publication/8533625/file/8533654.pdf

Zhang, Xiaoming. 2010. "Deng Xiaoping and China's Decision to Go to War with Vietnam." *Journal of Cold War Studies* 12 (3): 3–29.

Zhao, Quansheng. 2018. "The influence of Confucianism on Chinese Politics and Foreign Policy." *Asian Education and Development Studies* 7 (4): 321–328.

Zhao, Suisheng. 2004a. "Chinese Foreign Policy: Pragmatism and Strategic Behavior." In Zhao Suisheng (ed.) *Chinese Foreign Policy: Pragmatism and Strategic Behavior* (pp. 3–20). New York: M.E. Sharpe.

———. 2004b. "Beijing's Perception after the Tiananmen Incidence." In Zhao Suisheng (ed.) *Chinese Foreign Policy: Pragmatism and Strategic Behavior* (pp. 140–150). New York: M.E. Sharpe.

———. 2004c. "The Making of China's Periphery Policy." In Zhao Suisheng (ed.) *Chinese Foreign Policy: Pragmatism and Strategic Behavior* (pp. 256–275). New York: M.E. Sharpe.

———. 2012. "Hu Jintao's Foreign Policy Legacy." Retrieved from https://www.e-ir.info/2012/12/08/hu-jintaos-foreign-policy-legacy/

———. 2013. "Chinese Foreign Policy as a Rising Power to find its Rightful Place." *Perceptions* 18 (1): 101–128.

———. 2016. "Xi Jinping's Maoist Revival." *Journal of Democracy* 27 (3): 83–97.

Zhao, Yali, and John D. Hoge. 2006. "Countering Textbook Distortion: War Atrocities in Asia, 1937–1945." *Social Education* 70 (7), pp. 424–430.

Zhao, Ye. 2016. "*Waijiaobu Qianhongshan: Zhonghanhezuoshouzushizhongguobaixingduihanfangushusadedeziranfanying* (外交部钱洪山：中韩合作受阻是中国百姓对韩方部署"萨德"的自然反应)." *Huanqiu Shibao.* Retrieved from http://world.huanqiu.com/hot/2016-11/9742609.html?agt=1

Zheng, Yongnian. 1999. *Discovering Chinese Nationalism in China: Modernization, Identity, and International Relations.* Cambridge: Cambridge University Press.

Zhong, Weifeng, and Julian T. Chan. 2018. "Policy Change Index: A Simulated Example." Retrieved from https://www.aei.org/articles/policy-change-index-a-simulated-example/

Zhou, Fangyin. 2011. "Equilibrium Analysis of the Tributary System." *The Chinese Journal of International Politics* 4 (2): 147–178.

Zhu, Feng. 2017. "China's North Korean Liability: How Washington Can Get Beijing to Rein in Pyongyang." *Foreign Affairs*, July 11. Retrieved from https://www.foreignaffairs.com/articles/china/2017-07-11/chinas-north-korean-liability

Zhu, Lin. 2016. "A Comparative Look at Chinese and American Stereotypes: A Focus Group Study." *Journal of Intercultural Communication* 42 (1). Retrieved from https://immi.se/intercultural/nr42/zhu.html

Zoellick, Robert B. 2005. "Whither China: From Membership to Responsibility?" U.S. Department of State Archive. Retrieved from https://2001-2009.state.gov/s/d/former/zoellick/rem/53682.htm

Zuo, Bin. 1997. *Zhongguorendelianyumianzi: bentushhuixinlixuetansuo* (中国人的脸与面子：本土社会心理学探索). Wuhan: Central China Normal University Press (华中师范大学出版社).

Index

Note: **Bold** page numbers refer to tables; *italic* page numbers refer to figures and page numbers followed by "n" denote endnotes.

Abe Shinzo (Japanese Prime Minister) 13–14, 42, 47, 81–82
Aristotle 52
ASEAN Regional Forum (ARF) 116
Asian financial crisis (1997–1999) 25
Asia-Pacific Economic Cooperation (APEC) summit 42
Association of Southeast Asian Nations (ASEAN) 116
authoritarianism 53

Ballistic Missile Defense (BMD) 80
Ban Ki-moon (South Korean Foreign Minister) 114
Bedford, Olwen 4
Beijing Review (news magazine) 66
Belt and Road Initiative 66
Biological Weapons Convention 27
"blood alliance" 30, 50n25, 51n26
Boxer Rebellion, 1900 60
Brazil: as great power in developing world 22; major developing country 22
Bush, George W. (U.S. President) 114, 116

Carter, Ashton B. (U.S. Assistant Secretary of Defense) 114
"Century of Humiliation" 1, 20, 50n17
Chang Wanquan (Chinese Defense Minister) 93
Chemical Weapons Convention 27
Chi Haotian (Chinese Defense Minister) 37
China: anarchy 42–46; anti-missile issues 93–94; bans Korean culture, *Xianhanling* 97; "the best period in

history" 97; "century of humiliation" 1; characteristics 63; China National Tourism Administration 97; companies in South Korean 98; Confucianism 63; controversy, "sick man of Asia" 1, 140; currency swap agreement with South Korea 39; definition 38, 42; hypotheses **132, 137**; and North Korea, relations between 3; offensive realism 54; Official Statements on South Korea **100**; policymaking 62; proclaimed identity 9; puzzling behavior **3**; retaliation 95–99; Six-Party Talks (SPT) regime 7; and South Korea, relations between 3–4, **101**; tourists to South Korea 97; traditional friendship, with North Korea 29; treaty of alliance with North Korea 130; tribute system 58
China Central Television (CCTV) 42
China Digest (Hong Kong) 66
China Victory Day parade 88
Chinese Communist Party (CCP) 62
Chinese core national interests: definition of 9n5, 126; Japan's THAAD radar deployment (case study) 86–87, 136; North Korea's Taepodong-2 launch and first nuclear test (case study) 126–128, **127**, 136; null hypotheses 48, 136; South Korea's THAAD system deployment (case study) 104–107, **105, 106,** 136
Chinese face culture: anti-corruption measures 64; China and Koreas, relations between 71–75; culture and foreign policy 52–54; defining face

178 *Index*

55–57; dynamics of 57–62; effect on foreign policy 62–71, **69, 71**, 134, *135*; face dynamics 64; losing face 3, 6, 9, 60–62; *mianzi* and *lian*, distinction between 56–57, 69–70; naming and shaming strategy 65; relationship between dynamics of *61*; saving face 9, 59–60; seeking face 6, 8–9, 57–59; *Taoguangyanghui* 67, 71

Chinese Foreign Ministry Spokesperson Archive (CFMSA) 21–22, *22*, 48

Chinese nationalism 4

Chinese People's Liberation Army (PLA) 30

Chinese People's Political Consultative Conference 32

Chosun dynasty 20

Cho Sung-tae (South Korean Defense Minister) 37

Christensen, Thomas J. 146

Chun Doo-hwan (South Korean President) 16

The Civic Culture (Almond and Verba) 52

Cold War 12, 16, 40, 46, 66

collective identity 12, 13

Complete, Verifiable, and Irreversible Dismantlement (CVID) 111

Confucian-Mencian paradigm 54

constructivism 11

constructivist social theory 11

corporate identity 12

Cultural Revolution 30

culture: in foreign policy analysis 8, 52–53, 54, 63; future of Chinese foreign policy 140; influence of culture on foreign policy 53–54; political 52–54; strategic culture 54

Dai Bingguo (chief deputy minister for Foreign Affairs of China) 112

14th Dalai Lama 3

Democratic People's Republic of Korea (DPRK) *see* North Korea

Deng, Xiaoping 22, 24, 35, 37

Durkheim, Emile 52

face: defining 55–57; face-saving excuses 77n8; losing face 60–62; mutual face 76n2; other-face 76n2; saving face 59–60; seeking face 57–59; self-face 76n2; translation of *mianmao* 77n5

Feng, Huiyun. 54

First Opium War 20

Foreign Policy Analysis (FPA) 12; Chinese, effect of face culture 62–71; culture in 52–53; identity in 11–12; influence of culture on 53–54; Japanese Case 134; North Korean Case 132–133; South Korean Case 133–134

Free Trade Agreement (FTA): monumental event 91

friendship trade 40

The Garlic War: aftermath of 76; background 72; between China and South Korea, 2000 7, 9, 71; China's strange behavior 73–74; developments 72–73

General Security of Military Information Agreement (GSOMIA) 46

global economic crisis (2007–2008) 25

global identity 49n2

Gong Ro-myung (head of South Korean representative and foreign minister) 36

great power, Chinese tradition 19–22; big and small states, dichotomy of 19–21; "Century of Humiliation" 20; Chinese Foreign Ministry Spokesperson Archive (CFMSA) 21–22, *22*; conceptions of national power 20; identity 19; *On Protracted War* 20–21; Sinocentrism 20

Gries, Peter Hays 4, 77

Gross Domestic Product (GDP) 23

Gu Mu (Chinese Vice Premier) 41

Hagel, Chuck (U.S. Defense Secretary) 82

Hallstein Doctrine 35

Han Min-gu (South Korean Defense Minister) 93

hanran (flagrant or brazen) 2

Ho, Benjamin Tze Ern. 4

Huang Hua (Chinese Foreign Minister) 35

Huang, Yi-Hui 4

Hui Liangyu (Chinese Vice Premier) 129n10

Hu Jintao (Chinese President) 66–67, 89, 90, 112, 114, 117, 122, 124

Hwang Kyoahn (South Korean Prime Minister) 95, 102

Ichiro Ozawa (former secretary-general of the Liberal Democratic Party in Japan) 49n5

identification of self 12

identity: China's 4; collective 12, 13; definition of 12; endogenous 4; in foreign policy analysis 11–12, 132–134; future of Chinese foreign policy 140; great power's identity 19; imagined 49n2; inter-state relations 5; in IR 4; of North Korea 17, **18**, 33; perceived (*see* perceived identity); personal/corporate 12; proclaimed (*see* proclaimed identity); realist approach 43–48; role 12, 13; self-identity 49n2; of South Korea 3, 17, **18**; type 12

imagined identity 49n2

inter-ethnic violence 53

International Atomic Energy Agency (IAEA) 7

International Relations (IR): expressions of intimacy 29; national friendship, notion of 28–29; reputation discourse 14–15, 63–64; social bonds 28–29; social contacts 29; Western 4

Ishihara Shintaro (Governor of Tokyo) 42, 85

Japan 40–43; Agreement Concerning Japanese Participation in Research for SDI 78; counter infiltration 40; missile defense system 79; partner for economic growth 40–41; peace state 13; perceived identity 40–43; proclamation of normal state identity 14; rival, close to enemy 41–43; Shariki and Kyogamisaki, X-band radars 2; THAAD (*see* THAAD radar deployment (case study), Japan's); unforgettable history 40; X-band radar 80

Jiang Zemin (Chinese President) 23, 32, 37, 50n23, 66–67

Johnston, Alastair Iain. 54

Kang Sok-ju (North Korea's First Vice Foreign Minister) 74, 117

Kelley, James (U.S. Assistant Secretary of State for Asia and the Pacific) 7, 74

Kim Dae-jung (South Korean President) 16, 17, 37, 50n15

Kim Dong-shin (South Korean Defense Minister) 37

Kim Gye-gwan (North Korean Deputy Foreign Minister) 113, 121

Kim, Heungkyu. 32

Kim Il-sung–Kim Jong-il Constitution 13

Kim Yong Sik (South Korean Foreign Minister) 35

Kim Young-sam (South Korean President) 16

Kofi Annan (U.N. Secretary General) 44, 114

Koizumi Junichiro (Japanese Prime Minister) 41, 84

Korea Air and Missile Defense (KAMD) 92

Korea-China Free Trade Agreement (FTA) 90, 133

Korea-China Joint Statement on Future Vision 90

Korea Institute for Defense Analyses (KIDA) 91

Korean Central News Agency (KCNA) 116

Korean Integrated News Database System (BIGKINDS) 25

Korean War 30, 32, 34, 36, 51n29, 64

Korea Trade Commission (KTC) 72

Kuomintang (KMT) 29

Kyogamisaki, second radar at 2, 81–82

Lee Myung-bak (South Korean President) 1, 17, 38, 89, 98, 108n3

Leninism 4

Liang Guanglie (Chinese Defense Minister) 83

Li Keqiang (Chinese Premier) 102

Li Qinggong (deputy secretary of China Council for National Security Policy Studies) 83

Liu Jianchao (Chinese Assistant Minister of Foreign Affairs) 93

Li Zhaoxing (Chinese Foreign Minister) 114, 117

losing face 6, 9, 60–62; dynamics of 68; internal and/or external 60–61; *see also* China

Machimura Nobutaka (Minister of Foreign Affairs) 80

Maoism 4

Mao Zedong 30

Marxism 4

Marx, Karl 52

Mexico: as great power in Latin America 22; major country 22

Mianzi/Lian in CFMSA Database **71**

Ming dynasty 58

Ministry of Finance and Economy (MOFE) 72

180 *Index*

modernization 53
Moon Jae-in (South Korean President) 88, 98, 99, 103, 107
"Mount Baekdu bloodline," notion of 49n6
My Country and My People (Lin Yutang) 55

Nakasone Yasuhiro (Japanese Prime Minister) 41
naming and shaming strategy 65
Nathan, Andrew J. 4
nationalism 53
National Missile Defense (NMD) 87n1
neoclassical realism 11, 44–45
normal state 14, 49n5
Northeast Project: between China and South Korea 76
North Korea: 1994 Agreement 74; "axis of evil" 15, 74; building of "blood alliance" 29–30; comprehensive approach 112; "forged in blood" China as 29; identity of 17, **18**; missile test 121; nuclear crises 4, 111; nuclear weapons development 9, 33, 74; oscillating but still friendly 30–32; perceived identity 29–34; second nuclear crisis 7; strategic asset and liability 32–34; Taepodong-2 launch (*see* Taepodong-2 launch (case study), North Korea's); traditional friendship, China 29; "verifiable and irreversible dismantlement" method 111
North Korean People's Army (NKPA) 30
nuclear state 49n6
nuclear weapons: bombs 5–6; in North Korea 5, 9, 12; in possession of United Kingdom 5
Nugata (Japanese Defense Minister) 81, 82

Obama, Barack (U.S. President) 81, 94, 106
offensive realism 54
Ohno Yoshinori (Japanese Minister of State for Defense) 80
One Belt, One Road program 66
Onodera Itsunori (Japanese Defense Minister) 42
ontological security 49n3
organizing or ordering principle 43

Pacific War 85
Panetta, Leon (U.S. Defense Secretary) 81

Park Bong-Ju (North Korean Premier) 122
Park Chung-hee (South Korean President) 16
Park Geun-hye (South Korean President) 1–2, 17, 88–93, 99, 102, 103, 108n5, 108n6, 109n11, 130
Patriot Advanced Capability (PAC)-3 79
People's China (newspaper) 66
People's Daily (newspaper) 24–25, 31, 34, 35, 48, 53, 67, 90, 94, 95, 104, 106, 118, 127–128
People's Republic of China (PRC) *see* China
People's Volunteer Army 64
perceived identity 6, 8, 11, 12–19; formation of 15; Japan 40–43; North Korea 29–34; South Korea 34–39; of three neighbors by China 27–43
Perry, William J. (U.S. former Defense Secretary) 114
personal/corporate identity 12
personal identity 12
Plato 52
political culture 52
Powell, Colin (U.S. Secretary of State) 126
proclaimed identity 6, 8, 11, 12–19, 49n2; China 9; formation of 15; great power, notion of 19–22; normal state 13; of North Korea 13; "Responsible China" or "China Great Power" *26*; responsible great power, rise of 22–27, *25*; self-identification 13; Word Cloud of *23*
psychological security 49n3
Pueblo Incident, in 1968 North Korea 31
Putin, Vladimir (Russian President) 88, 94

Qian Hongshan (assistant minister of Foreign Affairs) 96
Qin dynasty 59
Qing Dynasty 20
Qin, Yaqing. 62

realist approach 43–48; neoclassical realism 11, 44–45; structural realism 11, 43–44; unrealistic realism 45–48
Red Guards in China 30
Republic of Korea (ROK) *see* South Korea
reputation, concept of 49n8
responsible great power, rise of 22–27, *25*

Rhee Syngman (South Korean President) 16
Rice, Condoleezza (U.S. Secretary of State) 80, 114
Rodong Sinmun (newspaper) 29
Rodrigo Duterte (Philippine President) 98
Roh Moo-hyun (South Korean President) 17, 50n11, 89–90
role identity 12, 13
Rose, Gideon. 165
Rumsfeld, Donald (U.S. Secretary of Defense) 80, 82
Ryu Jae-seung (South Korean deputy minister for National Defense Policy) 2

Sarkozy (French President) 3
Sato Eisaku (Japanese Prime Minister) 40–41
saving face 9, 59–60; defensive mechanism 6; *see also* China
Scobell, Andrew 4
Scud and Nodong missiles 115
second nuclear crisis of North Korea: background 74; China's strange behavior 75; developments 74–75; hypothesis 75
Second World War 13, 84, 88, 90
seeking face 6, 8–9, 57–59; *see also* China
self-identity 49n2
2010 Senkaku Boat Collision Incident 77n14; between China and Japan 77n14
Shariki, first radar at 2, 79–81
Sino-Japanese relations 8, **8,** 28
Sino-North Korean Mutual Aid and Cooperation Friendship Treaty 30, 33–34, 119, 122
Sino-North Korean relations 8, **8,** 28, 130, *135*
Sino-South Korean relations 8, **8,** 28, 130–131, *135*
Sino-Soviet Treaty of Friendship, Alliance and Mutual Assistance 40
Sino-Vietnamese War 69
Six-Party Talks (SPT) regime 7, 70
social category 12
Socrates 52
South Korea 34–39; Agreement with Japan 46; and China, trade volume between *38*; Chinese Visitors to *39*; friend's enemy 34–35; middle power diplomacy 27; *nanchaoxian* (south

of Chosun) 36; national security and interests 93; perceived identity 34–39; probable good neighbor 35–37; THAAD (*see* THAAD system deployment (case study), South Korea's); win-win friend 37–39
South Korea's Air Defense Identification Zone (KADIZ) 98
Standard Missile (SM)-3 79–80
state identity: changes in 5; formation of 50n9; *see also* identity
Strategic Defense Initiative (SDI) 78
strategic state 49n6
structural realism 11, 43–44
"sunshine policy" of engagement 16, 50n12, 131

Taepodong-2 launch (case study), North Korea's: China's Official Statements **119**; Chinese core national interests 126–128, **127,** 136; failure to save face 120–122; features of **138**; first nuclear test 115–117; *Hanran,* in Official Press Conferences 124, **125**; highlevel officials **118**; launch of 2, 3, 81, 114, 121, 131; Launch of Taepodong-2 113–115; lost face, China's 119–120; North Korea's identity to China 117–119; origin of the SPT 110–113; restoring lost face 123–126; test results of hypotheses **137**
Taepodong-2 missile, launch of 2, 3
Tang Jiaxuan (Chinese Foreign Minister Tang Jiaxuan) 114, 126
Terminal High Altitude Area Defense (THAAD) system 2
THAAD-linked Army Navy/ Transportable Radar Surveillance (AN/TPY-2) systems 78
THAAD radar deployment (case study), Japan's: background 78–79; Chinese core national interests 86–87, 136; developments 79–84; features **138**; first radar at Shariki 79–81; Japan's identity to China 84–86; losing face 86; North Korean Missile threat **79**; response, China's 82–84; second radar at Kyogamisaki 81–82; test results of hypotheses **137**
THAAD system deployment (case study), South Korea's: back to normal 91–92; best relationship in history 89–91; Chinese core national interests

104–107, **105, 106,** 136; failure to save face 102–103; features of **138**; losing face, China's 101–102; restoring lost face 103; retaliation, China's 95–99; South Korea's identity to China 99–101, **100, 101**; strong opposition from China 92–95; test results of hypotheses **137**; "three no's principle" 102, 103
Theater Missile Defense (TMD) 87n1
Thomas Vandal (commander of U.S. Eighth Army in South Korea) 2
Three-Party Talks 111–112, 120, 128n2
Tiananmen incident 67
traditional friendship 51n27
Treaty of Friendship and Cooperation 69
Treaty on the Non-Proliferation of Nuclear Weapons (NPT) 7
Trump, Donald (U.S. President) 5–6, 16, 98
type identity 12

United Nations General Assembly Resolution 2758 68
United Nations Security Council (UNSC) 23–24
unrealistic realism 45–48
U.S.-Japan alliance 80
U.S. Missile Defense Agency 80
U.S. News and World Report 27
U.S. X-Band radar system 80

Verb in Context System (VICS) 54
Vietnam War 30
Voice of America (VOA) 108n7
*Voice of China (*magazine) 65

*Wall Street Journal (*newspaper) 1, 140
Waltz, Kenneth 11, 44, 46
Wang Yi (Chinese Foreign Minister) 24, 63, 90, 94, 103, 104, 106
Wang Yi (Foreign Minister) 98

Weber, Max 52
Wendt, Alexander 5, 11
Wen Jiabao (Chinese Premier) 3, 108n3, 115, 121
Work, Robert O. (U.S. Deputy Secretary of Defense) 92
Wu Dawei (Chinese Vice Foreign Minister) 114, 121, 123
Wu Dawei (Vice Minister) 94

X-band radars 82; AN/TPY-2 81; Japan 80; Shariki and Kyogamisaki 2, 93; THAAD system (*see* Terminal High Altitude Area Defense (THAAD) system); "United States–Japan Roadmap for Realignment Implementation," 80
*Xianfeng (*magazine) 77n10
Xi Jinping (Chinese President) 2, 21, 22, 24, 32, 42, 50–51n26, 50n19, 50n26, 62, 65–68, 88–92, 94, 95, 98, 99, 102–103, 106, 130

Yang Jiechi (Chinese Foreign Minister) 24, 32–33, 92
Yang Yujun (China's Defense Ministry Spokesperson) 91
Yoo Il-ho (South Korean Deputy Prime Minister and Finance Minister) 95
Yoo Jeh-Seung (South Korean Deputy Defense Minister for Policy) 94, 95
Yoshida Shigeru (Japanese Prime Minister) 40

Zhang, Feng. 62
Zhao, Quansheng. 62
Zheng Zeguang (Vice Minister of Foreign Affairs) 94
Zhou Enlai (Chinese Premier) 29, 31, 40
Zhu Rongji (Chinese Premier) 37
Zoellick, Robert B. (U.S. Deputy Secretary of State) 26, 129n8

Printed in the United States
By Bookmasters